WarCraft III: Reign of Chaos

OFFICIAL STRATEGY GUIDE

By Bart G. Farkas

WARCRAFT® III REIGN OF CHAOS™

©2002 PEARSON EDUCATION

BradyGAMES is a registered trademark
of Pearson Education, Inc.

BradyGAMES®

An Imprint of Pearson Education
201 West 103rd Street
Indianapolis, Indiana 46290

ISBN: 0-7440-00807-7

Library of Congress No.: 2002107822

Printing Code: The rightmost double-digit number is the year of the book's printing; the rightmost single-digit number is the number of the book's printing. For
example, 02-1 shows that the first printing of the book occurred in 2002.

05 04 03 02   4 3 2 1

Manufactured in the United States of America.

BradyGAMES Staff

PUBLISHER
David Waybright

EDITOR-IN-CHIEF
H. Leigh Davis

MARKETING MANAGER
Janet Eshenour

CREATIVE DIRECTOR
Robin Lasek

ASSISTANT LICENSING MANAGER
Mike Degler

ASSISTANT MARKETING MANAGER
Susie Nieman

Credits

SENIOR PROJECT EDITOR
David B. Bartley

GRAPHICS EDITORS
Michael Owen
Christian Sumner

PRODUCTION DESIGNERS
Bob Klunder
Jane Washburne

LEAD DESIGNER
Dan Caparo

DESIGN TEAM
Ann-Marie Deets
Carol Stamile
Chris Luckenbill

Special thanks to Melissa Edwards, Kelly Chun, Zach Callanan, Susan Sams, Jeremy Cargilo, Geoff Fraizer, Mike Hein, Jeff Chamberlain, Tim Campbell, James McCoy, Matt Householder, Ken Williams, Christian Arretche, and Len Harrison at Blizzard. Your time and expertise in reviewing this guide made it the best it could be.

ACKNOWLEDGEMENTS

As always I must thank David Bartley at BradyGames for being the rudder of the ship. I can always count on him in any situation. I'd also like to thank Leigh Davis, David Waybright, Christian Sumner, and Tim Cox (also of Brady) for their help and expertise.

As usual, working with Blizzard is a treat. The list of folks that helped me out is long, so I'll go ahead and list them. Before I do, however, I must take pains to specifically point out Melissa Edwards, Elaine Di Iorio, Mike Hein, and Geoff Fraizer for their logistical help.

Thanks also to:

John Lagrave	Brian Love	Mike Kramer
Eric Dodds	Ron Frybarger	Zach Allen
Ian Welke	Mike Schaeffer	Nicholas Pisani
Kenny Zigler	Jim Chadwick	Michelle Elbert
Tim Campbell	Derek Simmons	Manuel Gonzales
Rob Pardo	Ted Park	Dennis Lam
Pete Underwood	Mike Nyguyen	Andrew Brownell
Zach Callanan		John Yoo

DEDICATION

For Derek and Adam (Rugrati Diaperi)

TABLE OF

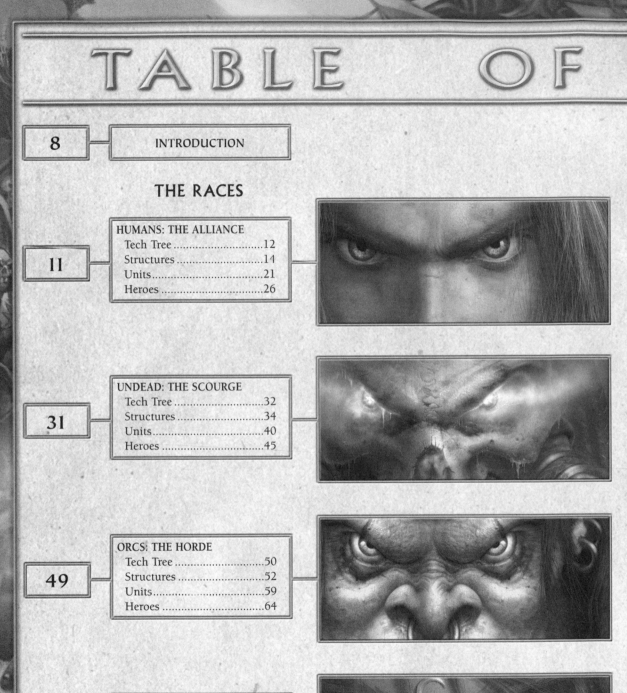

CONTENTS

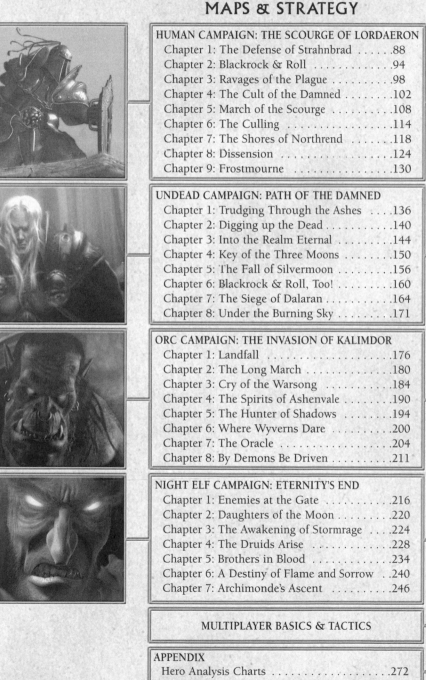

MAPS & STRATEGY

INTRODUCTION

The Warcraft franchise is one of the most beloved in all of computer gaming. It has been a long spell between *Warcraft® II: The Tides of Darkness™* and *Warcraft® III: Reign of Chaos™*. I am here to tell you that the wait has most definitely been worth it! This is the finest game of its kind *ever*, and I suspect that it will not be supplanted from its throne until Blizzard creates a future incarnation of the Warcraft franchise.

Warcraft III is the complete package. The single-player campaigns are absolutely engrossing and have the depth and complexity we've come to expect from the folks at Blizzard. For many, however, the real treat will be the multiplayer aspect on Battle.net® with an unlimited number of maps (these can be created with the World Editor that ships with *Warcraft III*). Like its cousin, *StarCraft®*, *Warcraft III* will live far past the life of most computer games, and will continue to be an enjoyable and popular game for years to come.

Because of the game's vast complexity and rich world, a guide like this helps us get the most out of the Warcraft experience. This book focuses on the details of the individual races and the strategies for the single-player missions, but there are also many tips, tactics, and overall strategies for multiplayer action.

USING THIS GUIDE

This book has been divided into a few fundamental sections: The Races, Maps & Strategy, Multiplayer Basics & Tactics, and an Appendix focusing on Hero Analysis.

The Races portion details every unit and structure for the four playable races, including the Tech Trees and extensive coverage of the Heroes. This is an invaluable source for statistical and strategic information, featuring everything from spell cooldown times to specific tactics for using magic.

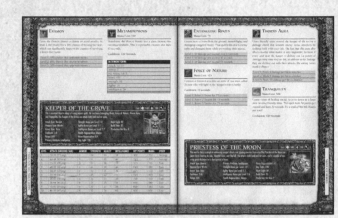

The **Maps & Strategy** section features tactical maps and in-depth strategies for each of the 36 single-player chapters in the Human, Undead, Orc, and Night Elf Campaigns. Each mission walkthrough contains a thorough step-by-step description of what must be done to satisfy the mission's victory requirements. We also provide a detailed map that contains key information for formulating strategies, as well as locations of significant areas and secret or hidden items.

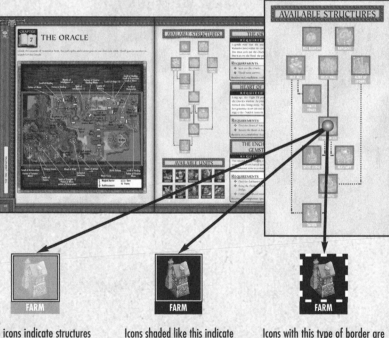

These icons indicate structures that are not available in the mission.

Icons shaded like this indicate structures that may be built in the mission.

Icons with this type of border are structures you start the mission with.

To get the most out of the *Warcraft III* experience, we suggest that you use the walkthrough descriptions only when you're stuck and need to know how to complete the mission. That said, we also suggest that you employ the use of the detailed maps for *every* mission so that you can take full advantage of any hidden items or bonuses that you otherwise may have missed!

Multiplayer Basics & Tactics delves into Battle.net strategies and other important details such as Mercenaries, Items, and Neutral structures. It contains several exclusive hints, tips, and strategies straight from the game designers and Blizzard Entertainment's fantastic QA department.

Finally, the **Appendix** provides an unprecedented level of Hero Analysis, comparing the Heroes of each race to one another, as well as cross-evaluating the overall Hero effectiveness between the four races. We've also repeated all of the Tech-trees in this section for quick reference.

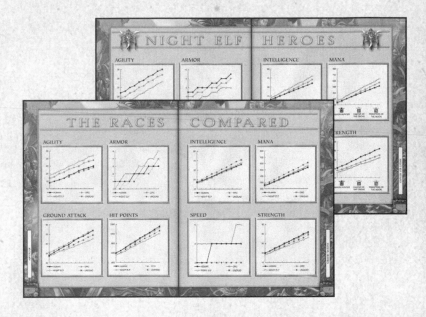

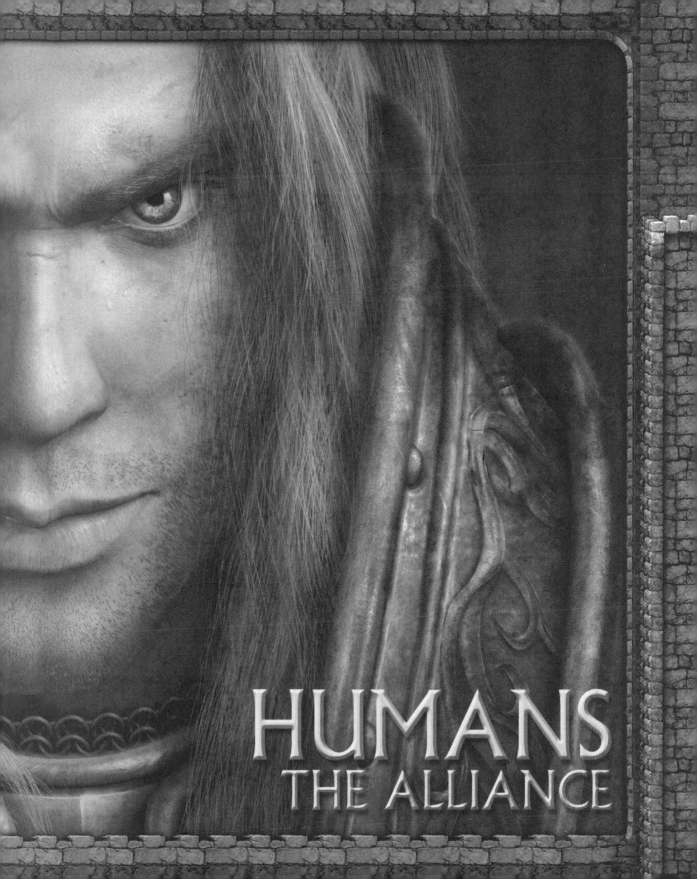

HUMANS
THE ALLIANCE

HUMAN TECH TREE

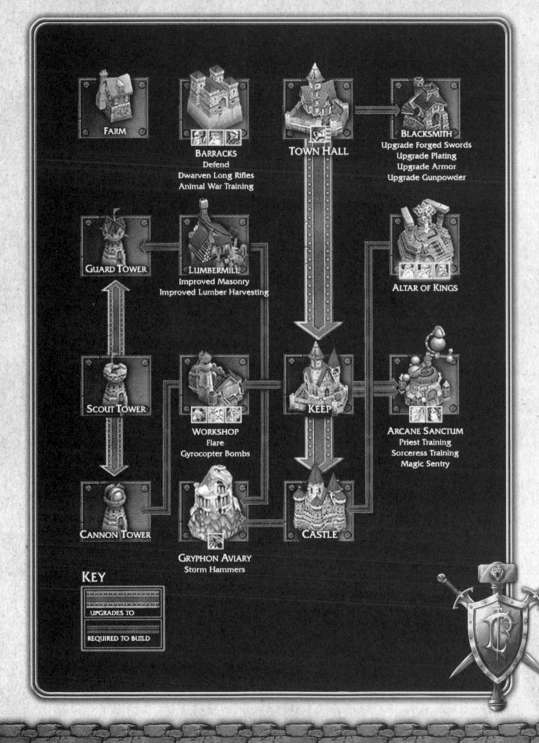

FARM

BARRACKS
Defend
Dwarven Long Rifles
Animal War Training

TOWN HALL

BLACKSMITH
Upgrade Forged Swords
Upgrade Plating
Upgrade Armor
Upgrade Gunpowder

GUARD TOWER

LUMBERMILL
Improved Masonry
Improved Lumber Harvesting

ALTAR OF KINGS

SCOUT TOWER

WORKSHOP
Flare
Gyrocopter Bombs

KEEP

ARCANE SANCTUM
Priest Training
Sorceress Training
Magic Sentry

CANNON TOWER

GRYPHON AVIARY
Storm Hammers

CASTLE

KEY

UPGRADES TO

REQUIRED TO BUILD

HUMANS: THE ALLIANCE

HUMAN TRUISMS

Here are a few thoughts to consider when playing as the Alliance:

❖ Humans have the unique ability to put more than one Peasant on a structure that's being built. The lengthy construction time for a Town Hall can be expidited considerably by putting four Peasants on it at once. Of course, you will incur an extra Gold and Lumber cost when you employ this technique.

❖ Call to Arms is a great way to quickly increase the defensive ability of your base. If the enemy attacks an undefended base, using this ability (in the Town Hall) instantly gives you Militia fighters that can hold off the enemy long enough for your main force to save the day.

❖ The Archmage's Mass Teleport ability is an excellent way to instantly drop an attack force right in the middle of an enemy's base. The only difficulty with this tactic is that you must have a ground unit in the area where you want to teleport. If you use the Sorceress' Invisibility, you can run a cloaked unit into the enemy's base, and then cast Mass Teleport—instant surprise attack!

❖ To set up a quick defensive perimeter, form two groups of four Peasants and have them work together at building Guard Towers. Assuming the resources are available for this, a strong defensive perimeter of Guard Towers can be constructed quickly in this way.

❖ Steam Tanks destroy enemy structures with great efficiency, so use them in groups of three or four as a secondary attack wave behind your melee units.

HUMAN TECH TREE

HUMAN STRUCTURES

TOWN HALL

Cost: ⬤ 450 🔺 150

The Town Hall is the primary structure for the Human race. It trains Peasants and acts as the receptacle for gathered resources. Build them near remote Gold Mines to accelerate the collection of this precious metal. If you strive to harvest gold from remote Gold Mines, then you can expect to build multiple Town Halls. This structure also has the unique ability to turn nearby Peasants into Militia with the Call to Arms skill, briefly transforming them into fierce fighting machines.

Upgrades: N/A
Building Upgrades: Keep, Castle
Creates: Peasants
Starting Hit Points: 1500
Armor: 5
Provides: 12 Food

CALL TO ARMS

This ability turns your everyday Peasants into Militia that vigorously defend your turf. When your forces are wearing thin, summon some Peasants near the home camp by using Call to Arms and they'll set their pedestrian tasks aside mommentarily to fight for your survival! Select Back to Work to call all nearby Militia to the Town Hall for conversion back into Peasants. This ability is also available to the Keep and the Castle.

KEEP

Cost: ⬤ 320 🔺 110

Upgrading a Town Hall to a Keep unlocks the production of additional Human structures and units.

Building Upgrades: Castle
Creates: Peasants
Starting Hit Points: 1800
Armor: 5
Provides: 12 Food
Requires: Town Hall

CASTLE

Cost: ⬤ 390 🔺 130

Upgrading a Keep to a Castle unlocks the production of additional Human structures and units.

Creates: Peasants
Starting Hit Points: 2000
Armor: 5
Provides: 12 Food
Requires: Keep, Altar of Kings

BARRACKS

The Barracks is the primary troop production facility for the Alliance. This building trains Footmen, Riflemen, and Knights. It also contains the Defend Upgrade for Footmen, Long Rifles for Riflemen, and Animal War Training for Knights and Gryphon Riders.

Cost: 240 / 80

Upgrades: Defend, Long Rifles, Animal War Training
Creates: Footmen, Riflemen, Knights
Starting Hit Points: 1500
Armor: 5

DEFEND

Research Cost: 150 Gold, 100 Lumber

Increases defensive capabilities of Footmen against ranged and piercing attacks.

LONG RIFLES

Research Cost: 125 Gold, 75 Lumber

Increases the attack range of Riflemen. This upgrade is especially critical when the enemy has an upgraded attack range!

Requires: Workshop

ANIMAL WAR TRAINING

Research Cost: 250 Gold, 200 Lumber

Increases the maximum hit points of Knights and Gryphon Riders by 150. This is arguably the most important upgrade in the Barracks—without Animal War Training, the considerable resource investment in creating Knights and Gryphon Riders could be in jeopardy.

Requires: Lumber Mill, Blacksmith, Castle

LUMBER MILL

The Lumber Mill serves as the drop point for harvested lumber. Even though a Town Hall accepts deposits of Lumber as well as Gold, the Lumber Mill is the preferred repository for Lumber. For highest efficiency, build a Lumber Mill in close proximity to large Lumber resources. The Lumber Mill also contains upgrades for Lumber collection and masonry, which increases the hit points of your buildings.

Cost: 170 / 0

Upgrades: Improved/Advanced Lumber Harvesting, Improved/Advanced/Imbued Masonry
Creates: N/A
Starting Hit Points: 900
Armor: 5

IMPROVED LUMBER HARVESTING

Research Cost: 100 Gold

Increases the amount of lumber a Peasant can carry by 5. Although it may not seem like a great deal, this advantage can be significant during the course of an entire game.

ADVANCED LUMBER HARVESTING

Research Cost: 200 Gold

Further increases the amount of lumber a Peasant can carry by another 5. This second boost makes a significant impact on your lumber supplies.

Requires: Castle

IMPROVED MASONRY

Research Cost: 100 Gold, 100 Lumber

Increases the armor and hit points for all of your buildings. Pursue this upgrade quickly to prepare for the inevitable enemy attack.

ADVANCED MASONRY

Research Cost: 150 Gold, 150 Lumber

Further increases the armor and hit points for all of your buildings by roughly 15%.

Requires: Keep

IMBUED MASONRY

Research Cost: 200 Gold, 200 Lumber

This final boost to your buildings again bumps your structures' hit points up another 15%.

Requires: Castle

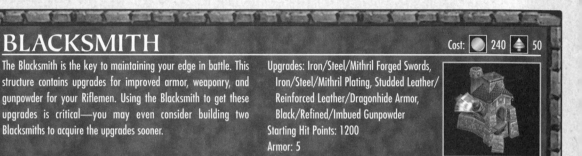

BLACKSMITH

Cost: 🪙 240 🪵 50

The Blacksmith is the key to maintaining your edge in battle. This structure contains upgrades for improved armor, weaponry, and gunpowder for your Riflemen. Using the Blacksmith to get these upgrades is critical—you may even consider building two Blacksmiths to acquire the upgrades sooner.

Upgrades: Iron/Steel/Mithril Forged Swords, Iron/Steel/Mithril Plating, Studded Leather/ Reinforced Leather/Dragonhide Armor, Black/Refined/Imbued Gunpowder
Starting Hit Points: 1200
Armor: 5
Requires: Town Hall

 NOTE •

A common tactic in team multiplayer action is for one player to upgrade only Footmen and Knights, while another upgrades only the Riflemen abilities. The two players then join together for a well-balanced and fully upgraded force in half the time it would take them to accomplish this individually.

IRON FORGED SWORDS

Research Cost: 100 Gold, 50 Lumber

Increases the melee attack damage of Footmen, Knights, Militia, and Gryphon Riders. This upgrade is the first step of three to upgrade these units' attack abilities.

STEEL FORGED SWORDS

Research Cost: 250 Gold, 100 Lumber

This further increases the melee attack damage of Footmen, Knights, Militia, and Gryphon Riders. Cost begins to become an issue at this point, especially if you are trying to build a base, assemble an attack force, and improve your upgrades.

Requires: Keep

MITHRIL FORGED SWORDS

Research Cost: 400 Gold, 150 Lumber

This is the top level for Footmen, Knights, Militia, and Gryphon Riders for attack upgrades, but it comes at a high price.

Requires: Castle

IRON PLATING

Research Cost: 125 Gold, 75 Lumber

Increases the armor of Footmen, Knights, Gyrocopters, Steam Tanks, and Militia. This is another upgrade that you should acquire as soon as your resources allow.

HUMANS: THE ALLIANCE

STEEL PLATING

Research Cost: 200 Gold, 125 Lumber

Further increases the armor of Footmen, Knights, Gyrocopters, Steam Tanks, and Militia.

Requires: Keep

MITHRIL PLATING

Research Cost: 275 Gold, 175 Lumber

This is the highest upgrade for the armor of Footmen, Knights, Gyrocopters, Steam Tanks, and Militia.

Requires: Castle

STUDDED LEATHER ARMOR

Research Cost: 100 Gold, 100 Lumber

Increases the armor of Riflemen, Mortar Teams, and Gryphon Riders.

REINFORCED LEATHER ARMOR

Research Cost: 150 Gold, 150 Lumber

Further increases the armor of Riflemen, Mortar Teams, and Gryphon Riders.

Requires: Keep

DRAGONHIDE ARMOR

Research Cost: 200 Gold, 200 Lumber

The highest armor upgrade for Riflemen, Mortar Teams, and Gryphon Riders.

Requires: Castle

BLACK GUNPOWDER

Research Cost: 100 Gold, 50 Lumber

Increases the ranged attack damage of Riflemen, Mortar Teams, Steam Tanks, and Gyrocopters.

REFINED GUNPOWDER

Research Cost: 250 Gold, 100 Lumber

Further increases the ranged attack damage of Riflemen, Mortar Teams, Steam Tanks, and Gyrocopters.

Requires: Keep

IMBUED GUNPOWDER

Research Cost: 400 Gold, 150 Lumber

Further increases the ranged attack damage of Riflemen, Mortar Teams, Steam Tanks, and Gyrocopters. This is the highest upgrade for the attack abilities of these units.

Requires: Castle

FARM

Cost: ⬤ 80 ⬆ 20

The Farm is the backbone of the Human economy. It provides the food that you'll need to manage your armies, and indeed, without them your unit production will halt completely. Always be careful not to get caught short on food supply when quickly trying to prepare an attack (or defense) force.

Upgrades: N/A
Provides: 6 Food
Starting Hit Points: 700
Armor: 5

 TIP

The number of Farms needed to get 90 food is 13 (15 if you don't have a Town Hall), so you must build that many to obtain the largest army possible.

ARCANE SANCTUM

Cost: 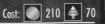 210 70

The Arcane Sanctum creates your spell-casters, the Priests and Sorceresses. It also contains the Magic Sentry upgrade, as well as specific training for each of these enchanted units.

Upgrades: Magic Sentry, Sorceress
  Adept/Master Training, Priest
  Adept/Master Training
Creates: Priests, Sorceresses
Starting Hit Points: 1050
Armor: 5
Requires: Keep

MAGIC SENTRY

Research Cost: 100 Gold

Enables towers to see invisible units. Magic Sentry is useful in multiplayer games when enemies try to sneak invisible units into your camp. In these situations, place one Tower inside your camp, and at least a pair on the perimeter to spot invisible enemy units moving into your area.

SORCERESS ADEPT TRAINING

Research Cost: 150 Gold

Increases the Sorceress' Mana capacity and regeneration rate. Adept Training also boosts the Sorceress' hit points and attack damage. Once she has acquired this training, the Invisibility spell is available.

SORCERESS MASTER TRAINING

Research Cost: 250 Gold, 100 Lumber

Much like the Adept Training, Master Training increases Mana regeneration, Mana capacity, hit points, and attack damage. Completing this upgrade also gives the Sorceress the ability to cast Polymorph.

Requires: Castle

PRIEST ADEPT TRAINING

Research Cost: 150 Gold

Just like the Sorceress' training, this increases the Priest's Mana capacity, Mana regeneration rate, hit points, and attack damage. Adept Training also gives him the ability to cast Dispel Magic.

PRIEST MASTER TRAINING

Research Cost: 250 Gold, 100 Lumber

Increases the Priest's Mana capacity, Mana regeneration rate, hit points, and attack damage. It also gives him the ability to cast Inner Fire.

Requires: Castle

ALTAR OF KINGS

Cost: 300 100

The Altar of Kings summons the Human Heroes—reviving slain Heroes and serving as their entry point. The Altar of Kings is also necessary before you can upgrade your Town Hall to a Castle.

Upgrades: N/A
Creates: Paladin, Archmage, Mountain King
Starting Hit Points: 900
Armor: 5

NOTE

When a Human Hero has been vanquished, he can be revived at the Altar of Kings for a price. This cost depends on the level of the Hero, and is always represented only in Gold, not Lumber.

WORKSHOP

Cost: 240 | 50

The Workshop is the production facility for Steam Tanks, Mortar Teams, and Gyrocopters, and also contains the Flare and Gyrocopter Bomb upgrades.

Upgrades: Gyrocopter Bombs, Flare
Creates: Gyrocopter, Mortar Team, Steam Tank
Starting Hit Points: 1200
Armor: 5
Requires: Keep, Blacksmith

GYROCOPTER BOMBS

Research Cost: 150 Gold, 100 Lumber

Allows Gyrocopters to attack ground units. Before attaining this upgrade, these Human flying machines are completely vulnerable to attacks from the ground. Get this upgrade as soon as you can, so your Gyrocopters can defend themselves.

Requires: Castle

FLARE

Research Cost: 100 Gold, 50 Lumber

Flare gives Mortar Teams a one-time shot at revealing any area on the map. This ability is useful when preparing an attack against the enemy because it can identify your adversary's weak spots.

NOTE

The Flare ability also allows you to see invisible enemy units, so it can be used near your own base if you haven't invested in Magic Sentinel and fear that invisible units (such as immobile Night Elves in the darkness) may be near your camp.

SCOUT TOWER

Cost: 80 | 20

The Scout Tower is a key structure to any Human encampment's survival. Not only does it provide a considerably greater line of sight (both during the day and at night), but it can also be upgraded to a Guard Tower (shoots arrows at enemies) and ultimately a Cannon Tower (fires cannons at enemies). In conjunction with the Magic Sentry upgrade, they can also spot invisible units moving inside their sphere of vision. When Magic Sentry is activated, a blue shimmering icon appears above the Scout/Guard/Cannon Towers to alert you that it's working.

Building Upgrades: Guard Tower, Cannon Tower
Upgrades: N/A
Creates: N/A
Starting Hit Points: 500
Armor: 5
Abilities: Magic Sentry (if upgraded in Arcane Sanctum)

> **NOTE**
>
> You can upgrade to either a Guard Tower or a Cannon Tower from the Scout Tower, but once you've converted a Scout Tower into one or the other, that's it. You cannot upgrade a Guard Tower to a Cannon Tower or vice versa. Once the choice is made, you've committed for good.

GUARD TOWER

Cost: 140   60

The Guard Tower is a solid defender against both land *and* air units, making it important if you have a lot of aerial attacks swooping in on your encampment. Once the Scout Tower has been upgraded to Guard Tower status, it cannot be upgraded to a Cannon Tower.

Building Upgrades: N/A
Upgrades: N/A
Starting Hit Points: 500
Armor: 5
Abilities: Magic Sentry (if upgraded in Arcane Sanctum)
Requires: Scout Tower, Lumber Mill

CANNON TOWER

Cost: 200   100

The Cannon Tower is the granddaddy of defensive towers. Its shots do area of effect damage that can quickly vanquish large groups of enemies. However, this tower cannot attack air units.

Building Upgrades: N/A
Upgrades: N/A
Starting Hit Points: 600
Armor: 5
Abilities: Magic Sentry (if upgraded in Arcane Sanctum)
Requires: Scout Tower, Workshop

GRYPHON AVIARY

Cost: 250   120

The Gryphon Aviary trains Gryphon Riders and also contains the Storm Hammers upgrade.

Building Upgrades: N/A
Upgrades: Storm Hammers
Creates: Gryphon Rider
Starting Hit Points: 1200
Armor: 5
Requires: Castle, Lumber Mill

STORM HAMMERS

Research Cost: 200 Gold, 150 Lumber

Storm Hammers allows the Gryphon Rider's hammer attack to blow through the first target and deal damage to the enemy *behind* it. This is especially important when attacking large groups of land units.

HUMANS: THE ALLIANCE

HUMAN UNITS

PEASANT

Cost: ⬤ 90 🔺 0 🔔 1

The Peasant is the basic worker of the Human race. This unit is capable of harvesting both Gold and Lumber equally well, and can even repair damaged buildings. Four Peasants can work together to build a Farm in mere seconds. You can also use your Peasants as weapons by converting them into Militia with the Call to Arms, but we recommend resorting to this tactic only when absolutely necessary.

Armor: 0
Damage: 5-6
Speed: Slow
Range: Melee
Hit Points: 220
Mana: N/A

Abilities: Repair, Build Structure, Gather, Call to Arms (from Town Hall)

CALL TO ARMS

This ability turns your everyday Peasants into Militia that vigorously defend your turf. When your forces are wearing thin, summon some Peasants near the home camp by using Call to Arms and they'll set their pedestrian tasks aside mommentarily to fight for your survival!

MILITIA

Cost: ⬤ 80 🔺 0 🔔 1

Peasants can be turned into Militia by using the Call to Arms skill in the Town Hall/Keep/Castle. Once converted to Militia, the Peasants remain in that form for 45 seconds. If your Footmen and Knights have their sword and armor upgrades, the Militia will also benefit from these!

Armor: 4
Damage: 12-13
Speed: Average

Range: Melee
Hit Points: 220
Mana: N/A

FOOTMAN

Cost: ⬤ 160 🔺 0 🔔 2

The Footman is the base soldier for your army and will be used early in situations where you need a quick defense for your base, and later to comprise the bulk of a large attack force. The Footman can attack only land units, but uses just two food units, making this fighter far less costly than a Knight.

Armor: 2
Damage: 12-13
Speed: Average
Range: Melee

Hit Points: 420
Mana: N/A
Abilities: Defend

DEFEND

Research Cost: 150 Gold, 100 Lumber

Defend increases the defensive capabilities of the Footmen by 30% from ranged attackers, such as archers. The trade-off is that the Footmen, in turn, lose 30% of their movement speed, dropping their speed from average to slow. Still, this is an important skill in the heat of battle, especially when your Footmen are fighting ranged-weapon units like those of the Night Elves.

RIFLEMAN

Cost: ⬤ 240 🔺 30 🗡 3

Riflemen are ranged attackers that can attack enemy land units most effectively from hills. Because they can fire over distances, they are the first producible unit that can attack air units (Heroes excluded). The Riflemen are more expensive and require more resources (3 units of food each), but their attack damage is nearly double that of the Footmen.

Armor: 0	Range: 400
Damage: 18-24	Hit Points: 520
Speed: Average	Mana: N/A

TIP

Riflemen are excellent units for shooting at enemy air units. Enemies can fly over your camp with Gyrocopters or Hippogryphs (or even Druid Crows) to survey the situation. A few Riflemen firing from your base will most certainly discourage this. Although Guard Towers are also excellent for this purpose, they are immobile, whereas Riflemen can aggressively pursue the enemy.

KNIGHT

Cost: ⬤ 290 🔺 60 🗡 4

The Knight is the most powerful melee unit for the Human race. Mounted on a horse, this unit is capable of covering distances faster than the Footman. A large group of Knights will strike fear into the hearts of even seasoned warriors. Because of their quickness, it's usually beneficial to group Knights together or with other units that share a fast speed rating. Knights are excellent quick-response units for putting out fires or riding into the enemy's camp for a surprise attack.

Armor: 6	Range: Melee
Damage: 21-29	Hit Points: 800
Speed: Fast	Mana: N/A

PRIEST

Cost: ⬤ 160 🔺 10 🗡 2

The Priest is a spell-caster with the ability to Heal. He can also summon Inner Fire, a defensive spell used on friendly units to improve their damage by 10% and armor by +5. The Priest's Dispel Magic spell takes the teeth out of an enemy Hero's magical attack. As a rule, every group should have at least one Priest in it, if for no other reason than to heal heavily damaged (and expensive) units. Using the Heal skill saves precious resources over the course of a game. Dispel Magic should be used whenever engaging the enemy, because you never know when they may use magic on your group. With this spell active, your foes' magical attacks are useless.

Armor: 0	Mana: 200
Damage: 8-9	Abilities: Heal,
Speed: Average	Dispel Magic,
Range: 600	Inner Fire
Hit Points: 220	

NOTE

Inner Fire and Dispel Magic do not have a cooldown period, so as long as there is enough Mana, these spells can be cast continuously.

TIP

Priests can heal all non-mechanical units in your arsenal, as well as any allied units! Many successful multiplayer teams move groups of Priests around to heal their troops.

HEAL (AUTOCAST)

Mana Cost: 5

The ability to heal is absolutely invaluable. When invoked, every 5 units of Mana heals 25 hit points to the targeted unit. Heal does not work, however, against mechanical units like Steam Tanks.

DISPEL MAGIC

Research Cost: 150 Gold
Mana Cost: 75

Dispel Magic removes all magical spells within the targeted area (when the spell is cast, an area of effect must be chosen). This is, of course, very important when the enemy is pounding you into the Stone Age with a magical spell, but it also damages summoned creatures.

Requires: Priest Adept Training

INNER FIRE (AUTOCAST)

Research Cost: 250 Gold, 100 Lumber
Mana Cost: 25

Inner Fire increases a friendly unit's attack rating by 10% and adds 5 points to its armor rating. It lasts 60 seconds and has no cooldown period, so it can be cast repeatedly to upgrade multiple units.

Requires: Priest Master Training

SORCERESS

This powerful magical unit can cast Slow, which decreases movement and attack speed on enemy units. The Sorceress can also learn Invisibility to temporarily cloak one of your units from enemy sight. With her Polymorph spell, the Sorceress can transform an enemy unit into an animal.

Cost: ⬤ 180 ♦ 20 🔹 2	
Armor: 0	Mana: 200
Damage: 11-14	Abilities: Slow,
Speed: Average	Invisibility,
Range: 600	Polymorph
Hit Points: 250	

SLOW (AUTOCAST)
Mana Cost: 50

Slow can be cast on individual enemy units only. When invoked, it slows the enemy unit's attack rate by 25% and its movement rate by 60%. Obviously, this spell is best used on powerful enemies, such as Heroes, to get the maximum effect. Slow lasts for 60 seconds and has no cooldown period, so it can be cast repeatedly.

INVISIBILITY

Research Cost: 150 Gold
Mana Cost: 50

This spell makes the target unit invisible for 120 seconds. The catch, however, is that the unit will be revealed if it attacks or uses any abilities during this time period.

Requires: Sorceress Adept Training

POLYMORPH

Research Cost: 250 Gold, 100 Lumber
Mana Cost: 220

Polymorph turns the targeted enemy unit (with the exception of Heroes) into a sheep. This wooly creature retains that unit's hit points and armor, but cannot attack. The spell lasts for 60 seconds.

Requires: Sorceress Master Training

> **TIP**
>
> Using the Invisibility spell in combination with the Archmage's Mass Teleport is a phenomenal strategic formula. Make a unit invisible, then send it into the middle of the enemy's camp. Once in place, cast Mass Teleport on that unit. When a bevy of your forces suddenly appear out of thin air, your adversary will be in for a *very* big surprise!

MORTAR TEAM

Cost: 210   70   3

The Mortar Team is a pair of Dwarves who fire long-range mortars for substantial siege damage. They are exceptionally effective against buildings, but less so against units. They are also very slow moving and vulnerable to enemy melee attacks. Although unable to attack air units, they can be used to clear dense forests to reach otherwise inaccessible areas.

Armor: 0
Damage: 52-64
Speed: Slow
Range: 1000
Hit Points: 380

Mana: N/A
Abilities: Flare
(researched at
Workshop)

> **TIP**
>
> Mortar Teams can blow apart areas of forest to allow your Peasants to access a hidden Gold Mine. Another more nefarious use for Mortar Teams is to destroy an enemy's forests to cut off their supply of Lumber. Although largely ineffective with Night Elf enemies because they don't chop down trees, this tactic works with diabolical success on the other three races—all of whom are very dependent on large tracts of forests.

FLARE

Research Cost: 100 Gold, 50 Lumber

Flare illuminates one area of the map, giving the Mortar Team a one-time shot to see what's going on somewhere on the map. Each Mortar Team gets only *one* Flare (once the Flare upgrade is researched at the Workshop), so use it wisely.

GYROCOPTER

Cost: 220 | 60 | 2

The Gyrocopter is a swift aerial reconnaissance machine that can attack only air units until it has been afforded the Gyrocopter Bomb upgrade. Initially, this flying machine is usually used for exploring or scouting enemy locations, but once upgraded, it can hold its own in battle. In fact, a group of five or six Gyrocopters can be very helpful for managing skirmishes all over the map. Because of their speed and lofty advantage, they can get across the map much quicker than ground units.

Armor: 2
Damage: 25-30
Speed: Fast
Range: 500

Hit Points: 350
Mana: N/A
Abilities: True Sight

TRUE SIGHT

True Sight is always active and enables Gyrocopters to see invisible enemy units.

GYROCOPTER BOMBS

Research Cost: 150 Gold, 100 Lumber

Allows Gyrocopters to attack ground units. Before attaining this upgrade, these Human flying machines are completely vulnerable to attacks from the ground. Get this upgrade as soon as you can, so your Gyrocopters can defend themselves.

Requires: Castle

STEAM TANK

Cost: 230 | 60 | 3

The Steam Tank is a heavily armored troop transport that can substantially damage enemy buildings, but cannot attack enemy units.

Armor: 2
Damage: 45-55
Speed: Slow

Range: 192
Hit Points: 700
Mana: N/A

GRYPHON RIDER

Cost: 330 | 70 | 4

The Gryphon Rider is the flying tank of the Human arsenal and is an awesome weapon when used in groups. This unit is mounted by a Dwarven hammer-thrower who can toss his weapons at either air or ground units, delivering a powerful blow. If Storm Hammers has been researched at the Gryphon Aviary, the hammer attack passes through the enemy and hits an enemy behind it. Attain Animal War Training in the Barracks to increase the hit points of these units.

Armor: 0
Damage: 45-55
Speed: Average

Range: 450
Hit Points: 650
Mana: N/A

HUMAN HEROES

NOTE •

The first Hero (for any race) is always free, with the only cost being the food cost of having the Hero active.

ARCHMAGE

Cost: ⬤ 500 ◭ 100 🔷 5

The Archmage is a mystical Hero, skilled at ranged assaults. He can learn Blizzard, Summon Water Elemental, Brilliance Aura, and Mass Teleport with the ability to attack both land and air units.

Weapon Type: Normal
Armor Type: Hero
Range: 600
Primary Attribute: Intelligence
Strength Bonus per Level: 1.8
Agility Bonus per Level: 1

Intelligence Bonus per Level: 3.2
Day Sight: 1800
Night Sight: 800
Build Time: 55
Move Speed: Fast
Production Hot Key: A

LEVEL	ATTACK (GROUND/AIR)	ARMOR	STRENGTH	AGILITY	INTELLIGENCE	HIT POINTS	MANA
1	21-27 [24 avg]	3	14	17	19	450	285
2	24-30 [27 avg]	3	15	18	22	475	330
3	27-33 [30 avg]	4	17	19	25	525	375
4	30-36 [33 avg]	4	19	20	28	575	420
5	33-39 [36 avg]	4	21	21	31	625	465
6	37-43 [40 avg]	5	23	22	35	675	525
7	40-46 [43 avg]	5	24	23	38	700	570
8	43-49 [46 avg]	5	26	24	41	750	615
9	46-52 [49 avg]	6	28	25	44	800	660
10	49-55 [52 avg]	6	30	26	47	850	705

BLIZZARD

Mana Cost: 75

Calls down blasts of freezing ice shards that damage units in a target area—excellent for pummeling tightly grouped bands of enemy units and structures.

Level 1: 6 waves of attack at 30 damage each
Level 2: 8 waves of attack at 40 damage each
Level 3: 10 waves of attack at 50 damage each

SUMMON WATER ELEMENTAL

Mana Cost: 140

Summons a Water Elemental to attack the Archmage's enemies; lasts for 60 seconds.

| Level 1: 450 hit points, light damage |
| Level 2: 675 hit points, moderate damage |
| Level 3: 900 hit points, heavy damage |

BRILLIANCE AURA

Gives additional Mana regeneration to nearby friendly units.

| Level 1: Adds 100% Mana regeneration |
| Level 2: Adds 200% Mana regeneration |
| Level 3: Adds 300% Mana regeneration |

MASS TELEPORT (ULTIMATE)

Mana Cost: 100

Teleports the Archmage and nearby friendly units to a target friendly non-flying unit. Best used in conjunction with Invisibility. By cloaking a unit and sneaking them into the enemy base, you can Mass Teleport a group of units in for the kill. This ability is not available until the Archmage reaches level 6.

MOUNTAIN KING

Cost: ⬤ 500 ⬛ 100 ▨ 5

This warrior Hero is adept at offensive combat and disrupting enemy troops. He can learn Storm Bolt, Thunder Clap, Bash, and Avatar. He can attack only land units.

Weapon Type: Normal
Armor Type: Hero
Range: Melee
Primary Attribute: Strength
Strength Bonus per Level: 3
Agility Bonus per Level: 1.5

Intelligence Bonus per Level: 1.5
Day Sight: 1800
Night Sight: 800
Build Time: 55
Move Speed: Average
Production Hot Key: M

LEVEL	ATTACK (GROUND/AIR)	ARMOR	STRENGTH	AGILITY	INTELLIGENCE	HIT POINTS	MANA
1	26-36 [31 avg]/None	2	24	11	15	700	225
2	29-39 [34 avg]/None	3	27	12	16	775	240
3	32-42 [37 avg]/None	3	30	14	18	850	270
4	35-45 [40 avg]/None	4	33	15	19	925	285
5	38-48 [43 avg]/None	4	36	17	21	1000	315
6	41-51 [46 avg]/None	4	39	18	22	1075	330
7	44-54 [49 avg]/None	5	42	20	24	1150	360
8	47-57 [52 avg]/None	5	45	21	25	1225	375
9	50-60 [49 avg]/None	6	48	23	27	1300	405
10	53-63 [52 avg]/None	6	51	24	28	1375	420

STORM BOLT

Mana Cost: 75

A magical hammer that causes damage and stuns the target when thrown. Often used to destroy an enemy Hero approaching in an attack wave.

Cooldown: 9 Seconds

Level 1: 100 damage and a 5-second stun
Level 2: 200 damage and a 7-second stun
Level 3: 300 damage and a 9-second stun

BASH

Gives a chance that the Mountain King's attack will do 25 bonus damage and stun his opponent for two seconds (one second for Heroes). This is a passive ability.

Level 1: 15% chance, damage +25
Level 2: 25% chance, damage +25
Level 3: 35% chance, damage +25

THUNDER CLAP
Mana Cost: 100

Slams the ground, damaging and slowing nearby enemy land units. Best used in fierce melee combat where your Mountain King is surrounded by foes.

Cooldown: 6 seconds

Level 1: 70 damage, 25% move, 25% attack
Level 2: 110 damage, 50% move, 50% attack
Level 3: 150 damage, 75% move, 75% attack

 ## AVATAR (ULTIMATE)

The Mountain King gets 5 bonus armor, 500 extra hit points, a boost of 20 damage, and spell immunity for 60 seconds. While in the form of an Avatar, the Mountain King is significantly larger in size. Best used in the thick of battle. This ability is not available until the Mountain King reaches level 6.

Mana Cost: 150
Cooldown: 120 seconds

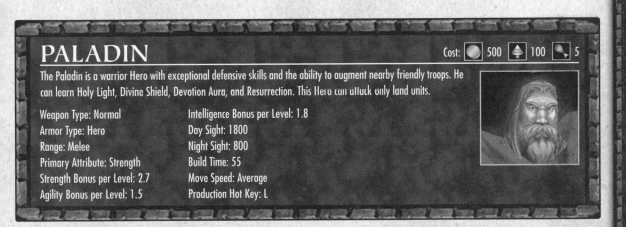

PALADIN

Cost: 500 100 5

The Paladin is a warrior Hero with exceptional defensive skills and the ability to augment nearby friendly troops. He can learn Holy Light, Divine Shield, Devotion Aura, and Resurrection. This Hero can attack only land units.

Weapon Type: Normal
Armor Type: Hero
Range: Melee
Primary Attribute: Strength
Strength Bonus per Level: 2.7
Agility Bonus per Level: 1.5

Intelligence Bonus per Level: 1.8
Day Sight: 1800
Night Sight: 800
Build Time: 55
Move Speed: Average
Production Hot Key: L

LEVEL	ATTACK (GROUND/AIR)	ARMOR	STRENGTH	AGILITY	INTELLIGENCE	HIT POINTS	MANA
1	24-34 [29 avg]/None	4	22	13	17	650	255
2	26-36 [31 avg]/None	4	24	14	18	700	270
3	29-39 [34 avg]/None	5	27	16	20	775	300
4	32-42 [37 avg]/None	5	30	17	22	850	330
5	34-44 [39 avg]/None	6	32	19	24	900	360
6	37-47 [42 avg]/None	6	35	20	26	975	390
7	40-50 [45 avg]/None	7	38	22	27	1050	405
8	42-52 [47 avg]/None	7	40	23	29	1100	435
9	45-55 [50 avg]/None	8	43	25	31	1175	465
10	48-58 [53 avg]/None	8	46	26	33	1250	495

HUMAN HEROES

HOLY LIGHT

Mana Cost: 75

Summons energy that can mete out half-damage to an undead enemy unit or heal a living friendly unit. The power of this spell increases as points are put into it. It's especially useful against undead opponents.

Cooldown: 5 Seconds

Level 1: Heals for 200 Hit Points
Level 2: Heals for 400 Hit Points
Level 3: Heals for 600 Hit Points

DEVOTION AURA

Gives additional armor to nearby friendly units. Armor is always important, so an extra armor level of +3 for all units near the Paladin can truly make the difference in a close battle.

Level 1: Increases base armor by 1
Level 2: Increases base armor by 2
Level 3: Increases base armor by 3

DIVINE SHIELD

Mana Cost: 125

An impenetrable shield surrounds the Paladin, protecting him from all damage and spells for 10 seconds. Putting more points into Divine Shield increases its duration. This spell can turn the tide of a battle, especially at level 3. This is particularly true when the enemy focuses their attacks on your Paladin, which is common in multiplayer action. Casting Divine Shield in this situation forces the enemy to redirect its attack while your other forces take advantage of this opportunity.

Cooldown: 75 Seconds

Level 1: Lasts 10 Seconds
Level 2: Lasts 20 Seconds
Level 3: Lasts 30 Seconds

RESURRECTION (ULTIMATE)

Restores life to the corpses of up to six friendly ground units within a target area. This is a crucial skill when you're losing in the heat of a battle. Position the Paladin near the corpses of Knights and other high-level units before you use it. This ability is not available until the Paladin reaches level 6.

Mana Cost: 250
Cooldown: 240 Seconds

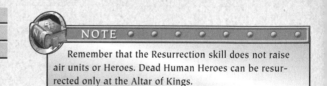

NOTE

Remember that the Resurrection skill does not raise air units or Heroes. Dead Human Heroes can be resurrected only at the Altar of Kings.

UNDEAD
THE SCOURGE

UNDEAD TECH TREE

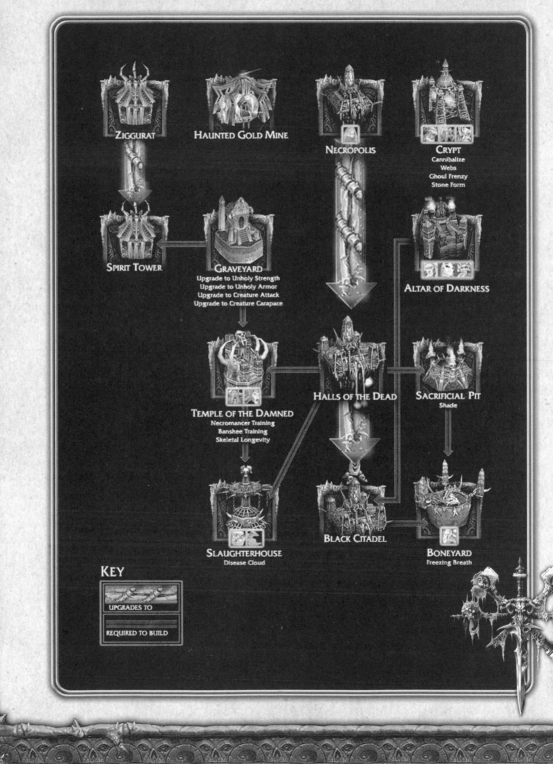

ZIGGURAT

HAUNTED GOLD MINE

NECROPOLIS

CRYPT
Cannibalize
Webs
Ghoul Frenzy
Stone Form

SPIRIT TOWER

GRAVEYARD
Upgrade to Unholy Strength
Upgrade to Unholy Armor
Upgrade to Creature Attack
Upgrade to Creature Carapace

ALTAR OF DARKNESS

TEMPLE OF THE DAMNED
Necromancer Training
Banshee Training
Skeletal Longevity

HALLS OF THE DEAD

SACRIFICIAL PIT
Shade

SLAUGHTERHOUSE
Disease Cloud

BLACK CITADEL

BONEYARD
Freezing Breath

KEY

UPGRADES TO

REQUIRED TO BUILD

UNDEAD TRUISMS

Here are a few thoughts to consider when playing as the Scourge:

❖ Remember that Critter carcasses can also be used by your Necromancers for Raise Dead. One Critter body gives a Necromancer two Skeleton Warriors.

❖ Use Meat Wagons to carry bodies to the battlefield for your Necromancers. This supplies them with a load of carcasses to raise into Skeleton Warriors.

❖ In battle, keep the Necromancers safe behind the front lines and place Raise Dead on Autocast. This ensures that plenty of Skeleton Warriors will join your cause as the battle proceeds.

❖ The Undead's ability to Haunt remote Gold Mines without having to build a primary building nearby gives them a distinct advantage when it comes to harvesting this precious resource. When moving around a map to capture Gold Mines, take an Acolyte along with your attack group so that they can summon Haunt Gold Mine after the Creeps or enemies have been destroyed.

❖ Because Undead structures are summoned, and not built, you can save plenty of resources (and food) by creating only as many Acolytes as are needed to collect Gold. Technically, you need just *one* Acolyte to summon an entire base!

❖ The Death Knight's Unholy Aura is important to the success of the Undead. Like the Orc's Endurance Aura, Unholy Aura also increases movement speed, but the real bonus comes in hit point regeneration. At level 3, hit points regenerate at a rate of 150%, which means less money spent on replacement units.

UNDEAD TECH TREE

UNDEAD STRUCTURES

NOTE

With the exception of the Necropolis and Haunted Gold Mines, all Undead structures must be built on Blighted ground. This is created by building near the edge of existing Blight. Building a Necropolis on healthy turf very quickly spreads Blight to the soil around it, clearing the way for further Scourge development.

NECROPOLIS

Cost: 350 0

The Necropolis is the primary structure for the Undead Scourge. It trains Acolytes and receives Lumber gathered by Ghouls. Upgrading to the Halls of Dead and the Black Citadel enables the production of additional types of units and structures. The Necropolis does not need to be near a Gold Mine in order for Gold to be collected—this is different from all the other races, and gives the Undead a unique advantage for gathering this precious metal from remote areas.

Upgrades: N/A
Building Upgrades: Halls of the Dead, Black Citadel
Creates: Acolytes
Hit Points: 1500
Armor: 5

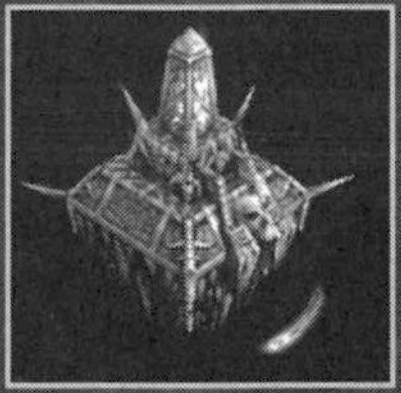

HALLS OF THE DEAD

Cost: 300 150

Upgrading a Necropolis to the Halls of the Dead unlocks the production of additional Undead structures and units.

Upgrades: N/A
Building Upgrades: Black Citadel
Creates: Acolytes
Abilities: Can attack land and air units
Hit Points: 2000
Armor: 5
Damage: 41-50

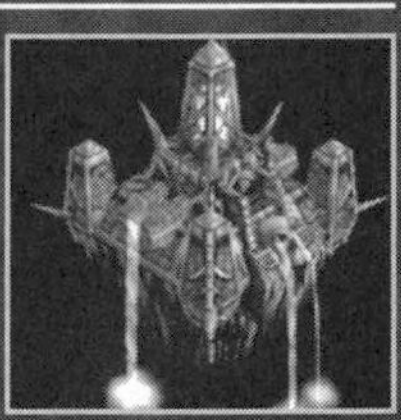

BLACK CITADEL

Cost: 345 150

Upgrading the Halls of the Dead to a Black Citadel unlocks the production of additional Undead structures and units.

Upgrades: N/A
Creates: Acolytes
Abilities: Can attack land and air units
Hit Points: 2300
Armor: 5
Damage: 49-60

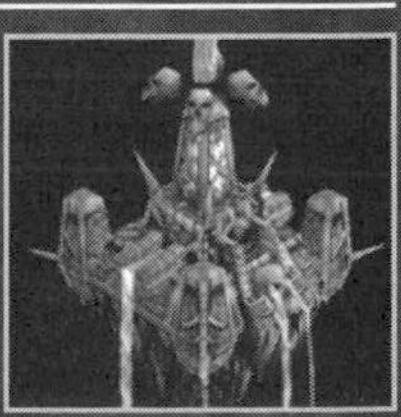

CRYPT

Cost:  280 ⬆ 50

The Crypt is the primary troop production building for the Undead. It trains Ghouls, Crypt Fiends, and Gargoyles. The Crypt also contains the upgrades Ghoul Frenzy, Cannibalize, Stone Form, and Web. As with the other races, you may want to build two Crypts to increase troop production and upgrade more quickly.

Upgrades: Cannibalize, Ghoul Frenzy, Web, Stone Form
Creates: Ghouls, Crypt Fiends, Gargoyles
Armor: 5
Hit Points: 1300

CANNIBALIZE

Research Cost: 75 Gold, 0 Lumber

Cannibalize allows Ghouls to eat corpses to heal themselves. This important ability can extend the life of a Ghoul considerably, but don't delay these grisly health-boosting meals, because corpses quickly decompose and become unusable after falling to the ground.

WEB (AUTOCAST)

Research Cost: 100 Gold, 50 Lumber

Web is a skill that binds a targeted enemy air unit to the ground so that it can be attacked by ground units. Use it if your forces lack any ground-to-air attack abilities. It's even a good idea to keep at least one Crypt Fiend at your base to bring down enemies attacking from the sky.

Requires: Graveyard, Halls of the Dead

GHOUL FRENZY

Research Cost: 150 Gold, 100 Lumber

Ghoul Frenzy increases both the movement speed and attack rate of Ghouls. The 25% boost to the attack rate is a significant amount, especially when using a pack of Ghouls as an attack/defense force.

Requires: Graveyard, Black Citadel

STONE FORM

Research Cost: 150 Gold, 75 Lumber

Transforms the Gargoyle into a statue with a very high armor and regeneration rating. Although unable to attack or move when in Stone Form, the Gargoyle can regenerate quickly to fight again with restored health. When a group of Gargoyles takes significant damage, move them to safety and invoke Stone Form so they can recuperate.

Requires: Graveyard, Black Citadel

HAUNTED GOLD MINE

Cost:  300 ⬆ 170

While not a traditional structure, a Haunted Gold Mine is the only non-Necropolis structure that can exist on Blight-free ground. Haunting a Gold Mine corrupts it so that Acolytes may enter and collect its treasures.

Upgrades: N/A
Armor: 5
Hit Points: 800

GRAVEYARD

Cost: ○ 250 ◭ 0

The Graveyard is the place to gain attack and armor upgrades for the Undead units. This building also produces bodies that can be raised to fight for the Necromancer, and serves as a Lumber drop-off point for harvesting Ghouls.

Upgrades: Unholy/Improved/Advanced Unholy Strength, Creature/Improved/ Advanced Creature Attack, Unholy/Improved/Advanced Unholy Armor, Creature/Improved/ Advanced Creature Carapace
Armor: 5
Hit Points: 900

 ### UNHOLY STRENGTH

Research Cost: 125 Gold, 50 Lumber

Increases the attack damage of Ghouls, Abominations, Meat Wagons, and Skeleton Warriors.

 ### IMPROVED UNHOLY STRENGTH

Research Cost: 250 Gold, 100 Lumber

Further increases the attack damage of Ghouls, Meat Wagons, Abominations, and Skeleton Warriors.
Requires: Halls of the Dead

 ### ADVANCED UNHOLY STRENGTH

Research Cost: 375 Gold, 150 Lumber

The highest upgrade for the attack damage of Ghouls, Meat Wagons, Abominations, and Skeleton Warriors.
Requires: Black Citadel

 ### CREATURE ATTACK

Research Cost: 150 Gold, 50 Lumber

Increases the attack damage of Crypt Fiends, Gargoyles, and Frost Wyrms.

 ### IMPROVED CREATURE ATTACK

Research Cost: 225 Gold, 100 Lumber

Further increases the attack damage of Crypt Fiends, Gargoyles, and Frost Wyrms.
Requires: Halls of the Dead

 ### ADVANCED CREATURE ATTACK

Research Cost: 300 Gold, 150 Lumber

The highest upgrade to increase the attack damage of Crypt Fiends, Gargoyles, and Frost Wyrms.
Requires: Black Citadel

 ### UNHOLY ARMOR

Research Cost: 125 Gold, 50 Lumber

Increases the armor of Ghouls, Abominations, and Skeleton Warriors.

 ### IMPROVED UNHOLY ARMOR

Research Cost: 250 Gold, 100 Lumber

Further increases the armor of Ghouls, Abominations, and Skeleton Warriors.
Requires: Halls of the Dead

 ### ADVANCED UNHOLY ARMOR

Research Cost: 375 Gold, 150 Lumber

The highest upgrade for an increase in the armor of Ghouls, Abominations, and Skeleton Warriors.
Requires: Black Citadel

 ### CREATURE CARAPACE

Research Cost: 150 Gold, 75 Lumber

Increases the armor of Crypt Fiends, Gargoyles, and Frost Wyrms.

 ### IMPROVED CREATURE CARAPACE

Research Cost: 250 Gold, 150 Lumber

Further increases the armor of Crypt Fiends, Gargoyles, and Frost Wyrms.
Requires: Halls of the Dead

ADVANCED CREATURE CARAPACE

Research Cost: 350 Gold, 225 Lumber

The highest upgrade to increase the armor of Crypt Fiends, Gargoyles, and Frost Wyrms to their maximum levels.
Requires: Black Citadel

ZIGGURAT

Cost: ⬤ 150 ⬆ 50

This is the backbone of the Undead economy. The Ziggurat provides food to the Scourge, and can also be upgraded to a Spirit Tower, assuming an additional role as a defensive structure that can attack land and air units.

Building Upgrades: Spirit Tower
Upgrades: N/A
Armor: 5
Hit Points: 550

SPIRIT TOWER

Cost: ⬤ 120 ⬆ 40

The Spirit Tower is the primary defensive structure for the Undead. Because there are usually several Ziggurats in your town, it's easy (although expensive) to upgrade them all into Spirit Towers that will work to defend, as well as feed.

Armor: 5
Hit Points: 550
Damage: 27-32
Requires: Graveyard

SLAUGHTERHOUSE

Cost: ⬤ 240 ⬆ 80

Produces Abominations and Meat Wagons, and contains the Disease Cloud upgrades. Abominations are the heavy-duty attack units of the Undead Scourge, so a Slaughterhouse is essential to prevail in melee combat.

Upgrades: Disease Cloud
Creates: Meat Wagon, Abomination
Armor: 5
Hit Points: 1200
Requires: Halls of the Dead, Graveyard

 ## DISEASE CLOUD
Research Cost: 225 Gold, 125 Lumber

Abominations with this upgrade passively infect nearby enemy units with a disease. Disease Cloud also leaves behind a deadly gas when an Abomination dies or a Meat Wagon attacks.

Requires: Black Citadel

ALTAR OF DARKNESS

Cost: 300 ⬆ 100

Creates and revives the Undead Heroes. It's a good idea to place more than one Altar of Darkness on the map to resurrect slain Heroes in alternate locations (other than the main base). This may be costly, however, since the Altar of Darkness must be constructed on Blighted ground.

Upgrades: N/A
Creates: Death Night, Dreadlord, Lich
Abilities: N/A
Armor: 5
Hit Points: 900

TEMPLE OF THE DAMNED

Cost: 225 ⬆ 80

This is a spell-caster production building. The Temple of the Damned trains and upgrades Necromancers and Banshees. It also provides Skeletal Longevity.

Upgrades: Skeletal Longevity, Necromancer
   Adept/Master Training, Banshee
   Adept/Master Training
Creates: Necromancer, Banshee
Armor: 5
Hit Points: 1100
Requires: Halls of the Dead, Graveyard

SKELETAL LONGEVITY
Research Cost: 100 Gold, 75 Lumber

Increases the duration of raised Skeleton Warriors by 15 seconds. That may not seem like a great deal of time, but it can make a huge difference in combat. Many battles are resolved in less than 30 seconds, so having the extra longevity for these units is very valuable.

NECROMANCER ADEPT TRAINING
Research Cost: 150 Gold, 0 Lumber

Adept Training for the Necromancer increases his Mana capacity and regeneration rate, as well as hit points and attack damage. It also enables the Necromancer to cast Unholy Frenzy.

BANSHEE ADEPT TRAINING
Research Cost: 150 Gold, 0 Lumber

Adept Training for the Banshee increases her Mana capacity and regeneration rate, as well as hit points and attack damage. It also enables her to cast Anti-Magic spell.

NECROMANCER MASTER TRAINING
Research Cost: 250 Gold, 100 Lumber

Further increases Necromancer's Mana capacity and regeneration rate, as well as hit points and attack damage. It also enables him to cast Cripple.
Requires: Black Citadel

BANSHEE MASTER TRAINING
Research Cost: 250 Gold, 100 Lumber

Master Training for the Banshee further increases her Mana capacity and regeneration rate, as well as hit points and attack damage. It also enables her to cast Possession.
Requires: Black Citadel

BONEYARD

Cost: 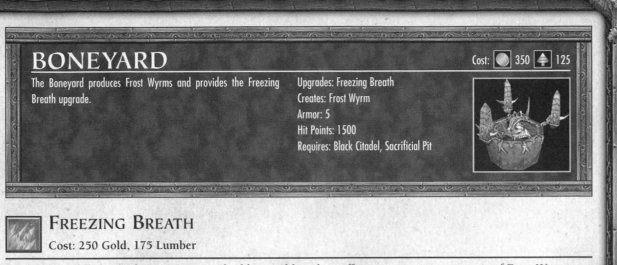 350 | 125

The Boneyard produces Frost Wyrms and provides the Freezing Breath upgrade.

Upgrades: Freezing Breath
Creates: Frost Wyrm
Armor: 5
Hit Points: 1500
Requires: Black Citadel, Sacrificial Pit

FREEZING BREATH

Cost: 250 Gold, 175 Lumber

Freezing Breath halts production in enemy buildings. Although its effects are temporary, a group of Frost Wyrms can severely limit an enemy's production of key units when attacking in unison.

SACRIFICIAL PIT

Cost: 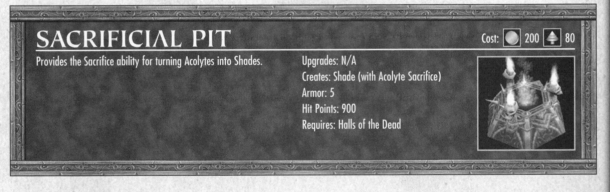 200 | 80

Provides the Sacrifice ability for turning Acolytes into Shades.

Upgrades: N/A
Creates: Shade (with Acolyte Sacrifice)
Armor: 5
Hit Points: 900
Requires: Halls of the Dead

SACRIFICE

Cost: 1 Food, Life of an Acolyte

Sacrifice is achieved by targeting an Acolyte for sacrifice and turning it into a Shade. Shades are lightly armored, cloaked spirits that can see invisible units, but cannot attack.

UNDEAD UNITS

UNDEAD: THE SCOURGE

ACOLYTE

Cost: 🔘 90 ⚔ 0 ⛏ 1

The Acolyte is the basic worker for the Undead Scourge. It can summon structures, harvest gold, and repair buildings. Acolytes can also be sacrificed to create Shades at a Sacrificial Pit.

Armor: 0
Damage: 9-10
Speed: Slow
Range: Melee
Hit Points: 180
Mana: N/A

Abilities: Summon Building, Unsummon Building, Repair, Sacrifice

SUMMON BUILDING

Summons the creation of a new structure. Once the building summoning process has been initiated, the Acolyte is free to move to another area to summon a new structure.

REPAIR (AUTOCAST)

Cost: Variable

Repairs Undead structures and mechanical units. Restore has an auto-cast ability that ensures any damage is repaired when an Acolyte is present.

UNSUMMON BUILDING

This ability is unique to the Scourge. Unsummon enables an Acolyte to reclaim 50% of the resources that originally went into the creation of a structure. This skill is vital when resources are scarce and just a small amount of Gold and/or Lumber can facilitate the revival of a Hero or the haunting of a Gold Mine.

SACRIFICE

Cost: The Life of the Acolyte

Sacrifice turns an Acolyte into a Shade at a Sacrificial Pit. Shades are invisible spirits that can see invisible enemy units.

SHADE

Cost: Sacrifice Acolyte at Sacrificial Pit

Shades can detect invisible foes. Although unable to attack, they are as effective as sentries that monitor enemy troop movement.

Armor: 0
Damage: No attack
Speed: Average

Hit Points: 250

GHOUL

Cost: 140 0 2

Although primarily the Undead's basic attack unit against enemy land units, Ghouls can also harvest Lumber. This effective gatherer and fierce fighter can also use the Cannibalize ability to heal itself.

Armor: 0
Damage: 12-14
Speed: Average
Range: Melee

Hit Points: 330
Mana: N/A
Abilities: Cannibalize, Ghoul Frenzy

CANNIBALIZE

Research Cost: 75 Gold

Consumes the nearest corpse to heal the Ghoul at a rate of 10 hit points per second. Research this skill as soon as possible if you have Ghouls in your plans.

GHOUL FRENZY

Research Cost: 150 Gold, 100 Lumber

Ghoul Frenzy increases both the movement speed and attack rate of Ghouls. The 25% boost to the attack rate is a significant amount, especially when using a pack of Ghouls as an attack/defense force.

CRYPT FIEND

Cost: 250 40 3

The Crypt Fiend is a combat support beast with a ranged attack. This unit can learn the Web ability, and attacks only ground units.

Armor: 0
Damage: 27-32
Speed: Average
Range: 550

Hit Points: 550
Mana: N/A
Abilities: Web
Requires: Graveyard

WEB (AUTOCAST)

Research Cost: 100 Gold, 50 Lumber

Binds an air unit in webbing, bringing it to the ground so that land units can attack it. Web lasts for 20 seconds and should be set for Autocast to automatically bring down your prey

Requires: Graveyard, Halls of the Dead

GARGOYLE

Cost: 220 30 2

These flying beasts can attack both land and air units. Gargoyles can improve their defenses with the Stone Form ability.

Armor: 5
Damage: 46-57 Melee (land), 16-18 Magic (air)
Speed: Average
Range: 300 (for ranged attack)

Hit Points: 400
Mana: N/A
Abilities: Stone Form
Requires: Graveyard, Black Citadel

STONE FORM

Research Cost: 150 Gold, 75 Lumber

Transforms the Gargoyles into a statue with high armor rating and a significantly improved regeneration rate. The catch is that it cannot attack while in this form. Be aware that once in Stone Form, a Gargoyle cannot immediately return to its true state until a cooldown of 30 seconds has transpired. The regeneration rate is 8 hit points per second and the armor rating is 15 while in Stone Form.

Requires: Graveyard, Black Citadel

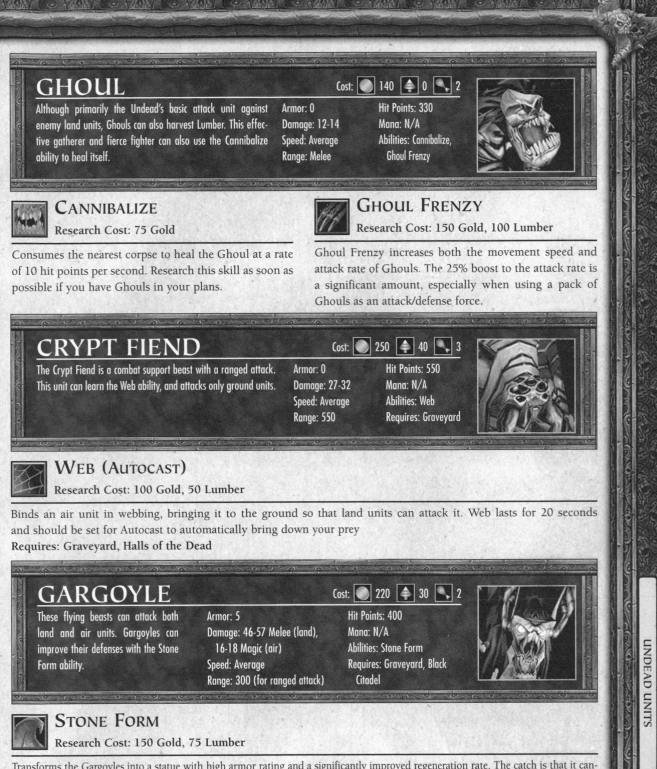

UNDEAD UNITS

SKELETON WARRIOR

Cost: 75 Mana from Necromancer

Skeleton Warriors are created from the Graveyard by the Necromancer. The Necromancer raises them from the dead at a cost of 75 Mana per pair. The brief life of these creatures can be increased by 15 seconds with the Skeletal Longevity upgrade in the Temple of the Damned.

Armor: 1	Range: Melee
Damage: 14-15	Hit Points: 180
Speed: Average	Mana: N/A

MEAT WAGON

Cost:  270 65 4

The Meat Wagon is a corpse storage machine that also serves as a catapult, vaulting portions of diseased bodies at the enemy and dealing significant damage. This effective weapon against land units and trees has three core uses. First, it's an excellent siege weapon on its own. Secondly, it can be used in combination with a Necromancer to create a group of skeletal warriors by loading the Meat Wagon up with corpses from a Graveyard, then transporting them to the attack site, and dropping the corpses for the Necromancer to create an Undead army. Finally, the Meat Wagon can greatly benefit Ghouls with the Cannibalize upgrade by supplying fresh corpses for the battling Ghouls to replenish their health.

Armor: 2	Mana: N/A
Damage: 82-102	Abilities: Get
(Flinging Corpses	Corpse, Drop all
with a Meat-a-Pult)	Corpses,
Speed: Slow	Disease Cloud
Range: 1000	
Hit Points: 450	

DISEASE CLOUD

Research Cost: 225 Gold, 125 Lumber

Adds a deadly gaseous force to Meat Wagon attacks, heaping extra damage on the enemy.
Requires: Black Citadel

ABOMINATION

Cost: 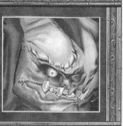 280 70 4

This eviscerated, hook- and claw-wielding melee unit is a powerful force against enemy land units. When upgraded with Disease Cloud Aura, this horrible beast will strike fear into the enemy's heart.

Armor: 2	Hit Points: 1080
Damage: 33-39	Mana: N/A
Speed: Average	Abilities: Disease
Range: Melee	Cloud

DISEASE CLOUD

Research Cost: 225 Gold, 125 Lumber

Spreads a deadly gas in proximity to the Abomination, damaging enemy units.
Requires: Black Citadel

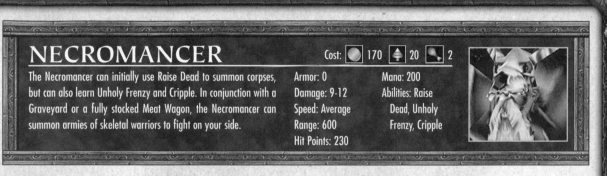

NECROMANCER

Cost: ⬤ 170 ⛰ 20 🔨 2

The Necromancer can initially use Raise Dead to summon corpses, but can also learn Unholy Frenzy and Cripple. In conjunction with a Graveyard or a fully stocked Meat Wagon, the Necromancer can summon armies of skeletal warriors to fight on your side.

Armor: 0
Damage: 9-12
Speed: Average
Range: 600
Hit Points: 230

Mana: 200
Abilities: Raise Dead, Unholy Frenzy, Cripple

RAISE DEAD

Mana Cost: 75

Raises two Skeleton Warriors to fight at the Necromancer's side. This spell has an auto-casting option that allows these minions to be raised repeatedly and automatically as the Necromancer's Mana level allows. Right-click on the Raise Dead icon if you want to deactivate Autocasting.

UNHOLY FRENZY

Research Cost: 150 Gold
Mana Cost: 50

Unholy Frenzy increases the attack rate of a targeted unit by 75% at a cost of four hit points per second to that unit. Despite the trade-off, Unholy Frenzy is definitely worthwhile.

CRIPPLE

Research Cost: 250 Gold, 100 Lumber
Mana Cost: 175, Cooldown: 10 Seconds

Reduces movement speed by 75%, attack rate by 50%, and damage by 50% of a targeted enemy unit. This is best used against powerful enemies, such as Heroes.

BANSHEE

Cost: ⬤ 180 ⛰ 30 🔨 2

This flying spell-caster can initially use Curse, which causes enemy units to miss their targets in combat. Banshees can also learn Anti-Magic Shell and Possession.

Armor: 0
Damage: 11-15
Speed: Average
Range: 500
Hit Points: 210

Mana: 200
Abilities: Curse, Anti-Magic Shell, Possession

CURSE (AUTOCAST)

Mana Cost: 50

This spell curses an enemy unit, causing it to suffer a 25% chance of missing their targets for 60 seconds. Cast it upon several of the tougher enemies in a melee battle to significantly reduce the amount of damage dealt to your frontline units.

ANTI-MAGIC SHELL

Research Cost: 150 Gold
Mana Cost: 75

Creates a barrier that stops spells from affecting the targeted unit for 90 seconds—very effective when used on Heroes or other valuable/expensive units.
Requires: Banshee Adept Training

TIP ● ● ● ● ● ● ● ● ● ● ● ● ● ● ● ● ● ●

Enemies often target your most powerful units when a battle begins. In your adversary's mind, eliminating your Heroes puts them one step closer to raising their victory flag, because magical support is critical to your success. The Anti-magic shell protects your Heroes from the enemy's magical attacks. The hope is that the enemy will waste a significant amount of Mana while futilely attempting to defeat your magic-safe Heroes.

POSSESSION

Research Cost: 250 Gold, 100 Lumber
Mana Cost: 250

Displaces the soul of a targeted unit, giving you control of it, but destroying the caster's body. The only caveat to Possession is that it cannot be used on Heroes or on flying units. Still, it's an effective way to rip away a powerful (and expensive) unit from the enemy.

Requires: Banshee Master Training, Black Citadel

TIP

The Possession spell of the Banshee can be used not only on enemy units, but also creeps, putting creatures like Ogres and Troll Berserkers under your control.

FROST WYRM

The Frost Wyrm is basically a flying, heavy assault weapon capable of dealing huge amounts of damage to the enemy, while also slowing its targets. Its ability to attack land and air units makes it well worth the considerable Gold and Food cost. When Freezing Breath has been upgraded, Frost Wyrm's attacks on enemy buildings stop production for 5 seconds. A continuous attack from the Frost Wyrm essentially prevents the targeted structure from producing anything during its final moments before complete destruction!

Cost: 450 · 120 · 7

Armor: 0	Hit Points: 1100
Damage: 85-105	Mana: N/A
Speed: Slow	Abilities: Freezing
Range: 300	Breath

FREEZING BREATH

Stops production of targeted structure for 5 seconds with each attack of Freezing Breath. You can also use this ability to freeze Towers so they cannot fire back.

UNDEAD HEROES

DEATH KNIGHT

Cost: ⬤ 500　⬆ 100　⛏ 5

This warrior Hero is the evil counterpart to the Human Paladin. He can learn Death Coil, Death Pact, Unholy Aura, and Animate Dead. Although able to attack only land units, the Death Knight is a strong melee fighter.

Weapon Type: Normal
Armor Type: Hero
Range: Melee
Primary Attribute: Strength
Strength Bonus per Level: 2.7
Agility Bonus per Level: 1.5

Intelligence Bonus per Level: 1.8
Day Sight: 1800
Night Sight: 800
Build Time: 55
Move Speed: Fast
Production Hot Key: D

LEVEL	ATTACK (GROUND/AIR)	ARMOR	STRENGTH	AGILITY	INTELLIGENCE	HIT POINT	MANA
1	25-35 [30 avg]/None	4	23	12	17	675	255
2	27-37 [32 avg]/None	4	25	13	18	725	270
3	30-40 [35 avg]/None	5	28	15	20	800	300
4	33-43 [39 avg]/None	5	31	16	22	875	330
5	35-45 [40 avg]/None	5	33	18	24	925	360
6	38-48 [43 avg]/None	6	36	19	26	1000	390
7	41-51 [46 avg]/None	6	39	21	27	1075	405
8	43-53 [48 avg]/None	7	41	22	29	1125	435
9	46-56 [51 avg]/None	7	44	24	31	1200	465
10	49-59 [54 avg]/None	8	47	25	33	1275	495

 ### DEATH COIL

Mana Cost: 75, Cooldown: 5 Seconds

A coil of death that can damage a living enemy unit or heal a friendly Undead unit.

Level 1: Heals for 200 Hit Points
Level 2: Heals for 400 Hit Points
Level 3: Heals for 600 Hit Points

 ### DEATH PACT

Mana Cost: 75, Cooldown: 30 Seconds

Kills targeted unit, converting 60% of its hit points into hit points for the Death Knight. Death Pact is a gruesome but effective way for this Hero to heal his battered body quickly. With additional points in this skill, the conversion of target unit hit points to health for the Death Knight increases greatly.

Level 1: 60% conversion
Level 2: 125% conversion
Level 3: 200% conversion

UNHOLY AURA

Increases the movement speed and life regeneration rate of nearby friendly units. As with any aura, Unholy Aura is passive, which means it's active at all times once you've invested some points in it.

| Level 1: 10% movement, 50% regeneration |
| Level 2: 20% movement, 100% regeneration |
| Level 3: 30% movement, 150% regeneration |

ANIMATE DEAD

Mana Cost: 300, Cooldown: 240 Seconds

Raises up to six dead units in an area to fight for the Death Knight for 120 seconds. This spell is best used in heavy-duty melee combat where plenty of bodies are littering the ground—ensure you have an adequate supply of Mana to invoke it when the opportunity arises. Animate Dead can be used near graveyards, as well as in conjunction with Meat Wagons as a way to augment an attack force. Animate Dead is not available until the Death Knight reaches level 6.

DREADLORD

Cost: 500 100 5

This is the Undead's cunning Hero, adept at controlling combat. The Dreadlord can learn Carrion Swarm, Sleep, Vampiric Aura, and Inferno, but can attack only land units.

Weapon Type: Normal
Armor Type: Hero
Range: Melee
Primary Attribute: Strength
Strength Bonus per Level: 2.5

Agility Bonus per Level: 1
Intelligence Bonus per Level: 2.5
Day Sight: 1800
Night Sight: 800
Build Time: 55

Move Speed: Average
Production Hot Key: E

LEVEL	ATTACK (GROUND/AIR)	ARMOR	STRENGTH	AGILITY	INTELLIGENCE	HIT POINTS	MANA
1	22-32 [27 avg]/None	3	20	16	18	600	270
2	24-34 [29 avg]/None	3	22	17	20	650	300
3	27-37 [32 avg]/None	3	25	18	23	725	345
4	29-39 [34 avg]/None	4	27	19	25	775	375
5	32-42 [37 avg]/None	4	30	20	28	850	420
6	34-44 [39 avg]/None	4	32	21	30	900	450
7	37-47 [42 avg]/None	5	35	22	33	975	495
8	39-49 [44 avg]/None	5	37	23	35	1025	525
9	42-52 [47 avg]/None	5	40	24	38	1100	570
10	44-54 [49 avg]/None	6	42	25	40	1150	600

CARRION SWARM

Mana Cost: 110, Cooldown: 10 Seconds

Sends a mob of bats to damage enemies in a line. Deals 100 damage to each enemy land unit, up to 300 damage total. This is best used when among a large group of enemies.

Level 1: 100 damage per unit, max 300
Level 2: 150 damage per unit, max 550
Level 3: 200 damage per unit, max 800

 # VAMPIRIC AURA

Units around the Dreadlord gain hit points when they strike a unit. Basically, Vampiric Aura sucks the life out of enemies (with every hit) and gives it to the nearby friendly units. This aura is extremely powerful, preserving vast amounts of resources throughout the course of a game by healing the Dread Lord's army.

Level 1: Gains 15% of attack damage.
Level 2: Gains 30% of attack damage.
Level 3: Gains 45% of attack damage.

 # SLEEP

Mana Cost: 100, Cooldown: 6 Seconds

Puts a target unit to sleep—a sleeping unit can be awakened by attacking it. It should also be noted that enemy Heroes are not immune to the Sleep spell, although they may have magic resistance that shortens the spell's effect. Still, it's very handy to be able to put an enemy's Hero to sleep while you attack the rest of the troops.

Level 1: 20-second sleep for 100 Mana
Level 2: 40-second sleep for 75 Mana
Level 3: 60-second sleep for 50 Mana

 # INFERNO

Mana Cost: 175, Cooldown: 180 Seconds

Inferno causes an Infernal to fall from the sky, raining down 50 points of damage and stunning nearby enemy units for four seconds. The Infernal will continue to thrash the opposition for 180 seconds and is also immune to magic! This ability is not available until the Dread Lord reaches level 6.

INFERNAL
Damage 49-60
Armor: 6
Range: Melee
Speed: Fast
Hit Points 1500
Abilities: Spell Immunity, Permanent Immolation

LICH

Cost: 🔵 500 🌲 100 👥 5

This mystical Hero is particularly adept at cold magic. The Lich can learn Frost Nova, Frost Armor, Dark Ritual, and Death and Decay, and can attack both land and air units.

Weapon Type: Normal
Armor Type: Hero
Range: 600
Primary Attribute: Intelligence
Strength Bonus per Level: 1.6

Agility Bonus per Level: 1
Intelligence Bonus per Level: 3.4
Day Sight: 1800
Night Sight: 800
Build Time: 55

Move Speed: Average
Production Hot Key: L

LEVEL	ATTACK (GROUND/AIR)	ARMOR	STRENGTH	AGILITY	INTELLIGENCE	HIT POINTS	MANA
1	22-28 [25 avg]/None	2	13	14	20	425	300
2	25-31 [28 avg]/None	3	14	15	23	450	345
3	28-34 [31 avg]/None	3	16	16	26	500	390
4	32-38 [35 avg]/None	3	17	17	30	525	450
5	35-41 [38 avg]/None	3	19	18	33	575	495
6	39-45 [42 avg]/None	4	21	19	37	625	555
7	42-48 [45 avg]/None	4	22	20	40	650	600
8	45-51 [48 avg]/None	4	24	21	43	700	645
9	49-55 [52 avg]/None	5	25	22	47	725	705
10	52-58 [55 avg]/None	5	27	23	50	775	750

FROST NOVA

Mana Cost: 125, Cooldown: 8 Seconds

Blasts units around the Lich with a wave of frost that deals 100 damage to the target, and 50 Nova damage. Cold damage slows the target unit's movement and attack rate for four seconds.

| Level 1: 100 Target damage, 50 Nova damage |
| Level 2: 100 Target damage, 100 Nova damage |
| Level 3: 100 Target damage, 150 Nova damage |

FROST ARMOR

Mana Cost: 50, Cooldown: 2 Seconds

Creates a shield of frost around a target unit. The shield adds 3 armor and slows melee units that attack it for 5 seconds. The actual Frost Armor spell lasts for 45 seconds.

| Level 1: Adds 3 armor, deals 5 seconds of cold |
| Level 2: Adds 5 armor, deals 5 seconds of cold |
| Level 3: Adds 7 armor, deals 5 seconds of cold |

DARK RITUAL

Mana Cost: 25, Cooldown: 15 Seconds

Sacrifices a target friendly unit to convert its hit points into Mana for the Lich.

| Level 1: 33% of hit points to Mana |
| Level 2: 66% of hit points to Mana |
| Level 3: 100% of hit points to Mana |

DEATH AND DECAY

Mana Cost: 250, Cooldown: 150 Seconds

Damages everything in its area of effect by 4 percent of its base hit points per second, including trees. This powerful spell lasts for 35 seconds and can even be used to clear a path through trees or to deny the enemy Lumber resources. Death and Decay can immediately decimate an entire area of forest, but is not available until the Lich reaches level 6.

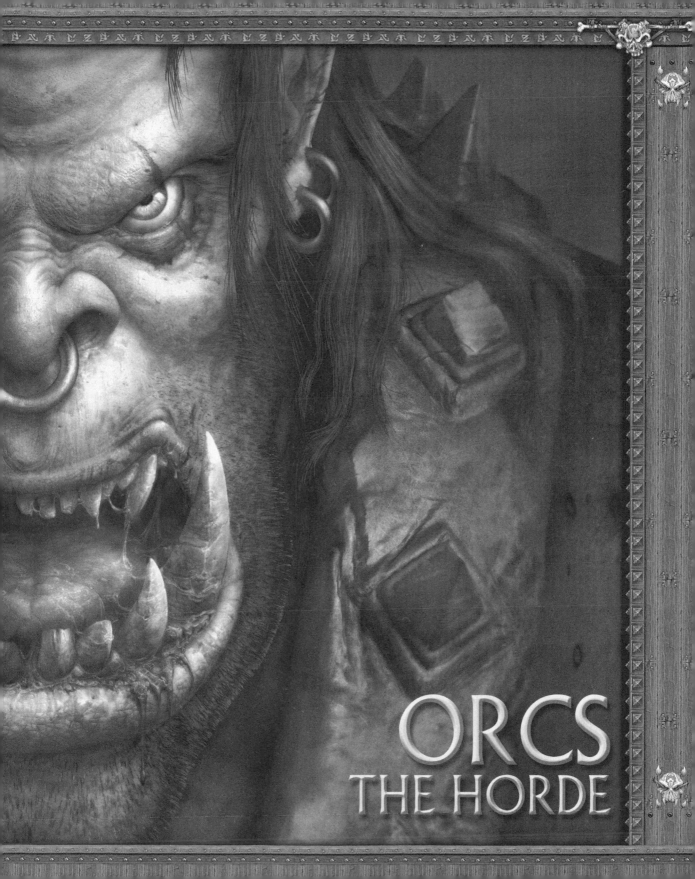

ORCS
THE HORDE

ORC TECH TREE

ORC BURROW

BARRACKS
Troll Regeneration
Berserker Strength

GREAT HALL
Pillage

ALTAR OF STORMS

WATCH TOWER

WAR MILL
Upgrade Melee Weapons
Upgrade Unit Armor
Upgrade Ranged Weapons
Upgrade Barricades

BEASTIARY
Weighted Nets
War Drums
Envenomed Weapons

STRONGHOLD

SPIRIT LODGE
Shaman Training
Witch Doctor Training

TAUREN TOTEM
Pulverize

FORTRESS

KEY

UPGRADES TO

REQUIRED TO BUILD

ORC TRUISMS

Here are a few thoughts to consider when playing as the Horde:

- It's possible to use Orc Burrows as an offensive weapon. Because the Peons that build them can immediately enter the Burrow and attack the enemy, these structures are often constructed in or near enemy bases!

- Intersperse Orc Burrows around your base. When the enemy attacks, have your Peons immediately get inside the Burrows both to protect themselves and also to defend the base. Once laden with Peons, Burrows are very effective at defense.

- When attacking an enemy base, the Far Seer's Earthquake is a very powerful spell that can destroy their food supply in one fell swoop. Use it to level food-producing structures, rendering your foe unable to build new units!

- The Far Seer's Chain Lightning is an excellent weapon to use on Wisps, Peons, Peasants, and Acolytes. When upgraded to level 3, one cast of Chain Lightning can simultaneously fry four or five of these units!

- Always take advantage of Auras, such as the Tauren Chieftain's Endurance Aura, which increases both the movement speed and the attack punch of Orc units.

- Use the Spiked Barricades upgrades. They are like a Thorns Aura for the Orc buildings—when the enemy hits them, the attacker takes damage, too!

- Always research the Pillage upgrade, because even if Orcs have depleted their resources, they can always attack an enemy building to increase their haul. This comes in handy when you're short on funds in a tight game and need just a small amount of Gold or Lumber to build an important unit or structure (like reviving a slain Hero). By attacking an enemy building, you may be able to recover the necessary resources you need.

ORC STRUCTURES

GREAT HALL

Cost: ⬤ 450 ▲ 150

The Great Hall is the primary Orc structure. It's used to train Peons and store resources that the Horde glean from the land. It can also be upgraded to a Stronghold and then subsequently to a Fortress, which enables the production of additional types of structures and units.

Upgrades: Pillage
Building Upgrades: Stronghold, Fortress
Starting Hit Points: 1400
Starting Armor: 5
Creates: Peons
Food Provided: 10

PILLAGE

Research Cost: 75 Gold, 25 Lumber

Allows Peons, Grunts, and Raiders to gather resources from enemy structures when attacking them. This skill becomes critical when your resources are depleted.

TIP

The Pillage ability can be used to gather valuable resources when you're in a pinch. It's best used against poorly-defended enemy outposts with a few buildings that your troops can loot without getting killed in the process. Sometimes, all you need is 30 Lumber to build a key unit or 100 Gold to revive a slain Hero—the Pillage upgrade is invaluable in those situations.

STRONGHOLD

Cost: ⬤ 310 ▲ 90

Upgrading a Great Hall to a Stronghold unlocks the production of additional Orc structures and units.

Upgrades: Pillage
Building Upgrades: Fortress
Starting Hit Points: 1600
Starting Armor: 5
Creates: Peons
Food Provided: 10

FORTRESS

Cost: ⬤ 345 ▲ 110

Upgrading a Stronghold to a Fortress unlocks the production of additional Orc structures and units.

Upgrades: Pillage
Starting Hit Points: 1800
Starting Armor: 5
Creates: Peons
Food Provided: 10

BARRACKS

Cost: ⬤ 260 ▲ 70

This is the primary troop production building for the Orcs. It trains Grunts, Troll Headhunters, and Catapults. The Berserker Strength and Troll Regeneration upgrades can be acquired here, as well.

Upgrades: Berserker Strength, Troll Regeneration
Creates: Grunts, Troll Headhunters, Catapults
Starting Hit Points: 1200
Armor: 5

BERSERKER STRENGTH

Research Cost: 200 Gold, 50 Lumber

Increases the damage Grunts inflict, while increasing their hit points. It's an important upgrade if you are planning on using these units extensively.

Requires: Fortress

TROLL REGENERATION

Research Cost: 125 Gold, 75 Lumber

Increases the hit point regeneration rate of both Headhunters and Witch Doctors. Your Headhunters will undoubtedly take damage while fending off aerial attacks on your base. The ability to regenerate quicker enables them to live longer, more effective lives.

Requires: Stronghold, War Mill

WAR MILL

Cost: ⬤ 240 ▲ 0

The War Mill serves as a drop-off point for harvested Lumber, but it's also an upgrade hub for increased armor, melee and ranged weapons, and Spiked Barricades. It never hurts to have more than one War Mill (each one by a large area of forest). Multiple mills increase your Lumber harvesting and enables you to upgrade your forces more quickly.

Upgrades: Steel/Thorium/Arcanite Melee Weapons, Steel/Thorium/Arcanite Range Weapons, Steel/Thorium/Arcanite Unit Armor, Spiked/Improved/Advanced Spiked Barricades
Creates: N/A
Armor: 5
Hit Points: 1000

STEEL MELEE WEAPONS

Research Cost: 100 Gold, 75 Lumber

Increases the attack damage inflicted by Raiders, Tauren, and Grunts.

THORIUM MELEE WEAPONS

Research Cost: 200 Gold, 125 Lumber

Further increases the attack damage inflicted by Raiders, Tauren, and Grunts.

Requires: Stronghold

ARCANITE MELEE WEAPONS
Research Cost: 300 Gold, 175 Lumber

The highest upgrade for increasing attack damage for Raiders, Tauren, and Grunts.

Requires: Fortress

 ## STEEL RANGED WEAPONS
Research Cost: 75 Gold, 75 Lumber

Increases the ranged attack damage of Headhunters, Wyverns, and Catapults.

 ## THORIUM RANGED WEAPONS
Research Cost: 150 Gold, 150 Lumber

Further increases the ranged attack damage of Headhunters, Wyverns, and Catapults.

Requires: Stronghold

 ## ARCANITE RANGED WEAPONS
Research Cost: 225 Gold, 225 Lumber

The highest upgrade to increase the ranged attack damage of Headhunters, Wyverns, and Catapults.

Requires: Fortress

 ## STEEL UNIT ARMOR
Research Cost: 150 Gold, 75 Lumber

Increases the armor of Raiders, Grunts, Tauren, Headhunters, Wyverns, and Catapults. It's a critical upgrade for the Orcs because it improves the defenses of almost every unit.

THORIUM UNIT ARMOR
Research Cost: 300 Gold, 150 Lumber

Further increases the armor of Raiders, Grunts, Tauren, Headhunters, Wyverns, and Catapults.

Requires: Stronghold

 ## ARCANITE UNIT ARMOR
Research Cost: 450 Gold, 225 Lumber

The highest upgrade for increases in the armor of Raiders, Grunts, Tauren, Headhunters, Wyverns, and Catapults.

Requires: Fortress

 ## SPIKED BARRICADES
Research Cost: 75 Gold, 25 Lumber

Surrounds Orc structures with spikes that damage enemies attacking your structures with melee attacks. This upgrade deals four points of damage per attack.

 ## IMPROVED SPIKED BARRICADES
Research Cost: 150 Gold, 75 Lumber

Spiked barricades deal 10 points of damage per attack.

Requires: Stronghold

 ## ADVANCED SPIKED BARRICADES
Research Cost: 225 Gold,125 Lumber

Spiked barricades deal 16 points of damage per attack.

Requires: Fortress

ORC BURROW

Cost: ⊙ 170 ⬚ 50

The Orc Burrow is critical to the Horde's economy. These structures provide Food, ultimately increasing the maximum number of units available for your army. It has the ability to garrison Peons inside it, which has two useful applications. First, Peons are protected while inside, and the enemy will even take damage trying to get at them if you have the Spiked Barricades upgrade. The second bonus is that Peons can actually attack the enemy (both air and land units) from inside the Orc Burrow, making this a very important structure from a defensive standpoint.

Abilities: Battle Stations
Creates: N/A
Armor: 2
Hit Points: 600
Food: 10
Damage: 34-41
Range: 700

BATTLE STATIONS

Commands nearby Peons to enter an Orc Burrow (each holds up to four at a time). Once inside, the Peons can then attack both air and land enemy units. If your base comes under fire, use Battle Stations to protect your Peons and gain the defensive bonus as they fight from within the safety of Orc Burrow walls.

> **TIP**
>
> You must build Orc Burrows to raise the food supply for a large attack force. Position them around your base to effectively use them as defensive structures. You need at least nine of them to maximize the number of units available, so give careful thought to where you build them to gain the greatest defensive benefit. When used in conjunction with Battle Stations and Spiked Barricades, Orc Burrows can be very effective against small attacks.

SPIRIT LODGE

Cost: ⊙ 255 ⬚ 90

This building produces the Orc spell-casters. It trains Shamans and Witch Doctors, and also contains the spell upgrades for these units.

Upgrades: Shaman Adept/Master Training, Witch Doctor Adept/Master Training
Creates: Shaman, Troll Witch Doctor
Armor: 5
Hit Points: 800
Requires: Stronghold

SHAMAN ADEPT TRAINING

Research Cost: 150 Gold

Increases the Shaman's hit points, Mana capacity, Mana regeneration rate, attack damage, and gives him the ability to cast Lightning Shield.

SHAMAN MASTER TRAINING

Research Cost: 250 Gold, 100 Lumber

Further increases the Shaman's hit points, Mana capacity, Mana regeneration rate, and attack damage. This extra level of training gives him the ability to also cast Bloodlust.

Requires: Fortress

WITCH DOCTOR ADEPT TRAINING

Research Cost: 150 Gold

Increases the Witch Doctor's Mana capacity, Mana regeneration rate, attack damage, hit points, and gives him the ability to cast Stasis Trap.

WITCH DOCTOR MASTER TRAINING

Research Cost: 250 Gold, 100 Lumber

Further increases the Witch Doctor's Mana capacity, Mana regeneration rate, attack damage, hit points, and gives the him the ability to cast Healing Ward. This important upgrade can save you a great deal of resources by healing badly damaged units before they succumb to persistent enemy attacks. It's always better to repair or heal rather than have to build/create from scratch.

ALTAR OF STORMS

Cost: ◯ 300 ⬆ 100

This structure creates Heroes and revives those who fall in battle. It not only serves these important functions, but without it, a Fortress cannot be constructed.

Upgrades: N/A
Creates: Blademaster, Far Seer,
  Tauren Chieftain
Armor: 5
Hit Points: 900

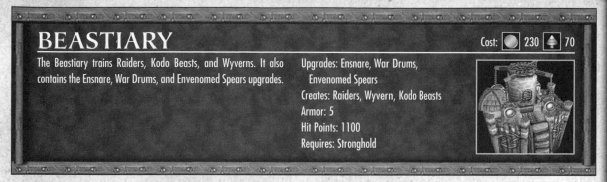

BEASTIARY

Cost: ◯ 230 △ 70

The Beastiary trains Raiders, Kodo Beasts, and Wyverns. It also contains the Ensnare, War Drums, and Envenomed Spears upgrades.

Upgrades: Ensnare, War Drums, Envenomed Spears
Creates: Raiders, Wyvern, Kodo Beasts
Armor: 5
Hit Points: 1100
Requires: Stronghold

ENSNARE

Research Cost: 100 Gold, 25 Lumber

Enables Raiders to tie a targeted enemy unit to the ground, rendering it immobile. This is an excellent skill to use against those enemy Heroes running around a battle to avoid confrontation, or retreating because they are heavily damaged. Ensnare also draws airborne enemies close enough to the ground to be attacked as ground units.

NOTE

Ensnare can save the day when you're without ground-to-air attack units and are facing a group of Chimeras or other dangerous airborne enemies. Have your Raiders use Ensnare to bring the enemy air units down one-by-one for quick disposal.

UPGRADE WAR DRUMS

Research Cost: 150 Gold, 100 Lumber

Increases the damage bonus that the Kodo's War Drums aura gives nearby units. This upgrade makes a significant difference to all units within range of the aura. Plan on using it if your troops include Kodo Beasts.

Requires: Fortress, War Mill

ENVENOMED SPEARS

Research Cost: 150 Gold, 100 Lumber

Adds an additional poison effect to Wyverns' attacks. A unit poisoned by Envenomed Spears takes damage over time. This upgrade doesn't hit the enemy like a napalm explosion, but rather provides a more long-term benefit by gradually eroding the enemy's health.

Requires: Fortress

WATCH TOWER

Cost: ◯ 180 △ 80

This defensive structure can attack both land and air units. It's very effective in conjunction with Orc Burrows filled with Peons, and also improves the line of sight around its location. When equipped with Spiked Barricades, the Watch Tower becomes a significant part of the Horde defense. Always have at least a pair of them in every camp.

Upgrades: N/A
Creates: N/A
Armor: 3
Hit Points: 500
Requires: War Mill
Damage: 19-22
Range: 800

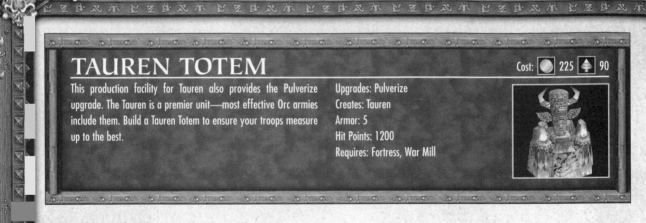

TAUREN TOTEM

Cost: 225 ⬢ 90

This production facility for Tauren also provides the Pulverize upgrade. The Tauren is a premier unit—most effective Orc armies include them. Build a Tauren Totem to ensure your troops measure up to the best.

Upgrades: Pulverize
Creates: Tauren
Armor: 5
Hit Points: 1200
Requires: Fortress, War Mill

PULVERIZE
Research Cost: 200 Gold, 150 Lumber

Gives Tauren the chance to deal area-of-effect damage on their attacks. Although this may not initially seem too helpful, the Pulverize ability can make a great deal of difference in close melee combat—especially if several Tauren use it at once.

ORC UNITS

PEON

Cost:  90 0 1

The Peon is the basic worker for the Orcish Horde. He can harvest Gold or Lumber, as well as build and repair structures. This versatile unit can also gather resources from the destruction of enemy buildings through the Pillage command. In tough defensive situations, send your Peons into Orc Burrows where they can attack both land and air units.

Armor: 0
Damage: 7-8
Speed: Slow
Range: Melee

Hit Points: 250
Mana: N/A
Abilities: Repair, Gather, Pillage

REPAIR (AUTOCAST)

Peons repair Buildings and Mechanical Units automatically when this ability is enabled. Repairing costs Gold and Lumber. You will be unable to perform this task if you're short on resources.

PILLAGE (PASSIVE)

Each attack that does damage to a building also gains resources, returning 50% of the building's hit points when you began to attack it. This ability is also available to Grunts and Raiders.

GRUNT

Cost: 235 0 3

This is the Horde's default melee unit. A brutish Orc warrior, the Grunt can learn the Berserker Strength ability at the Barracks, and can attack only land units.

Armor: 1
Damage: 18-21
Speed: Average
Range: Melee
Hit Points: 680

Mana: N/A
Ability: Pillage, Berserker Strength

BERSERKER STRENGTH (PASSIVE)

Research Cost: 200 Gold, 50 Lumber

Increases the damage Grunts inflict, while adding to their hit points. It's an important upgrade if you are planning on using these units extensively.

Requires: Fortress

TROLL HEADHUNTER

Cost: 160 20 2

The Troll Headhunter is a spear-throwing unit that's effective against both ground and air units. After it attains the Troll Regeneration at the Barracks, this adept warrior can self-heal its battle wounds.

Armor: 0
Damage: 23-27
Speed: Average
Range: 450
Hit Points: 280

Mana: N/A
Abilities: Troll Regeneration
Requires: War Mill

CATAPULT

Cost: ⬤ 260 ⬆ 70 🔨 4

The Catapult is the ultimate long-range siege weapon for the Orcs. It does exceptional damage to buildings and can also attack land units and trees. Because of the Catapult's vulnerability to melee attacks, it's important to always have some support units nearby to protect it. If an enemy unit is allowed to get close enough, the Catapult will be hopelessly unable to defend itself from the attack.

Armor: 2
Damage: 82-102
Speed: Slow
Range: 1000

Hit Points: 500
Mana: N/A
Requires: War
   Mill, Stronghold

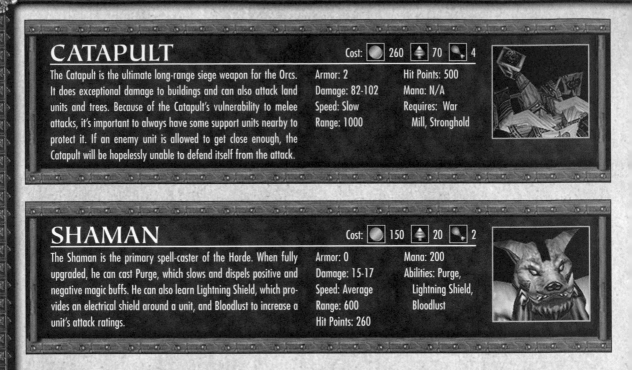

SHAMAN

Cost: ⬤ 150 ⬆ 20 🔨 2

The Shaman is the primary spell-caster of the Horde. When fully upgraded, he can cast Purge, which slows and dispels positive and negative magic buffs. He can also learn Lightning Shield, which provides an electrical shield around a unit, and Bloodlust to increase a unit's attack ratings.

Armor: 0
Damage: 15-17
Speed: Average
Range: 600
Hit Points: 260

Mana: 200
Abilities: Purge,
   Lightning Shield,
   Bloodlust

PURGE

Mana Cost: 75

Removes all magical buffs from a target unit and slows its movement speed initially by a factor of five. The affected unit will slowly regain its original speed over the course of 15 seconds. Purge is best used against enemy spell-casters and Heroes—in other words, enemies that use magic. Use this spell also against fast enemy units, such as Raiders.

> **NOTE**
>
> Purge can even damage summoned units. If your units are taking a beating from Skeleton Warriors or Water Elementals, use this ability to help combat them.

LIGHTNING SHIELD

Research Cost: 150 Gold
Mana Cost: 100

Forms a shield of electrical energy that surrounds a targeted unit, damaging all units around it at a rate of 20 points per second for 20 seconds. It's most effective when cast on a unit embroiled in heavy melee combat. Position your Shaman away from the battle and cast Lightning Shield on the Grunts, Tauren, and Heroes in the thick of the fight.

Requires: Shaman Adept Training

BLOODLUST (AUTOCAST)

Research Cost: 250 Gold, 100 Lumber
Mana Cost: 50

Increases the targeted unit's attack rate by 50% and movement speed by 25%. Use this spell in conjunction with Lightning Shield to support units in melee combat. Bloodlust lasts for 60 seconds.

Requires: Shaman Master Training

TIP

Sometimes, a unit needs to flee the battle to save its life. Since Bloodlust increases a unit's speed by 25%, it may be just what's needed to escape in this situation. Although primarily considered an offensive spell, Bloodlust can also be used in a defensive capacity.

TROLL WITCH DOCTOR

Cost: ⚪ 170 ⬆ 25 🔨 2

This supporting spell-caster can initially use Sentry Ward to summon an invisible detector. He can also learn Stasis Trap and Healing Ward at the Spirit Lodge.

Armor: 0
Damage: 12-14
Speed: Average
Range: 600
Hit Points: 240

Mana: 200
Abilities: Sentry Ward, Stasis Trap, Healing Ward

SENTRY WARD

Mana Cost: 100

Summons an invisible and immovable ward that temporarily reveals everything (including invisible units) in a particular area for 600 seconds (that's right, 10 minutes). This is a great spell to use in key map areas where you wish to keep an eye on the enemy's movements. Activate a Sentry Ward in a narrow pass or near an unclaimed Gold Mine to maintain surveillance without putting any units at risk.

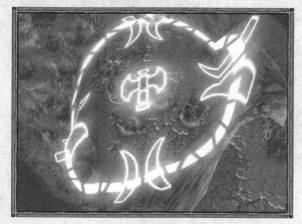

STASIS TRAP WARD

Research Cost: 150 Gold
Mana Cost: 100

Summons an invisible and immovable ward that stuns nearby land units. The trap activates when an enemy unit gets close enough to trigger it, and lasts for 150 seconds. The stun effect has a duration of 12 seconds, which is long enough for your forces to utterly spank your helpless foe. For optimal results, cast this spell near the entrance/exit to an enemy's base. When your adversary starts to move troops to or from their base, they will unwittingly step into your trap. Its ability to stun also makes Stasis Trap ideal for setting up ambushes.

Requires: Witch Doctor Adept Training

HEALING WARD

Research Cost: 250 Gold, 100 Lumber
Mana Cost: 200

Summons an immovable ward that heals nearby friendly units (non-mechanical only) at a rate of 2% per second. The Healing Ward is like having a portable Fountain of Life, albeit a watered-down version. Healing Ward is also effective in melee combat. Place it near the area of combat to heal the friendly units involved in battle while they fight.

Requires: Witch Doctor Master Training

RAIDER

Cost: ⊙ 210 ⬆ 40 ⬒ 3

The Raider is a highly-mobile wolf rider who can learn the Ensnare ability at the Beastiary. This unit's speed allows him to run down slower enemies, and his toughness makes him an excellent warrior against formidable enemy units and structures alike.

Armor: 0
Damage: 23-27
Speed: Fast
Range: Melee

Hit Points: 610
Mana: N/A
Abilities: Ensnare, Pillage

ENSNARE

Binds an enemy unit to the ground, rendering it immobile for 20 seconds. Airborne enemies can also be ensnared. This allows you to attack them as though they were land units.

PILLAGE (PASSIVE)

Research: Cost: 75 Gold, 25 Lumber

Each attack that does damage to a building also gains resources, returning 50% of the cost of the building if you destroy it at full health. This ability is also available to Grunts and Peons.

WYVERN

Cost: ⊙ 310 ⬆ 40 ⬒ 4

The Wyvern is a highly-mobile flying creature with excellent scouting abilities and ideal combat skills against enemy air units. It can learn Envenomed Spears to increase its attack ability. This is the Horde's key airborne weapon, but it's also able to attack enemies on the ground, making it even more valuable to the Orc cause. Use a few Wyverns as a quick-response team that can quickly come to the aid of your forces when they get in over their heads in remote areas of the map.

Armor: 0
Damage: 41-49
Speed: Fast
Range: 450
Hit Points: 500
Mana: N/A

Abilities:
   Envenomed
   Spears
Requires: Fortress

ENVENOMED SPEARS

Research Cost: 150 Gold, 100 Lumber

Adds an additional poison effect to Wyverns' attacks. A unit poisoned by Envenomed Spears takes damage over time. This upgrade doesn't hit the enemy like a bomb, but rather provides a more long-term benefit by gradually eroding the enemy's health.

Requires: Fortress

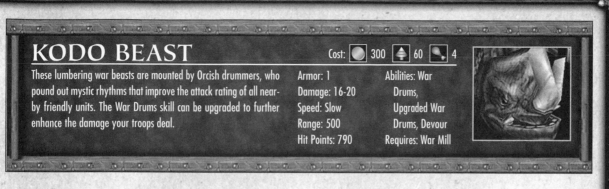

KODO BEAST

| Cost: | 🔵 300 | 🔺 60 | 🔨 4 |

These lumbering war beasts are mounted by Orcish drummers, who pound out mystic rhythms that improve the attack rating of all nearby friendly units. The War Drums skill can be upgraded to further enhance the damage your troops deal.

Armor: 1
Damage: 16-20
Speed: Slow
Range: 500
Hit Points: 790

Abilities: War Drums, Upgraded War Drums, Devour
Requires: War Mill

DEVOUR

Consumes a targeted unit. If the Kodo Beast is killed while still digesting the consumed unit, the victimized unit will pop out. Devour immediately removes the targeted unit from the game, then churns its prey inside the belly of the Kodo Beast, dealing it five points of damage per second until it (or the Kodo) is destroyed. This ability is always available. A Kodo may devour only one unit at a time.

WAR DRUMS AURA
(PASSIVE)

War Drums increases the attack rating of units near a Kodo Beast (+3 for Headhunters, +2 for Grunts). This ability has no cost and is always available. This aura can be upgraded at the Beastiary.

TAUREN

| Cost: | 🔵 325 | 🔺 80 | 🔨 5 |

This mighty warrior can learn the Pulverize ability at the Tauren Totem. Use Tauren en masse with this skill to produce a powerful force against enemy land units.

Armor: 3
Damage: 30-36
Speed: Average
Range: Melee

Hit Points: 1300
Mana: N/A
Abilities: Pulverize

PULVERIZE

Gives the Tauren a chance to deal area-of-effect damage on every attack. Several Tauren all fighting with the Pulverize ability can inflict massive damage, because of the likelihood that at least one of them will dish out area-of-effect damage. Pulverize is a must-have for your Tauren forces.

ORC HEROES

BLADEMASTER

Cost: ⬤ 500 ⬥ 100 ⬥ 5

This cunning Hero is adept at quickly killing individual units and creating confusion among enemies. The Blademaster can learn Wind Walk, Mirror Image, Critical Strike, and Bladestorm. All of these skills are very valuable to the Orcs, with Bladestorm being the ultimate destructive force that this Hero can summon.

Weapon Type: Normal
Armor Type: Hero
Range: Melee
Primary Attribute: Agility

Strength Bonus per Level: 2
Agility Bonus per Level: 1.75
Intelligence Bonus per Level: 2.25
Day Sight: 1800

Night Sight: 800
Build Time: 55
Move Speed: Fast
Production Hot Key: B

LEVEL	ATTACK (GROUND/AIR)	ARMOR	STRENGTH	AGILITY	INTELLIGENCE	HIT POINTS	MANA
1	25-47 [36 avg]/None	5	18	23	16	550	240
2	26-48 [37 avg]/None	5	20	24	18	600	270
3	28-50 [39 avg]/None	6	22	26	20	650	300
4	30-52 [41 avg]/None	6	24	28	22	700	330
5	32-54 [43 avg]/None	7	26	30	25	750	375
6	33-55 [44 avg]/None	7	28	31	27	800	405
7	35-57 [46 avg]/None	8	30	33	29	850	435
8	37-59 [48 avg]/None	9	32	35	31	900	465
9	39-61 [50 avg]/None	9	34	37	34	950	510
10	40-62 [51 avg]/None	9	36	38	36	1000	540

WIND WALK

Allows the Blademaster to become invisible for a set amount of time. Wind Walk has many uses, but when used in combination with Bladestorm (after the Blademaster has achieved level 6), it can be used for very effective ambushes of enemy forces. When an enemy force is moving, make the Blademaster invisible with Wind Walk, then move him into the middle of the enemy camp. Once in position, unleash Bladestorm as the rest of your troops attack. This ability also increases the Blademaster's speed.

Level 1: 100 Mana, +10% speed, 20 seconds
Level 2: 75 Mana, +40% speed, 40 seconds
Level 3: 25 Mana, +70% speed, 60 seconds

MIRROR IMAGE

Mana Cost: 150, Cooldown: 3 seconds

Confuses the enemy by creating a duplicate of the Blademaster. As points are invested into this spell, more duplicate Blademasters appear when this spell is invoked. Mirror Image can dramatically confuse the enemy because each illusion looks exactly like the real Blademaster.

Level 1: Creates 1 illusion
Level 2: Creates 2 illusions
Level 3: Creates 3 illusions

CRITICAL STRIKE (PASSIVE)

Gives the Blademaster a chance to do more damage on any given attack. When fully upgraded, the Blademaster has a 15% chance of doing 400% damage per hit!

| Level 1: 15% chance to do 2 times normal damage |
| Level 2: 15% chance to do 3 times normal damage |
| Level 3: 15% chance to do 4 times normal damage |

BLADESTORM (ULTIMATE)

Mana Cost: 250, Cooldown: 240 seconds

Causes a fury of destructive force around the Blademaster, dealing out 110 damage per second to all nearby enemy land-based units. This is the perfect spell to use just after the Blademaster runs into a large group of enemies. The Blademaster must reach level 6 before Bladestorm becomes available.

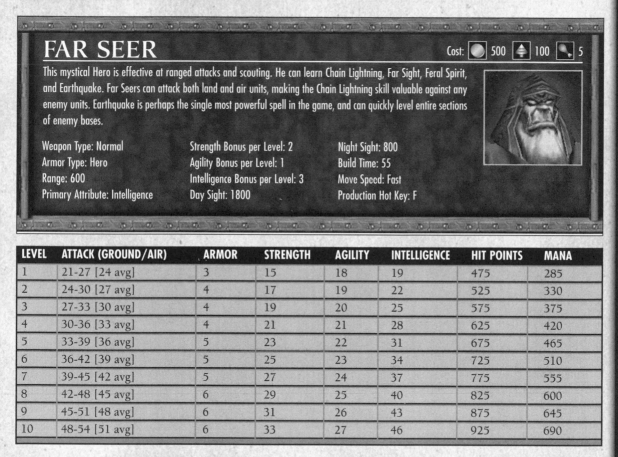

FAR SEER

Cost: ◯ 500 ⛰ 100 🔨 5

This mystical Hero is effective at ranged attacks and scouting. He can learn Chain Lightning, Far Sight, Feral Spirit, and Earthquake. Far Seers can attack both land and air units, making the Chain Lightning skill valuable against any enemy units. Earthquake is perhaps the single most powerful spell in the game, and can quickly level entire sections of enemy bases.

Weapon Type: Normal
Armor Type: Hero
Range: 600
Primary Attribute: Intelligence

Strength Bonus per Level: 2
Agility Bonus per Level: 1
Intelligence Bonus per Level: 3
Day Sight: 1800

Night Sight: 800
Build Time: 55
Move Speed: Fast
Production Hot Key: F

LEVEL	ATTACK (GROUND/AIR)	ARMOR	STRENGTH	AGILITY	INTELLIGENCE	HIT POINTS	MANA
1	21-27 [24 avg]	3	15	18	19	475	285
2	24-30 [27 avg]	4	17	19	22	525	330
3	27-33 [30 avg]	4	19	20	25	575	375
4	30-36 [33 avg]	4	21	21	28	625	420
5	33-39 [36 avg]	5	23	22	31	675	465
6	36-42 [39 avg]	5	25	23	34	725	510
7	39-45 [42 avg]	5	27	24	37	775	555
8	42-48 [45 avg]	6	29	25	40	825	600
9	45-51 [48 avg]	6	31	26	43	875	645
10	48-54 [51 avg]	6	33	27	46	925	690

CHAIN LIGHTNING

Mana Cost: 120, Cooldown: 9 seconds

Hurls a bolt of damaging lightning that jumps from target to target, inflicting massive damage to several nearby enemies. Chain Lightning is also a lot of fun to watch, especially when multiple foes are getting 'cooked' simultaneously.

| Level 1: 100 damage that hits up to 4 targets |
| Level 2: 140 damage that hits up to 6 targets |
| Level 3: 180 damage that hits up to 8 targets |

FAR SIGHT

Reveals the area of the map where this spell is cast upon, including invisible units. While it may not seem like a practical use of points when sharing distribution with Chain Lightning and Earthquake, the Far Sight spell can be well worthwhile in multiplayer games. Having the ability to view the enemy's positions at any time can be critical.

Level 1: Reveals a small area of map for 150 Mana
Level 2: Reveals a large area of map for 100 Mana
Level 3: Reveals a very large area of map for 50 Mana

FERAL SPIRIT

Mana Cost: 100, Cooldown: 15 Seconds

Summons up Spirit Wolves to fight alongside the Far Seer for 60 seconds. These canine mercenaries last for only a short time, but they are powerful and can also gain abilities like Critical Strike and become permanently invisible as points are poured into this spell!

Level 1: Two, 200 Hit Point wolves
Level 2: Two, 300 Hit Point wolves with Critical Strike
Level 3: Two, 400 Hit Point wolves with Critical Strike and permanent invisibility

EARTHQUAKE (ULTIMATE)

Mana Cost: 150, Cooldown: 90 Seconds

This ultimate Far Seer spell becomes available when he reaches level 6. Earthquake shakes the ground beneath the target point, dishing out 50 points of damage per second to buildings, and slowing all affected units by 75% if they're within the scope of the spell. Earthquake lasts for 25 seconds, so it can do 1250 points of damage to buildings! Indeed, this spell can cripple an enemy by demolishing closely grouped food/energy resources in just a few seconds.

TAUREN CHIEFTAIN

Cost: ⬤ 500 ◮ 100 🔨 5

The Tauren Chieftain is the warrior Hero of the Orcs. He is very skilled at absorbing damage from enemy attacks in melee combat, and can also dish out plenty of pain himself. The Tauren Chieftain can learn Shockwave, War Stomp, Endurance Aura, and Reincarnation.

Weapon Type: Normal
Armor Type: Hero
Range: Melee
Primary Attribute: Strength
Strength Bonus per Level: 3.2

Agility Bonus per Level: 1.5
Intelligence Bonus per Level: 1.3
Day Sight: 1800
Night Sight: 800
Build Time: 55

Move Speed: Average
Production Hot Key: T

LEVEL	ATTACK (GROUND/AIR)	ARMOR	STRENGTH	AGILITY	INTELLIGENCE	HIT POINTS	MANA
1	27-37 [32 avg]/None	2	25	10	14	725	210
2	30-40 [35 avg]/None	2	28	11	15	800	225
3	33-43 [38 avg]/None	3	31	13	16	875	240
4	36-46 [41 avg]/None	3	34	14	17	950	255
5	39-49 [44 avg]/None	4	37	16	19	1025	285
6	43-53 [48 avg]/None	4	41	17	20	1125	300
7	46-56 [51 avg]/None	5	44	19	21	1200	315
8	49-59 [54 avg]/None	5	47	20	23	1275	345
9	52-62 [57 avg]/None	6	50	22	24	1350	360
10	55-65 [60 avg]/None	6	53	23	25	1425	375

SHOCKWAVE

Mana Cost: 100, Cooldown: 8 seconds

A wave of force ripples out from the Hero, causing damage to enemy units that come into contact with it. This skill is very effective for melee combat situations.

Level 1: 75 damage
Level 2: 130 damage
Level 3: 200 damage

WAR STOMP

Mana Cost: 90, Cooldown: 6 seconds

The Chieftain slams the ground and deals out damage to all nearby enemies on the ground, stunning them briefly.

Level 1: 25 damage, 3-second stun
Level 2: 50 damage, 4-second stun
Level 3: 75 damage, 5-second stun

ENDURANCE AURA (PASSIVE)

Increases the movement speed and attack rate of nearby friendly units. When used with an attack group, the result is a faster and more ferocious group of units!

Level 1: Increases movement by 10, 5% attack bonus
Level 2: Increases movement by 20, 10% attack bonus
Level 3: Increases movement by 30, 15% attack bonus

REINCARNATION (ULTIMATE)

Cooldown: 240 Seconds

When killed, the Tauren Chieftain is automatically restored to full health, effectively granting this Hero a second life! This is especially effective if the Endurance Aura is active for other nearby friendly units. The Chieftain must reach level 6 before this powerful spell is available.

NIGHT ELVES
THE SENTINELS

NIGHT ELF TECH TREE

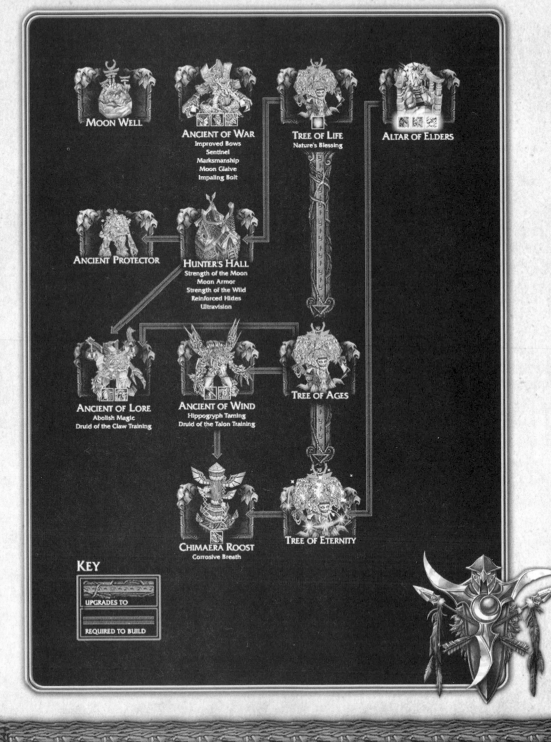

MOON WELL

ANCIENT OF WAR
Improved Bows
Sentinel
Marksmanship
Moon Glaive
Impaling Bolt

TREE OF LIFE
Nature's Blessing

ALTAR OF ELDERS

ANCIENT PROTECTOR

HUNTER'S HALL
Strength of the Moon
Moon Armor
Strength of the Wild
Reinforced Hides
Ultravision

ANCIENT OF LORE
Abolish Magic
Druid of the Claw Training

ANCIENT OF WIND
Hippogryph Taming
Druid of the Talon Training

TREE OF AGES

CHIMAERA ROOST
Corrosive Breath

TREE OF ETERNITY

KEY

UPGRADES TO

REQUIRED TO BUILD

NIGHT ELF TRUISMS

Here are a few thoughts to consider when playing as the Sentinels:

- ✥ Use the mobility of the Ancients, such as the Tree of Life, the Ancient Protector, the Ancient of Lore, and the Ancient of War, to relocate your base whenever necessary. The end result of this is a considerable saving in resources because it eliminates the need to rebuild key structures.

- ✥ Whenever your base is undefended and the enemy attacks, uproot your Ancients to fight your foes off until reinforcements arrive.

- ✥ Every Moon Well can replenish both Health and Mana. This ability, however, is by default turned off. We recommend turning the Autocast feature on so that your units will always be healed whenever they are near a Moon Well. This is very important when actively defending your base—the extra Health and Mana received from Moon Wells can certainly turn the tide of battle.

- ✥ Many of the Night Elf units have the ability to be hidden from the enemy during the night when stationary. Use this to your advantage to set up ambushes in well-traveled areas of the map, or near your base. It's also a good idea to camp near an enemy base, then hit their base with your hidden Night Elves when the enemy attack force leaves.

- ✥ The Keeper of the Grove's Tranquility is one of the most powerful spells in the game. It can heal an entire group of units to the tune of 20 hit points per second. When used in the middle of a battle, it can make all the difference.

- ✥ Wisps can harvest Lumber from any tree and from any location on the map! Sending a Wisp out to harvest Lumber in a remote location not only supplies you with this resource, but also provides an early-warning system of sorts. Enemies often move past a single Wisp in a tree without noticing it. Wisps do not need to be near a Tree of Life to harvest Lumber, so they can be placed anywhere.

NIGHT ELF STRUCTURES

TREE OF LIFE

Cost: ⬤ 400 🔺 150

The Tree of Life is the primary structure for the Night Elf race. It's not only used to train Wisps (which are the equivalent of the Human Peasants), but can also entangle Gold Mines, enabling Wisps to gather this precious resource. Upgrades to the Tree of Ages and ultimately the Tree of Eternity facilitate the production of additional units and structures. The Tree of Life is also a Treant, which means that it can uproot itself to actually battle enemies or simply relocate to another area on the map. Sometimes it's better to move the Tree of Life to a new Gold Mine rather than pouring more resources into building a second Tree of Life.

Upgrades: Nature's Blessing
Building Upgrades: Tree of Ages, Tree of
  Eternity
Creates: Wisps
Abilities: Entangle Gold Mine, Uproot,
  Eat Tree
Starting Hit Points: 1000
Starting Armor: 2
Food Provided: 10

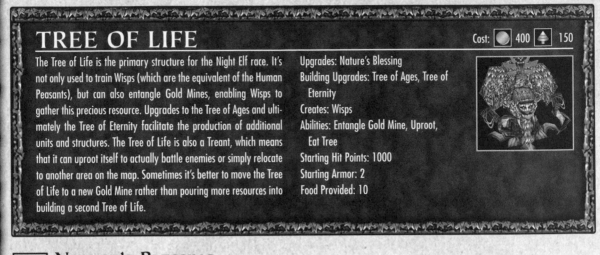

NATURE'S BLESSING

Research Cost: 200 Gold, 150 Lumber

Upgrades the movement speed for all of the Ancients (buildings that can uproot themselves and move independently). Nature's Blessing also upgrades Treant armor, making them more effective in combat. Pursue this upgrade after your base has been fully constructed and your units are sufficiently enhanced.

Requires: Tree of Eternity

Entangled Gold Mine
Gold: 2000

ENTANGLE GOLD MINE

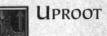

Enables the Tree of Life to burrow its roots into a Gold Mine and extract its resources from a few feet away.

UPROOT

Allows the Tree of Life/Ages/Eternity to lift its roots from the ground and move freely—to relocate or even fight the enemy.

EAT TREE

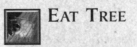

Night Elf Structures with this ability can heal themselves by feeding on nearby forests. Each tree consumed recovers 50 hit points to the Ancient.

TREE OF AGES

Cost: ⬤ 320 ⬆ 80

Upgrading a Tree of Life into a Tree of Ages unlocks the production of additional Night Elf structures and units.

Upgrades: Nature's Blessing
Building Upgrades: Tree of Eternity
Creates: Wisps
Abilities: Entangle Gold Mine, Uproot, Eat Tree

Starting Hit Points: 1400
Starting Armor: 2
Food Provided: 10

TREE OF ETERNITY

Cost: ⬤ 350 ⬆ 120

Upgrading a Tree of Ages into a Tree of Eternity unlocks the production of additional Night Elf structures and units.

Upgrades: Nature's Blessing
Creates: Wisps
Abilities: Entangle Gold Mine, Uproot, Eat Tree
Starting Hit Points: 1800

Starting Armor: 2
Food Provided: 10
Requires: Altar of Elders

ANCIENT OF WAR

Cost: ⬤ 230 ⬆ 70

The Ancient of War is the primary assault unit creator for the Night Elves. It trains Archers, Huntresses, and Ballista, and provides the upgrades for all these units. To expedite troop production and upgrades, consider having two Ancients of War working at the same time—one of them to produce units and the other for upgrades. Of course, operating two Ancients of War is predicated on whether or not resources are plentiful enough to do so.

Upgrades: Improved Bows, Sentinel, Marksmanship, Moon Glaive, Impaling Bolt

Creates: Archers, Huntresses, Ballistae
Abilities: Uproot, Eat Tree
Armor: 2
Hit Points: 800

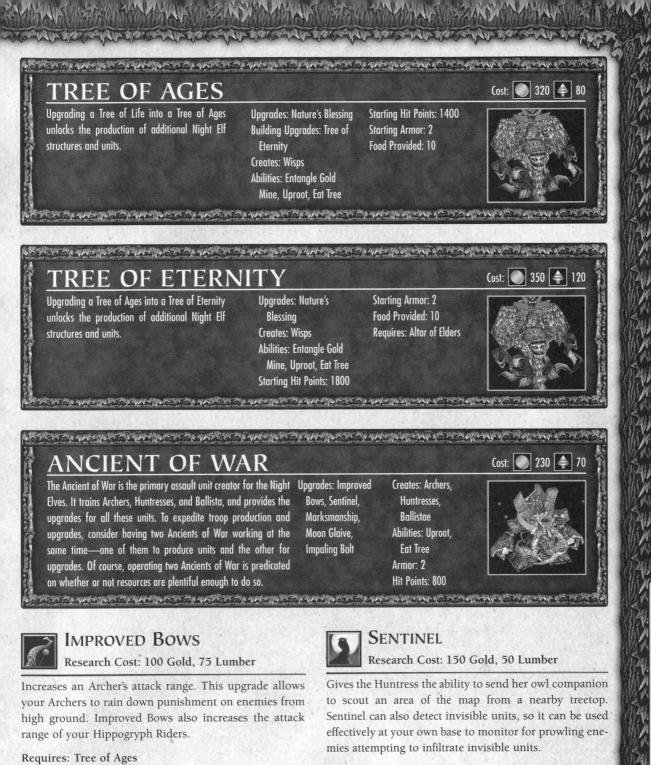

IMPROVED BOWS

Research Cost: 100 Gold, 75 Lumber

Increases an Archer's attack range. This upgrade allows your Archers to rain down punishment on enemies from high ground. Improved Bows also increases the attack range of your Hippogryph Riders.

Requires: Tree of Ages

SENTINEL

Research Cost: 150 Gold, 50 Lumber

Gives the Huntress the ability to send her owl companion to scout an area of the map from a nearby treetop. Sentinel can also detect invisible units, so it can be used effectively at your own base to monitor for prowling enemies attempting to infiltrate invisible units.

Requires: Hunter's Hall

MARKSMANSHIP

Research Cost: 150 Gold, 150 Lumber

Increases the damage of the Archer and Hippogryph attacks by +3. The extra damage provides a significant improvement for the Night Elves' bread-and-butter units.

Requires: Hunter's Hall, Tree of Eternity

MOON GLAIVE

Research Cost: 175 Gold, 125 Lumber

Without this ability, the Huntress can already strike two units with a single attack. Moon Glaive adds an additional victim to her attack, for a total of three strikes per attack. The damage really starts to accumulate when a group of Huntresses with Moon Glaive attacks a mob of enemies!

Requires: Hunter's Hall, Tree of Eternity

IMPALING BOLT

Research Cost: 150 Gold, 75 Lumber

Allows the bolts launched by the Ballista to pierce through initial ground targets and damage those behind. This skill is particularly powerful when the Ballista fires into a crowd of enemy units. Be cautious, however, to always protect your Ballistae by surrounding them with plenty of troops to prevent these long-range weapons from being shredded by enemy melee units.

Requires: Tree of Ages, Hunter's Hall

UPROOT

This skill quite literally uproots the Ancient of War so that it can move and fight.

> **TIP**
>
> When building an Ancient with a Wisp, beware that the Wisp will be lost during the process. Be prepared for this Wisp-loss as you are building up your Night Elf base or you could end up lacking sufficient numbers of this important unit.

HUNTER'S HALL

Cost: 245 | 100

This key structure provides the attack and armor upgrades for many Night Elf units. The Hunter's Hall is not a Treant, so it cannot be uprooted and moved. As with the Ancient of War, you may want to build two Hunter's Halls in order to upgrade quicker.

Upgrades: Strength of the Moon, Improved/Advanced Strength of the Moon, Strength of the Wild, Improved/Advanced Strength of the Wild, Ultravision, Moon Armor, Improved/Advanced Moon Armor, Reinforced Hides, Improved/Advanced Reinforced Hides

Armor: 2

Hit Points: 1100

Requires: Tree of Life

STRENGTH OF THE MOON

Research Cost: 125 Gold, 75 Lumber

Increases the damage of Archers, Huntresses, Ballistae, and Hippogryph Riders. This is a critical upgrade for all of your battle-ready units.

IMPROVED STRENGTH OF THE MOON

Research Cost: 250 Gold, 100 Lumber

Further increases the damage of Archers, Huntresses, Ballistae, and Hippogryph Riders.

Requires: Tree of Ages

ADVANCED STRENGTH OF THE MOON
Research Cost: 375 Gold, 125 Lumber

This is the ultimate upgrade for Archers, Huntresses, Ballistae, and Hippogryph riders, empowering these units with their maximum offensive damage potential.
Requires: Tree of Eternity

STRENGTH OF THE WILD
Research Cost: 100 Gold, 50 Lumber

Increases the damage that Druids of the Claw (in Bear form), Druids of the Talon (in Storm Crow form), Dryads, Hippogryphs, and Chimaeras inflict.

IMPROVED STRENGTH OF THE WILD
Research Cost: 250 Gold, 100 Lumber

Further juices up the damage that Druids of the Claw (in Bear form), Druids of the Talon (in Storm Crow form), Dryads, Hippogryphs, and Chimaeras inflict.
Requires: Tree of Ages

ADVANCED STRENGTH OF THE WILD
Research Cost: 400 Gold, 150 Lumber

This is the highest damage upgrade for Druids of the Claw (in Bear form), Druids of the Talon (in Storm Crow form), Dryads, Hippogryphs, and Chimaeras.
Requires: Tree of Eternity

ULTRAVISION
Research Cost: 75 Gold, 25 Lumber

Gives Night Elves the ability to see as far at night as they do during the day, providing Archers with a distinct advantage over the enemy.

MOON ARMOR
Research Cost: 150 Gold, 75 Lumber

Increases the armor of Archers, Huntresses, and Hippogryph Riders.

IMPROVED MOON ARMOR
Research Cost: 250 Gold, 100 Lumber

Further increases the armor of Archers, Huntresses, and Hippogryph Riders.
Requires: Tree of Ages

ADVANCED MOON ARMOR
Research Cost: 350 Gold, 125 Lumber

This is the highest armor upgrade for Archers, Huntresses, and Hippogryph Riders.
Requires: Tree of Eternity

REINFORCED HIDES
Research Cost: 150 Gold, 50 Lumber

Increases the armor of Druids of the Claw (in Bear form), Druids of the Talon (in Storm Crow form), Hippogryphs, Dryads, and Chimaeras.

IMPROVED REINFORCED HIDES
Research Cost: 250 Gold, 100 Lumber

Further increases the armor of Druids of the Claw (in Bear form), Druids of the Talon (in Storm Crow form), Hippogryphs, Dryads, and Chimaeras.
Requires: Tree of Ages

ADVANCED REINFORCED HIDES
Research Cost: 350 Gold, 150 Lumber

This is the highest armor upgrade for Druids of the Claw (in Bear form), Druids of the Talon (in Storm Crow form), Hippogryphs, Dryads, and Chimaeras.
Requires: Tree of Eternity

ANCIENT OF LORE

Cost: ⊙ 240 ⬆ 80

This is the keeper of spell-casters for the Night Elves. It trains Druids and Dryads. The Ancient of Lore is also capable of uprooting itself to relocate or fight!

Upgrades: Abolish Magic, Druid of the Claw Adept/
  Master Training
Creates: Dryad, Druid of the Claw
Abilities: Uproot, Eat Tree
Armor: 2
Hit Points: 750
Requires: Trees of Ages, Hunter's Hall

ABOLISH MAGIC

Research Cost: 75 Gold, 25 Lumber

Provides Dryads with the ability to dispel both positive (magic that improves enemy units) and negative (magic that damages your units) magical buffs. Abolish Magic also damages summoned units, such as the Horde's feral wolves.

DRUID OF THE CLAW ADEPT TRAINING

Research Cost: 150 Gold

Increases the Druid's Mana capacity when in Night Elf form. It boosts Mana regeneration, hit points, and attack damage, and also instills the ability for Druids of the Claw to rejuvenate any friendly non-mechanical unit.

DRUID OF THE CLAW MASTER TRAINING

Research Cost: 250 Gold, 100 Lumber

Further increases the Druid's Mana capacity when in Night Elf form. It further boosts Mana regeneration, hit points, and attack damage, and also instills the ability for Druids of the Claw to assume Bear form.

MOON WELL

Cost: ⊙ 175 ⬆ 40

This is the backbone of the Sentinel economy. The Moon Well provides food, which increases the maximum number of units that can be trained. Its added bonus is the Moon Well's power to replenish the Mana and hit points of nearby units. This built-in healing capability can be set to Autocast and inspires many to build Moon Wells in various locations throughout the map so that they can replenish their units without even returning to the home base.

Upgrades: N/A
Abilities: Replenish Mana and Life
  (Hit Points)
Armor: 2
Hit Points: 600
Mana: 300
Food Provided: 10

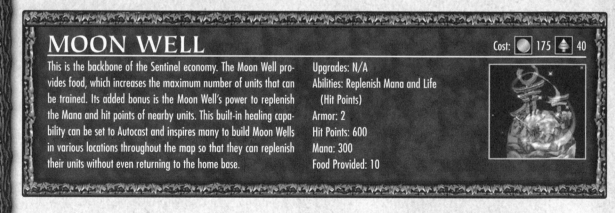

REPLENISH MANA AND LIFE

Enables the Moon Well to both heal and replenish Mana in a damaged or depleted unit. Although this can be achieved manually, right-clicking on the icon turns Autocasting on so that Moon Wells automatically heal nearby units with Life and Mana.

ANCIENT OF WIND

Cost: ⬤ 220 ▲ 80

The Ancient of Wind is the keeper of the Hippogryph aerial assault units. It's also where you create the Druid of the Talon, ground units that can also become Storm Crows and take flight with the Hippogryphs.

Upgrades: Hippogryph Taming, Druid of the Talon Adept/Master Training.
Creates: Hippogryph, Druid of the Talon
Abilities: Uproot, Eat Tree
Armor: 2
Hit Points: 750
Requires: Tree of Ages

HIPPOGRYPH TAMING

Research Cost: 100 Gold, 50 Lumber

Trains Hippogryphs to carry Archers, ultimately giving them the ability to also attack enemy ground units once an Archer has mounted.

DRUID OF THE TALON ADEPT TRAINING

Research Cost: 150 Gold

Increases the Night Elf form of the Druid's Mana capacity, Mana regeneration rate, hit points, attack damage, and gives them the ability to assume Storm Crow form.

DRUID OF THE TALON MASTER TRAINING

Research Cost: 250 Gold, 100 Lumber

Further increases the Night Elf form of the Druid's Mana capacity, Mana regeneration rate, hit points, and attack damage. It also gives them the ability to cast Cyclone.

Requires: Tree of Eternity

ALTAR OF ELDERS

Cost: ⬤ 300 ⬆ 100

This Night Elf structure summons and revives slain Heroes. It's often a good idea to have more than one Altar of Elders on the map so that slain Heroes can be revived in multiple places if necessary.

Upgrades: N/A
Creates: Heroes (Demon Hunter, Keeper of
      the Grove, Priestess of the Moon)
Armor: 2
Hit Points: 900

ANCIENT PROTECTOR

Cost: ⬤ 240 ⬆ 100

This defensive Ancient can attack both land and air units while rooted by throwing boulders. Uprooting adds a melee attack. It is the rough equivalent of the Human Watch Tower, although its ability to move makes it slightly more versatile.

Upgrades: N/A
Creates: N/A
Abilities: Uproot,
      Eat Tree
Armor: 2
Hit Points: 550

Damage: 43-65
Range: 700
Requires: Hunter's
      Hall

CHIMAERA ROOST

Cost: ⬤ 280 ⬆ 100

This structure trains Chimaeras and contains the Corrosive Breath upgrade.

Upgrades: Corrosive Breath
Creates: Chimaera
Abilities: N/A
Armor: 2
Hit Points: 1200
Requires: Tree of Eternity, Ancient of Wind

CORROSIVE BREATH

Research Cost: 200 Gold, 150 Lumber

Gives Chimaeras the ability to breathe corrosive bile on enemy buildings, bringing them to the ground much more quickly.

NIGHT ELF UNITS

WISP

Cost: ⬤ 70 ⬧ 0 🔨 1

The Wisp is similar in some ways to the Human Peasant, but there are substantial differences between the two. As the Sentinels' basic workers, Wisps can transform into Treants (Night Elf buildings). They also gather Gold and harvest Lumber, and it's their unique brand of Lumber harvesting that gives the Night Elves a decided edge. Because the Sentinels are in tune with nature, the Wisps' technique does not destroy the trees, making Lumber an unlimited resource for their race. Wisps can use Detonate to dispel magical buffs in an area, destroying themselves as well in the process. They can also use the Renew skill, which rebuilds damaged Night Elf and allied buildings, as well as friendly mechanical units.

Armor: 0
Damage: N/A
Speed: Slow
Range: N/A
Hit Points: 120

Mana: N/A
Abilities: Detonate,
    Renew, Gather,
    Create Building

DETONATE

The Wisp detonates, dispelling all the magical buffs and draining 50 Mana from each unit in the area. This destroys the Wisp, but may be well worth the sacrifice if the enemy is having a great deal of success with magical spells on your base. You may even want to detonate a few Wisps consecutively, both to remove the enemy's ability to use magic and to drain their Mana.

RENEW
(AUTOCAST)

Repairs Night Elf and allied buildings, as well as friendly mechanical units. This skill can be set to Autocast mode to ensure that Wisps renew damaged buildings/mechanical units automatically when nearby.

ARCHER

Cost: ⬤ 150 ⬧ 10 🔨 2

This combat attacker is the bread-and-butter combat unit for the Night Elves. Don't underestimate the capabilities of a pack of fully upgraded Archers—they are capable of attacking both land and air attacks, and can also learn the Mount Hippogryph upgrade to take their fight to the skies!

Armor: 0
Damage: 19-22
Speed: Average
Range: 500
Hit Points: 260

Mana: N/A
Ability: Mount
    Hippogryph,
    Hide

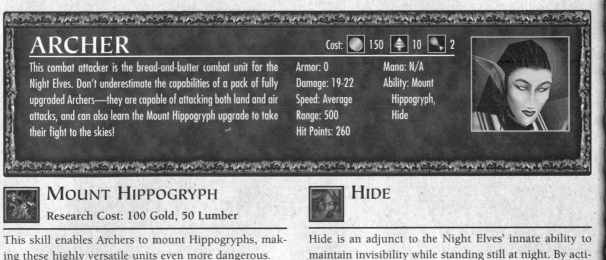

MOUNT HIPPOGRYPH

Research Cost: 100 Gold, 50 Lumber

This skill enables Archers to mount Hippogryphs, making these highly versatile units even more dangerous.

HIDE

Hide is an adjunct to the Night Elves' innate ability to maintain invisibility while standing still at night. By activating this skill, the Archer won't auto-acquire enemies, and thus remains hidden in the cloak of darkness while standing still. Use Hide when planning an ambush. This ability is also available to Huntresses.

HUNTRESS

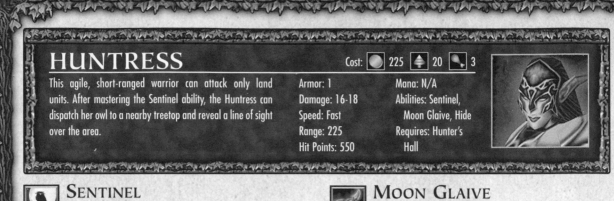

Cost: ⬤ 225 🔺 20 🪓 3

This agile, short-ranged warrior can attack only land units. After mastering the Sentinel ability, the Huntress can dispatch her owl to a nearby treetop and reveal a line of sight over the area.

Armor: 1
Damage: 16-18
Speed: Fast
Range: 225
Hit Points: 550

Mana: N/A
Abilities: Sentinel,
  Moon Glaive, Hide
Requires: Hunter's
  Hall

SENTINEL
Research Cost: 150 Gold, 50 Lumber

Sentinel sends an owl to a treetop. Her feathered scout reveals a line of sight that lasts for an unlimited amount of time. This gives you the ability to monitor an area of the map constantly. The trade-off is that each Huntress gets only one Sentinel (once this skill has been researched).
Requires: Hunter's Hall

MOON GLAIVE
Research Cost: 175 Gold, 125 Lumber

Without this ability, the Huntress can already strike two units with a single attack. Moon Glaive adds an additional victim to her attack, for a total of three strikes per attack. The damage really starts to accumulate when a group of Huntresses with Moon Glaive attacks a mob of enemies!
Requires: Hunter's Hall, Tree of Eternity

DRYAD

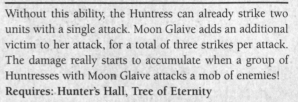

Cost: ⬤ 170 🔺 60 🪓 3

The Dryad can dispel enemy magic and is immune to spells. She is also capable of slowing land units using a poison attack. Abolish Magic gives her the ability to dispel all magic in an area.

Armor: 0
Damage: 15-17
Speed: Fast
Range: 500
Hit Points: 380

Mana: 200
Abilities: Abolish
  Magic, Slow
  Poison, Spell
  Immunity

ABOLISH MAGIC (AUTOCAST)
Research Cost: 75 Gold, 25 Lumber
Mana Cost: 50

Dispels all positive magical buffs on enemy units and negative buffs on friendly units. Abolish Magic also damages summoned units.

SLOW POISON (PASSIVE)

Slows targeted enemy's movement by 50% and reduces their attack by 25% for 5 seconds with the standard Dryad attack.

SPELL IMMUNITY (PASSIVE)

A passive skill that renders the Dryad immune to all magic.

BALLISTA

Cost: ⬤ 245 🔺 85 🪓 4

The Ballista is the long-range siege weapon for the Night Elves. This unit does exceptional damage against buildings, and can also attack land units and trees. Clearing forests is useful for limiting enemy resources or reaching an otherwise inaccessible Gold Mine.

Armor: 2
Damage: 56-69
Speed: Slow
Range: 1000
Hit Points: 450

Mana: N/A
Abilities: Impaling Bolt
Requires: Tree of Ages,
  Hunter's Hall

IMPALING BOLT (PASSIVE)

Research Cost: 150 Gold, 75 Lumber

A passive skill that allows the Ballista's attack to pass through the first unit it hits and damage the one behind it.
Requires: Tree of Ages, Hunter's Hall

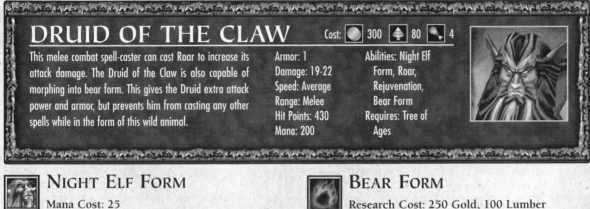

DRUID OF THE CLAW

Cost: 🔵 300 🔺 80 🔨 4

This melee combat spell-caster can cast Roar to increase its attack damage. The Druid of the Claw is also capable of morphing into bear form. This gives the Druid extra attack power and armor, but prevents him from casting any other spells while in the form of this wild animal.

Armor: 1
Damage: 19-22
Speed: Average
Range: Melee
Hit Points: 430
Mana: 200

Abilities: Night Elf Form, Roar, Rejuvenation, Bear Form
Requires: Tree of Ages

NIGHT ELF FORM

Mana Cost: 25

Transforms the Druid of the Claw (in Bear form) back into a Night Elf, allowing him to cast spells and regenerate Mana faster.

ROAR

Mana Cost: 100

Briefly provides a 25% increase to friendly unit attack damage. Use Roar in tight melee combat situations.

REJUVENATION

Research Cost: 150 Gold
Mana Cost: 125

BEAR FORM

Research Cost: 250 Gold, 100 Lumber
Mana Cost: 25

Transforms the Druid into a bear, slowing Mana regeneration, but turning him into a fighting machine. While in this state, he becomes a fighter and nothing more, losing his ability to cast spells until he returns to Druid form.

Armor: 3
Damage: 29-44
Speed: Average
Range: Melee
Hit Points: 960
Mana: 400

Requires: Druid of the Claw Master Training

Heals a targeted friendly unit with a maximum of 400 hit points. The catch is that it takes 12 seconds until the process is complete. Still, this is a very powerful healing ability and it's worth having at least a pair of Druids of the Claw nearby to both fight and heal.
Requires: Druid of the Claw Adept Training

DRUID OF THE TALON

Cost: 🔵 160 🔺 20 🔨 2

The Druid of the Talon is a secondary spell-caster in the Night Elf arsenal. He has the unique ability to turn himself into a Storm Crow, and can Autocast Faerie Fire, which lowers the enemy's armor rating. He can also immobilize enemy units with Cyclone.

Armor: 0
Damage: 11-15
Speed: Average
Range: 60
Hit Points: 225

Mana: 200
Abilities: Faerie Fire, Storm Crow Form, Cyclone

FAERIE FIRE

Mana Cost: 150

Reduces the targeted enemy's armor rating by 5 and lasts for 2 minutes.

CYCLONE

Research Cost: 250 Gold, 100 Lumber

Tosses an enemy unit into the air, rendering it unable to move, attack, or cast any spells for 30 seconds. This is an effective way to remove a dangerous foe from an intense battle.

Requires: Druid of the Talon Master Training

STORM CROW FORM

The Druid of the Talon has the innate ability to turn himself into a Storm Crow—a bird that can fly above any obstacle and move freely around the map. There is no limit to how long the Druid of the Talon can stay in Storm Crow form, but he cannot cast any magic when he is of the feather. This ability can be used for scouting, escape, or even as an emergency aerial attack.

Requires: Druid of the Talon Adept Training

Armor: 0
Damage: 24
Speed: Fast
Range: 60
Hit Points: 300
Mana: 200

HIPPOGRYPH

Cost: ◯ 190　⬚ 20　◣ 2

This flying melee attack unit is effective only against air units, such as Dragons or Gyrocopters. Once Hippogryph Taming has been learned, an Archer can ride on its back. The combined force of these units enables them to attack both air and ground units, making it one of the most important weapons in the Night Elf army.

Armor: 0	Mana: N/A
Damage: 38-46	Abilities: Pick up
Speed: Fast	Archer (requires
Range: Melee	Hippogryph
Hit Points: 500	Taming)

PICK UP ARCHER

Research Cost: 100 Gold, 50 Lumber

Allows the Hippogryph to saddle up an Archer, creating an air/ground attack unit.

Requires: Hippogryph Taming

CHIMAERA

Cost: ◯ 390　⬚ 70　◣ 5

This ranged flying siege creature is very effective against buildings and large groups of enemies. Although it can attack only ground units, this two-headed Dragon is a force to be reckoned with, especially in numbers. A group of six or seven Chimaeras can quickly destroy an enemy town.

Armor: 2	Hit Points: 900
Damage: 67-83	Mana: N/A
Speed: Slow	Abilities: Corrosive
Range: 450	Breath

CORROSIVE BREATH (PASSIVE)

Research Cost: 200 Gold, 150 Lumber

This passive ability turns the Chimaera's attack into a devastating substance that enhances damage to enemy buildings. A group of three or four Chimaeras with the Corrosive Breath upgrade can reduce an enemy building to ashes in just a few seconds.

NIGHT ELF HEROES

DEMON HUNTER

Cost: ◯ 500 ⬧ 100 🔨 5

This cunning Hero is adept at maneuvering through battles. He can learn Mana Burn, Immolation, Evasion, and Metamorphosis, but can attack only land units. Mana Burn is a key skill that can severely limit the enemy's ability to use magic over time, while Evasion often causes the enemy's attacks to miss this Hero.

Weapon Type: Normal
Armor Type: Hero
Range: Melee
Primary Attribute: Agility
Strength Bonus per Level: 2.4
Agility Bonus per Level: 1.5
Intelligence Bonus per Level: 2.1

Day Sight: 1800
Night Sight: 800
Build Time: 55
Move Speed: Fast
Production Hot Key: D

METAMORPHOSIS STATS

Cooldown: 1.6	
Range: 600	
Build Time: 60 seconds	
Weapon Type: Chaos	
Armor Type: Hero	
Move Speed: Fast	

LEVEL	ATTACK (GROUND/AIR)	ARMOR	STRENGTH	AGILITY	INTELLIGENCE	HIT POINTS	MANA
1	24-46 [35 avg]/None	5	19	22	16	575	240
2	25-47 [36 avg]/None	5	21	23	18	625	270
3	27-49 [38 avg]/None	6	23	25	20	675	300
4	28-50 [39 avg]/None	6	26	26	22	750	330
5	30-52 [41 avg]/None	6	28	28	24	800	360
6	31-53 [42 avg]/None	7	31	29	26	875	390
7	33-55 [44 avg]/None	7	33	31	28	925	420
8	34-56 [45 avg]/None	8	35	32	30	975	450
9	36-58 [47 avg]/None	8	38	34	32	1050	480
10	37-59 [48 avg]/None	9	40	35	34	1100	510

MANA BURN

Mana Cost: 75

Sends a bolt of negative energy that drains targeted enemy unit's Mana 100 points at a time. The Mana then combusts, dealing damage equal to the amount of Mana burned by the enemy. This double-pronged attack can be a *very* effective way to handle enemy Heroes. By draining their Mana and damaging them simultaneously, this spell can vastly improve your chances of victory over a particular Hero.

Level 1: Drains 100 Mana
Level 2: Drains 200 Mana
Level 3: Drains 300 Mana

IMMOLATION

Mana Cost: 35 (Mana continues to drain)

Engulfs the Demon Hunter in flames, causing damage to enemy units around him. Immolation drains Mana until deactivated, so one must be careful to turn it off if it's not needed. Immolation is best used when rushing headlong into a tight crowd of enemies where it can do the maximum damage.

Level 1: 10 damage per second
Level 2: 15 damage per second
Level 3: 20 damage per second

EVASION

Gives the Demon Hunter a chance to avoid attacks. At level 3, the enemy has a 30% chance of missing the Hero, which can significantly improve the chances of surviving a heavy duty battle.

Level 1: 10% chance that opponent misses
Level 2: 20% chance that opponent misses
Level 3: 30% chance that opponent misses

METAMORPHOSIS (ULTIMATE)

Mana Cost: 150, Cooldown: 120 Seconds

Transforms the Demon Hunter into a giant Demon that can shoot fireballs. This powerful creature has 500 additional hit points and lasts 60 seconds. Metamorphosis is not available until the Demon Hunter reaches level 6.

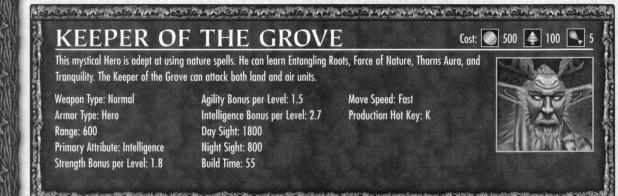

KEEPER OF THE GROVE

Cost: ◯ 500 ⬚ 100 🪓 5

This mystical Hero is adept at using nature spells. He can learn Entangling Roots, Force of Nature, Thorns Aura, and Tranquility. The Keeper of the Grove can attack both land and air units.

Weapon Type: Normal
Armor Type: Hero
Range: 600
Primary Attribute: Intelligence
Strength Bonus per Level: 1.8

Agility Bonus per Level: 1.5
Intelligence Bonus per Level: 2.7
Day Sight: 1800
Night Sight: 800
Build Time: 55

Move Speed: Fast
Production Hot Key: K

LEVEL	ATTACK (GROUND/AIR)	ARMOR	STRENGTH	AGILITY	INTELLIGENCE	HIT POINTS	MANA
1	20-26 [23 avg]	3	16	15	18	500	270
2	22-28 [25 avg]	3	17	16	20	525	300
3	25-31 [28 avg]	3	19	18	23	575	345
4	28-34 [31 avg]	4	21	19	26	625	390
5	30-36 [33 avg]	4	23	21	28	675	420
6	33-39 [36 avg]	5	25	22	31	725	465
7	36-42 [39 avg]	5	26	24	34	750	510
8	38-44 [41 avg]	6	28	25	36	800	540
9	41-47 [44 avg]	6	30	27	39	850	585
10	44-50 [47 avg]	6	32	28	42	900	630

ENTANGLING ROOTS

Mana Cost: 75

Causes roots to burst from the ground, immobilizing and damaging a targeted enemy. This spell holds down enemy units and damages them while preventing their retreat.

Level 1: 15 damage per second over 15 seconds	
Level 2: 15 damage per second over 30 seconds	
Level 3: 15 damage per second over 45 seconds	

FORCE OF NATURE

Mana Cost: 125, Cooldown: 20 seconds

Converts a forested area into an army of tree-men called Treants who will fight at the Keeper's side in battle.

Level 1: Raises 2 Treants for 75 seconds	
Level 2: Raises 3 Treants for 75 seconds	
Level 3: Raises 4 Treants for 75 seconds	

THORNS AURA

Gives friendly units around the Keeper of the Grove a damage shield that wounds enemy melee attackers by striking back with every hit. The fact that this aura also affects nearby units makes it very important, because if every unit near the Keeper is dishing out 12 points of damage every time they are hit, in *addition* to the damage they are dishing out with their attacks, the enemy won't stand a chance.

Level 1: Deals 4 damage per hit to attacker	
Level 2: Deals 8 damage per hit to attacker	
Level 3: Deals 12 damage per hit to attacker	

TRANQUILITY (ULTIMATE)

Mana Cost: 200, Cooldown: 120 Seconds

Causes rains of healing energy to pour down in a large area, healing friendly units. This spell heals 20 points per second and lasts 30 seconds, for a total of 600 hit points per unit! Tranquility is not available until the Keeper of the Grove reaches level 6.

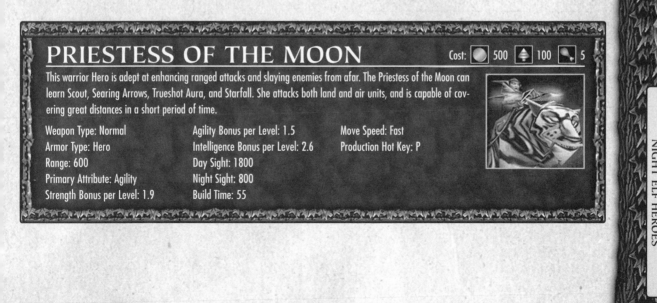

PRIESTESS OF THE MOON

Cost: ◯ 500　⬤ 100　🔨 5

This warrior Hero is adept at enhancing ranged attacks and slaying enemies from afar. The Priestess of the Moon can learn Scout, Searing Arrows, Trueshot Aura, and Starfall. She attacks both land and air units, and is capable of covering great distances in a short period of time.

Weapon Type: Normal	Agility Bonus per Level: 1.5	Move Speed: Fast
Armor Type: Hero	Intelligence Bonus per Level: 2.6	Production Hot Key: P
Range: 600	Day Sight: 1800	
Primary Attribute: Agility	Night Sight: 800	
Strength Bonus per Level: 1.9	Build Time: 55	

LEVEL	ATTACK (GROUND/AIR)	ARMOR	STRENGTH	AGILITY	INTELLIGENCE	HIT POINTS	MANA
1	21-31 [26 avg]	4	18	19	15	550	225
2	22-32 [27 avg]	4	19	20	17	575	255
3	24-34 [29 avg]	5	21	22	20	625	300
4	25-35 [30 avg]	5	23	23	22	675	330
5	27-37 [32 avg]	6	25	25	25	725	375
6	28-38 [33 avg]	6	27	26	28	775	420
7	30-40 [35 avg]	6	29	28	30	825	450
8	31-41 [36 avg]	7	31	29	33	875	495
9	33-43 [38 avg]	7	33	31	35	925	525
10	34-44 [39 avg]	8	35	32	38	975	570

SCOUT

Mana Cost: 100, Cooldown: 20 seconds

Summons an Owl that the player is able to control to scout any area. Each point into the skill increases the duration and sight radius of the Owl Scout, and lowers the Mana cost.

Level 1: Sees a small area for 100 Mana
Level 2: Sees a large area for 75 Mana
Level 3: Sees a huge area for 50 Mana

SEARING ARROWS

Mana Cost: 8

Increases the damage of the Priestess' attack by adding a fire damage bonus. Unfortunately, this skill also drains Mana with each shot, so it behooves the Priestess to have a Mana potion on hand at all times.

Level 1: 10 bonus damage
Level 2: 20 bonus damage
Level 3: 30 bonus damage

TRUESHOT AURA

Gives friendly units around the Priestess bonus damage to their ranged attacks.

Level 1: Increases best ranged damage by 10%
Level 2: Increases best ranged damage by 20%
Level 3: Increases best ranged damage by 30%

STARFALL (ULTIMATE)

Mana Cost: 200, Cooldown: 120 Seconds

Starfall calls down waves of falling stars that damage enemy units in a targeted area. This is a very powerful and destructive spell, against both enemy units and structures. It's ideal against enemy units that are pinned in battle and unable to flee it. Each wave of attacks deals 75 points of damage, and the spell lasts for 30 seconds. Starfall is not available until the Priestess of the Moon reaches level 6.

HUMAN CAMPAIGN

THE SCOURGE OF LORDAERON

Warcraft III: Reign of Chaos begins with the familiar, the Human Campaign. These initial chapters of the single-player game will ease you into the new features, fresh concepts, and latest eccentricities while drawing you ever deeper into the unfolding storyline. This section of the guide provides detailed maps and walkthroughs for each mission (chapter), including special tips, notes, and warnings wherever necessary.

CHAPTER 1

THE DEFENSE OF STRAHNBRAD

Despite a barrage of plague rumors and mounting political tensions, recent Orc uprisings in southern Lordaeron have forced the Alliance High Command to take decisive measures.

To contain the remaining Orcish threat, the Alliance has sent two of its greatest Paladins—the legendary Uther Lightbringer and Arthas, the young Prince of Lordaeron—to drive the Raiders back and ascertain the extent of the remaining Orc forces.

Slave Master

R

Start

Bloodhill Bandits

Strahnbrad Gates

Receive Bandit Quest

Strahnbrad Cemetery

R

Bandits

Bandits Camp

R

Receive Rescue Timmy Quest

Rescue Timmy Hero

- - - - - ▶ Enemy Path   ────▶ Path to Strahnbrad   **R** Reinforcements

AVAILABLE STRUCTURES

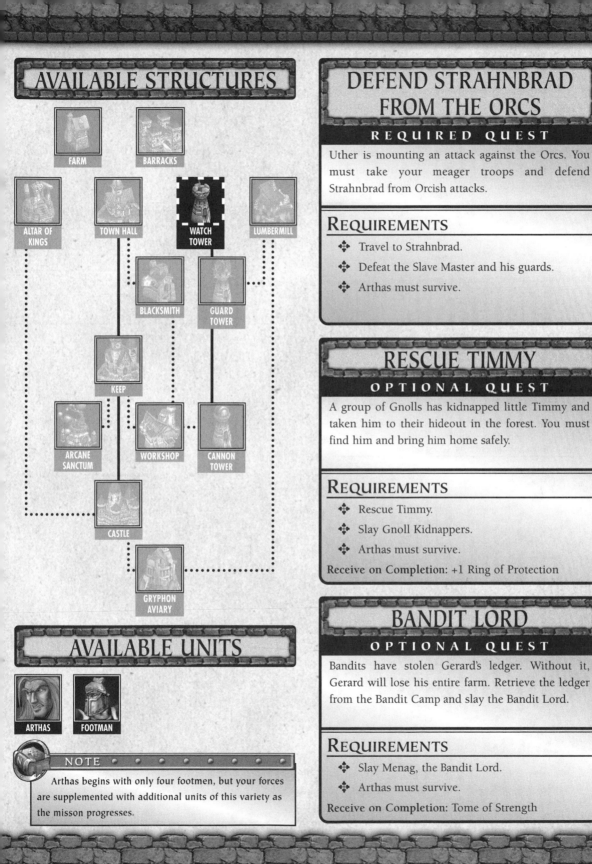

- FARM
- BARRACKS
- ALTAR OF KINGS
- TOWN HALL
- WATCH TOWER
- LUMBERMILL
- BLACKSMITH
- GUARD TOWER
- KEEP
- ARCANE SANCTUM
- WORKSHOP
- CANNON TOWER
- CASTLE
- GRYPHON AVIARY

AVAILABLE UNITS

- ARTHAS
- FOOTMAN

NOTE

Arthas begins with only four footmen, but your forces are supplemented with additional units of this variety as the misson progresses.

DEFEND STRAHNBRAD FROM THE ORCS

REQUIRED QUEST

Uther is mounting an attack against the Orcs. You must take your meager troops and defend Strahnbrad from Orcish attacks.

REQUIREMENTS

- ❖ Travel to Strahnbrad.
- ❖ Defeat the Slave Master and his guards.
- ❖ Arthas must survive.

RESCUE TIMMY

OPTIONAL QUEST

A group of Gnolls has kidnapped little Timmy and taken him to their hideout in the forest. You must find him and bring him home safely.

REQUIREMENTS

- ❖ Rescue Timmy.
- ❖ Slay Gnoll Kidnappers.
- ❖ Arthas must survive.

Receive on Completion: +1 Ring of Protection

BANDIT LORD

OPTIONAL QUEST

Bandits have stolen Gerard's ledger. Without it, Gerard will lose his entire farm. Retrieve the ledger from the Bandit Camp and slay the Bandit Lord.

REQUIREMENTS

- ❖ Slay Menag, the Bandit Lord.
- ❖ Arthas must survive.

Receive on Completion: Tome of Strength

THE PATH TO VICTORY

This mission begins with your Hero, Arthas, meeting with Uther in a crude encampment. Arthas informs his comrade that there's an Orc encampment nearby, and Uther vows to take it out while you (Arthas) and your forces move to protect the town of Strahnbrad.

Arthas and Uther meet as the first mission begins, but the young prince and his Footmen will be without the great Paladin when it comes to completing this mission.

Four footmen accompany Arthas, who is armed with Holy Light. This spell heals injured units for 200 hit points. The two optional quests in this mission can be wrapped up nicely before you even reach the gates of Strahnbrad.

> **NOTE**
> Don't be afraid to use Holy Light, because there are no Barracks to replace lost Footmen in this initial mission.

GET REINFORCEMENTS AND RESCUE TIMMY

Move southeast from the encampment and you'll soon encounter two Footmen battling a Rogue. Help them destroy the Rogue, and they'll join your forces. Use Holy Light to heal the injured warriors before proceeding. From this point, you can move directly to the gates of Strahnbrad (see map), but we recommend that you clear the entire map of enemies and complete the optional quests first.

Move toward the southwest corner of the map where you'll find some villagers who are willing to join your forces. These sturdy men become another pair of Footmen that you can add to your ranks. Various villagers greet you as you traverse the farms, but they have nothing particularly helpful to offer.

These men on the far western edge of the map join your ranks when you approach them.

Move southeast from here to meet Alicia. She reports that young Timmy has been captured by Gnoll Kidnappers and dragged into the forest. To rescue him, you must move to the east toward the Gnoll camp. Two Gnolls and a Gnoll Poacher await you there, but they're no match for your forces. Crush them and free Timmy. A gracious Alicia rewards your courage with a Ring of Protection +1, which also yields a Potion of Healing. Take the time to use Holy Light to heal any damaged Footmen in your ranks.

THE BLOODHILL BANDITS AND THE BANDIT LORD

There is one more optional quest remaining before you reach Strahnbrad, along with some non-quest related enemies that you should fight to increase Arthas' experience. The more experience he gets, the sooner he'll level up, allowing you to add to or improve his spells.

Fight every available battle on this map, and Arthas will level-up, earning him one Hero ability point for you to assign. You may then invest in either Divine Shield, which gives Arthas a brief impenetrable shield, or the Devotion Aura, which adds armor rating to all units near the Hero. Devotion Aura is the best choice right now, because it will immediately improve your Footmen by increasing their armor by +1.

An alcove of trees is accessible from the main path (see map) near the starting encampment. A villager named Benedict calls for help as you enter the enclosure, but it's a trap! When you approach him, he reveals himself to be a Bandit as the rest of the criminals in his posse hop out of the trees and attack your group! Dash their plans by using Holy Light to keep your men healthy and reduce these foes to a pile of skeletons. The Bandits leave a Scroll of Healing that Arthas can pick up and use to heal your troops later in the game.

Proceed down the path to meet up with Gerard and his wife, Matilda. You'll learn that some Bloodhill Bandits just waltzed off with an important ledger and you are charged with retrieving it.

Chase the fleeing Bandits to their base in the southeast corner of the map, where Menag and four of his brutes defy you to take back the ledger. A bloody battle ensues, so have Arthas judiciously use his Holy Light spell again. Gerard's stolen item and a potion of Mana are yours when you defeat the Bandits. Return the ledger to Gerard and you'll get a Tome of Strength in return, increasing Arthas' strength rating by +1.

The fight with Menag is tough, but Holy Light should enable your troops to prevail without any casualties.

Benedict turns out to be a wolf in sheep's clothing. The Bandits in this enclosure won't be anything that your Footmen and Arthas can't handle.

STRAHNBRAD

The time has come to visit Strahnbrad and defeat the Slave Master. Cross the bridge and approach the gates. Prepare to fight a pair of Orc Grunts. Strahnbrad is a large town that occupies most of the northeast quadrant of the map. There are four 'arms' that branch off from Strahnbrad's central square. The Slave Master is in the upper-left arm (see map), so save that area for last if you want to gain the most experience. Move through Strahnbrad, slaying the Orc enemies as they surface. When you get to the lower-left area of town, you'll find some Footmen fighting with Orcs—these soldiers join you, bolstering your ranks for the last time before you meet the Slave Master.

There is a group of reinforcements in the lower-left 'arm' of Strahnbrad.

Once your ranks are full and all the enemies have been destroyed, move up toward the upper-left 'arm' off the central square to meet the Slave Master. Before you can face your ultimate foe, some of the villagers must be unavoidably removed from the town. Throw everything you've got at the Slave Master and his two defending Grunts. When this fearsome crew has fallen to your forces, the mission is complete! Enjoy the victory, but don't get comfortable—your missions only become more challenging from this point forward.

The Slave Master is tough, but your Footmen can take him down without much trouble.

CHAPTER 2

BLACKROCK & ROLL

Shortly after your victory in Strahnbrad, Arthas reconvenes at Uther's camp. The great Paladin has sent two of his best Knights into parlay with the Orc leader, the Blademaster, but when two Knight horses return without their masters, Uther requests that you, Arthas, lead the attack on the Orc encampment.

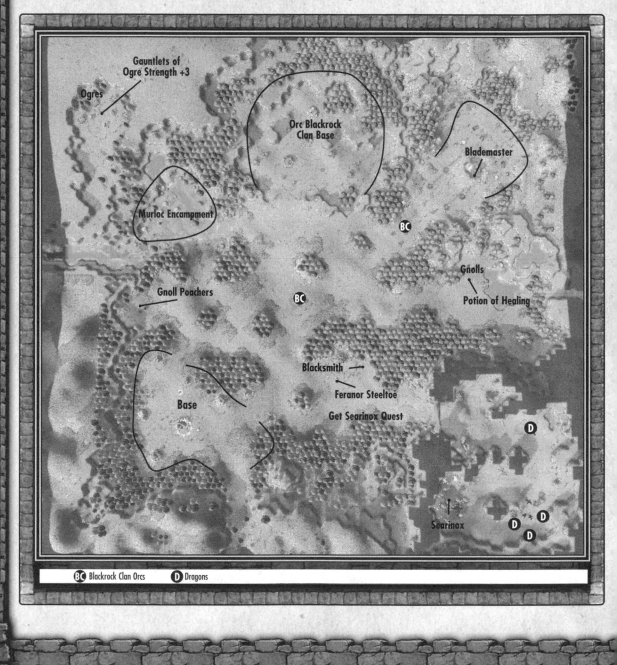

Gauntlets of
Ogre Strength +3

Ogres

Orc Blackrock
Clan Base

Blademaster

Murloc Encampment

BC

Gnolls

Potion of Healing

Gnoll Poachers

BC

Blacksmith

Feranor Steeltoe

Get Searinox Quest

Base

D

Searinox

D

D

D

BC Blackrock Clan Orcs   D Dragons

AVAILABLE STRUCTURES

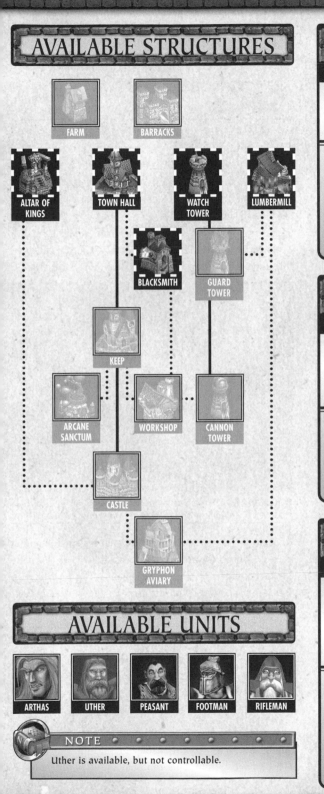

FARM

BARRACKS

ALTAR OF KINGS

TOWN HALL

WATCH TOWER

LUMBERMILL

BLACKSMITH

GUARD TOWER

KEEP

ARCANE SANCTUM

WORKSHOP

CANNON TOWER

CASTLE

GRYPHON AVIARY

AVAILABLE UNITS

ARTHAS

UTHER

PEASANT

FOOTMAN

RIFLEMAN

NOTE
Uther is available, but not controllable.

ESTABLISH BASE

REQUIRED QUEST

Uther has instructed you to establish a base by constructing buildings and producing units for the fight against the Orc menace.

REQUIREMENTS

* Construct a Barracks.
* Construct two Farms.
* Train six Footmen.

BLADEMASTER

REQUIRED QUEST

The Blademaster will not reason with Uther, and as a result violence has become the only solution to the problem. Arthas must lead an attack force into the Orc encampment and cleanse it of its Orcish presence.

REQUIREMENTS

* Defeat the Blademaster.
* Arthas must survive.

SEARINOX

OPTIONAL QUEST

Feranor Steeltoe is a Dragon hunter who's looking to capture the Dragon Searinox. Steeltoe says that if you can return the Heart of Searinox to him, he can create something that will bestow fiery abilities on Arthas.

REQUIREMENTS

* Bring the Heart of Searinox to Feranor Steeltoe.
* Slay Searinox the Black Dragon.

Receive on Completion: Orb of Fire

THE PATH TO VICTORY

This chapter in the Human saga requires you to complete two quests before advancing. You must first construct a base to the required level, then destroy the Blademaster. While this can be done without completing the optional quest or doing battle in the main Orc base, we recommend clearing the entire map to provide Arthas with valuable experience and items.

BUILD THE BASE

Add to your starting base by immediately building two Farms, a Barracks, and possibly even upgrading the Scout Towers to Guard Towers. While you don't necessarily need additional Peasants to complete this task, training a couple more certainly speeds up your efforts. Start churning out Footmen as soon as possible, because the Blackrock Clan will attack the eastern edge of your base as you attempt to build the base. Once you have six Footmen and the rest of the base is built, your first required quest is complete.

When the Blackrock Clan attacks, send Arhtas and Uther out to squelch the invasion.

SEARINOX, FERANOR STEELTOE, AND THE BLACKSMITH

Move your troops (the six Footmen and Arthas) east toward Feranor Steeltoe's encampment. When you meet him, you receive the Searinox quest and Steeltoe lends you the use of four Riflemen—an essential force to defeat the Dragons. Steeltoe also offers you the services of the Blacksmith, giving you access to the first four troop upgrades: Iron Forged Swords, Iron Plating, Black Gunpowder, and Studded Leather Armor. These are all valuable upgrades, so start improving your troops right away.

FERANOR STEELTOE: Now, I will reforge your weapons to strike with searing heat!

Feranor Steeltoe gives you some Riflemen and lets you use his Blacksmith to upgrade your troops.

To begin this quest, group your units into a single fighting force and head toward the southeast corner of the map. You'll encounter the first Black Dragon Welp after passing through an archway. Not surprisingly, the only units that can hit it are your Riflemen, but that doesn't mean you should forsake your Footmen (you'll need them soon). Work your way through the Welps until you get to Searinox (see map). Searinox summons Skeletal Archers to defend him, and this is where your Footmen earn their keep. Send the Footmen after the Skeletal Archers while your Riflemen bring down Searinox.

Return the Heart of Searinox to Feranor Steeltoe, and he forges an Orb of Fire for Arthas, giving him a whopping +12 damage rating! This optional quest is too good to pass up.

Have your Footmen focus their damage on the Skeletal Archers since they cannot attack Searinox. Your Riflemen can then concentrate on the big dragon.

NOTE

Arthas will likely level up again soon, earning him another point to add to his spells. How you spend this point is up to you, but we recommend investing in Holy Light. This spell heals 400 points with just two points in it, which is enough to restore full health to a Footman each time it's cast!

The Murloc Encampment and Gnoll Poachers

There's a Murloc Encampment in the northwest corner of the map, and a pair of Gnoll groups on its central edges (see map). Although it's not necessary to destroy these Creeps, doing so increases Arthas' experience points and helps him level up, ultimately making him more powerful. None of these enemies provides significant resistance, but monitor the battles closely to avoid casualties.

Blackrock Clan Base and the Blademaster

Two areas remain for you to sweep off the map. Although the mission can end by defeating the Blademaster at any time, it's better to gain the experience, so your next order of business should be to destroy the Blackrock Clan base in the northern area of the map. You'll battle several Grunts, some Troll Headhunters, and a Raider or two, so keep Arthas nearby and use his Holy Light.

The Orcs continually attempt to build units in the Barracks and the Beastiary, so go after those structures first, then clear out the Pig Farms. When the Blackrock Clan's base has been destroyed, you can turn your attention to the Blademaster and the end of this chapter.

The Blackrock Clan's base provides the toughest challenge for your troops in this chapter.

Defeating the Blademaster is your ultimate goal in this mission. He resides in a special area in the northeast corner of the map and is not well defended, other than a small group of Orcs near the entrance to his area. Move through the initial defense force to the point where you see the obelisks that mark the path to the Blademaster. When you reach the Orcish Hero, he'll try to throw you off by using a spell that produces two copies of him, creating a pair of Blademasters for you to fight. The catch is that only one is the real foe. You have no choice but to destroy them both, so have your troops attack with everything they've got!

The Blademaster duplicates himself, but only one is real.

RAVAGES OF THE PLAGUE

Arthas and his men wait near a crossroads to meet with an Archmage named Jaina. She appears, albeit late, and says that the villages along the King's road must be explored to discover the origins of the plague. Jaina joins you on this mission, bringing along her ability to summon Water Elementals.

Fountain of Health

Potion of Healing

Bandit Encampment

Murloc Base

U

U

U
U
R

M

U
U

U
U
U

Infected Granary

Bandits

Get Fountain Quest

U
U

Blighted Ground + Granary

R

Ring of Protection +2

R
U

Start

⚡⚡ Destroyed Bridge   R Reinforcements   M Murloc Tide Runners   U Undead

AVAILABLE STRUCTURES

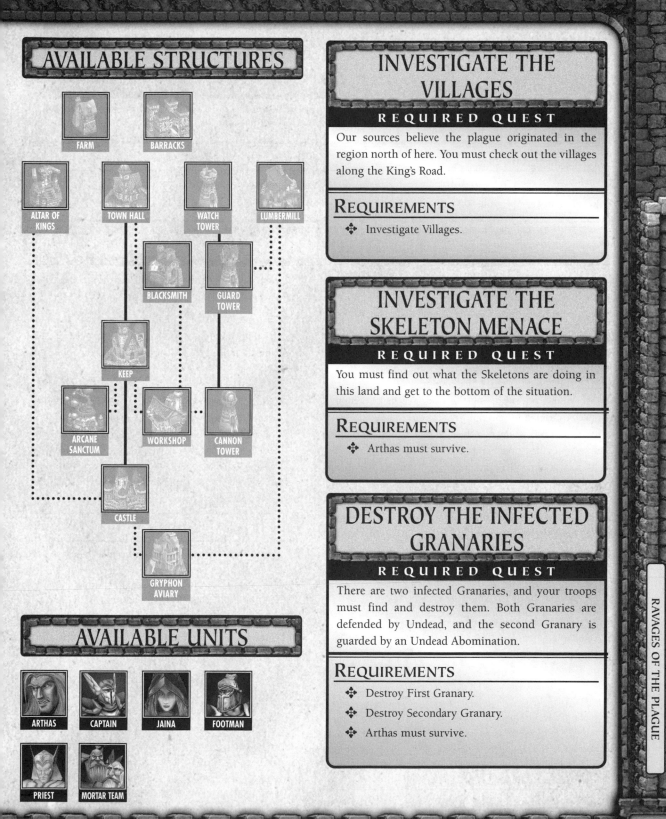

FARM

BARRACKS

ALTAR OF KINGS

TOWN HALL

WATCH TOWER

LUMBERMILL

BLACKSMITH

GUARD TOWER

KEEP

ARCANE SANCTUM

WORKSHOP

CANNON TOWER

CASTLE

GRYPHON AVIARY

AVAILABLE UNITS

ARTHAS

CAPTAIN

JAINA

FOOTMAN

PRIEST

MORTAR TEAM

INVESTIGATE THE VILLAGES

REQUIRED QUEST

Our sources believe the plague originated in the region north of here. You must check out the villages along the King's Road.

REQUIREMENTS

- ✣ Investigate Villages.

INVESTIGATE THE SKELETON MENACE

REQUIRED QUEST

You must find out what the Skeletons are doing in this land and get to the bottom of the situation.

REQUIREMENTS

- ✣ Arthas must survive.

DESTROY THE INFECTED GRANARIES

REQUIRED QUEST

There are two infected Granaries, and your troops must find and destroy them. Both Granaries are defended by Undead, and the second Granary is guarded by an Undead Abomination.

REQUIREMENTS

- ✣ Destroy First Granary.
- ✣ Destroy Secondary Granary.
- ✣ Arthas must survive.

FOUNTAIN OF HEALTH

OPTIONAL QUEST

There is an ancient fountain-shrine nearby. Legends say that the fountain's holy waters can restore health and heal grievous wounds. You must get your troops to the fountain to drink in its healing ways.

REQUIREMENTS

✦ Go to the Fountain of Health.

Receive on Completion: Restored Health (from the fountain)

THE PATH TO VICTORY

Jaina arrives and joins Arthas, two Footmen, and a Captain. Your forces begin to follow the King's Road to investigate all of the villages along the way. This mission meanders throughout the map and takes several unexpected turns.

BANDITS AND MURLOCS

Move your group up along the road (see map), keeping your eyes peeled for anything suspicious. You won't meet an enemy until you reach the first batch of Bandits near the second village. Beyond this point, you'll find Alric who tells you about the Fountain of Health quest. Continue into the river area—it looks as if you cannot pass through this area, but the water is shallow enough for your troops to make it. The river basin is rife with Murlocs, so expect some fighting along the way. There's a Murloc base in the

There's a Lightning Orb to be had if you destroy the Murloc Hut in the Murloc base.

northeast corner of the map; vanquish these troops and destroy the Murloc Hut to receive an Maul of Strength!

Keep moving toward the west until you come to a small Bandit camp along the upper path. Destroy everything there and then head down the southern river trail.

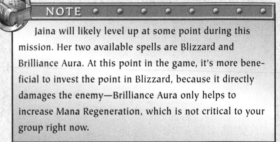

NOTE

Jaina will likely level up at some point during this mission. Her two available spells are Blizzard and Brilliance Aura. At this point in the game, it's more beneficial to invest the point in Blizzard, because it directly damages the enemy—Brilliance Aura only helps to increase Mana Regeneration, which is not critical to your group right now.

MEET THE UNDEAD

A group of Footmen join your cause in the next village. These soldiers are engaged with a group of Undead Skeleton Warriors and need your help. Throw all of your troops at the Scourge and keep an eye on how much damage your individual units are taking. The Undead tend to target one unit at a time, so be ready to use Holy Light to save your men.

After destroying the Skeleton Warriors, you get the next quest (Investigate Skeleton Menace). Move your troops toward the Fountain of Health in the northwest corner of the map. As you approach it, you face another battle with the Undead. There's a Potion of Mana in this area as well, but don't worry about it until the enemy has been neutralized. After clearing out the enemy, move up to the Fountain of Health and replenish your units.

The quest ends when you reach the Fountain of Health. This magical well replenishes all of your units' hit points when they stand beside it.

The Mortar Teams join your team when you help them out.

INVESTIGATE SKELETAL MENACE

Move your party south along the only road open to you. You discover that the Undead have taken over yet another village—crush the Skeleton Warriors there and keep moving south. Eventually, you encounter a Granary on Blighted ground. Demolish this unholy structure and two Priests join your effort. These magical Human clergy have the ability to heal your units and dispel enemy magic—adding a two-fold benefit to your ranks.

Follow the path on the map until you reach an undamaged village. Two Dwarven Mortar Teams need help as they struggle against an Undead attack. Move to the south to assist these troops and they join your army. You now have developed a fairly robust and varied attack force, including Arthas, Jaina, Footmen, Priests, and Mortar Teams.

Keep heading toward the southwest corner of the map. A few more Undead Skeletal Warriors stand in your path, but so does a Mantle of Intelligence +3. Add it to Arthas' inventory, then return to the town and prepare for a fight. The Undead are determined to defend their Granary, so concentrate on the Undead units first, then tackle their coveted structure. You definitely don't want the Scourge to have a free shot at your troops while you're trying to destroy a building.

THE FINAL GRANARY AND KEL'THUZAD

Move north to enter an area near the final Granary where a morbid mob of Undead are mulling around. Say hello to the horrific Kel'Thuzad—fortunately, he won't do anything to you in this mission. Kel'Thuzad vacates the area with his Undead minions, but leaves behind an Abomination to make your attempt at destroying the final Granary as difficult as possible. Throw everything you've got at this macabre beast, and he'll perish quickly under the strength of your attacks. Once the Abomination is restored to the pieces of corpses he was created from, level the Granary and close the book on this chapter of the Human campaign.

KEL'THUZAD
We've been discovered, my brothers! Flee and continue with the operation!

Kel'Thuzad dispatches an Abomination before he leaves.

CHAPTER 4

THE CULT OF THE DAMNED

The next day, Jaina and Arthas see cultists (Acolytes) starting to Haunt a Gold Mine on the outskirts of Andorhal. As a camp is being set up nearby, Kel'Thuzad shows up with a group of Ghouls and attacks Jaina. Arthas tries to rescue her, but it's too late, Jaina's dead.

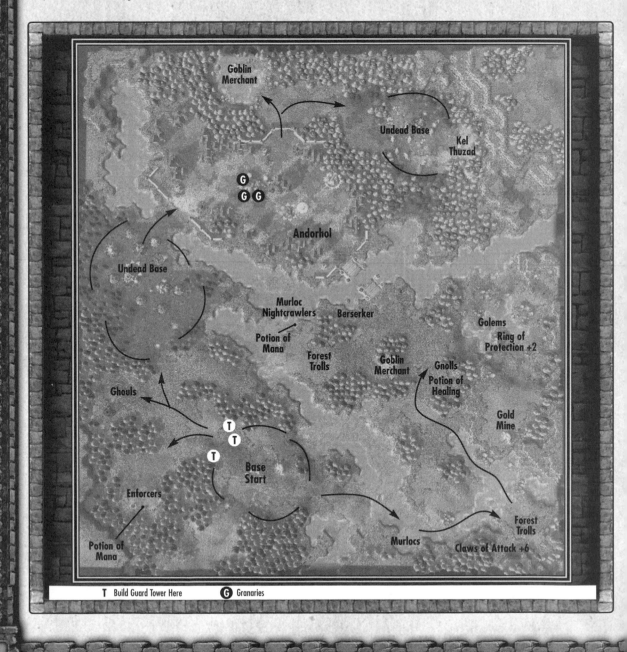

T Build Guard Tower Here   G Granaries

AVAILABLE STRUCTURES

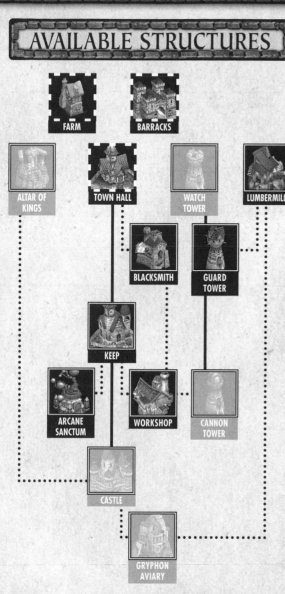

FARM

BARRACKS

ALTAR OF KINGS

TOWN HALL

WATCH TOWER

LUMBERMILL

BLACKSMITH

GUARD TOWER

KEEP

ARCANE SANCTUM

WORKSHOP

CANNON TOWER

CASTLE

GRYPHON AVIARY

AVAILABLE UNITS

ARTHAS

FOOTMAN

RIFLEMAN

PRIEST

MORTAR TEAM

JAINA

INVESTIGATE ANDORHAL

REQUIRED QUEST

The plagued crates of grain seem to have originated from Andorhal—the distribution center of Lordaeron's agricultural products. Investigate Andorhal and ascertain whether there is any link between the mysterious cultists and the dread plague.

REQUIREMENTS

✤ Expose Andorhal.

CONFRONT KEL'THUZAD

REQUIRED QUEST

The evil Necromancer, Kel'Thuzad, is apparently responsible for spreading the mysterious plague. Hunt him down and bring the renegade wizard to justice!

REQUIREMENTS

✤ Find Kel'Thuzad.

Receive on Completion: Mission Complete

THE PATH TO VICTORY

This chapter has a large map with plenty of areas for Arthas to increase his experience by fighting Creeps and the Undead. Ultimately, your Hero must leave no quadrant unexplored to advance to the next chapter of the saga, so get ready for plenty of fighting. Build your base to defend against the significant Undead force to the north, then move through the map to capture the second Gold Mine.

BUILD A TOWN

Arthas and Jaina immediately have their hands full, battling some Undead Ghouls that attack the base in waves. Defense is the first order of business—construct a pair of Guard Towers at the northwestern entrance to the base. The enemy eventually attacks this area, frequently, so the towers and a group of battle units are essential to ward off the Undead attacks.

Prepare a defense for frequent attacks on your base entrance.

Once the Guard Towers are in place and you're reasonably sure that you can fight off any attacks on your base, have your Peasants build more Farms, a Lumber Mill, and a Blacksmith—the latter allows you to upgrade both your Riflemen and Footmen. It's important to secure the other upgrades from this structure, as well, such as Long Rifles, Improved Masonry, and Advanced Lumber Harvesting. All of these make life easier when in combat later on.

VENTURING FORTH

With the work of building your town and upgrading your forces behind you, it's time to venture forth into the unknown. Begin with the three Enforcer Creeps in the camp just around the corner from your base. Move in and quickly annihilate the Enforcers to get a Potion of Mana.

Next, move back toward the southeastern corner of the camp, leaving your Guard Towers and a few Footmen behind to stave off the Undead attacks.

THE NEW GOLD MINE

Unfortunately, the Gold Mine that you begin with is not adequate for your needs in this mission. It's a good idea to secure another source of Gold and build a new Town Hall nearby to harvest it. Move your party to the east (see map) and keep an eye out for the Murlocs and various Creeps along the way. Keep Priests in your attack force to heal wounded units as you journey through the wilderness.

There are two Ghouls inside this building. You might as well get some experience by disposing of them.

The deadliest Creeps are the Stone and Mud Golems located just before the Gold Mine. Don't be afraid to use Holy Light to completely rejuvenate any unit in your party—it's always better to waste a little Mana ensuring that your troops have sufficient hit points than trying to save it and losing a unit needlessly.

The Creeps you meet en route to the Gold Mine are tough, but you're tougher.

> **NOTE**
>
> As you explore the map, hacking and slashing your way past enemies, Arthas and Jaina continue to gain experience and will likely level up again. It may be worthwhile to put a point into Divine Shield, which makes Arthas invulnerable to enemy attacks for 10 seconds.

Once you've secured the Gold Mine, move at least a pair of Peasants out to build a new Town Hall—you need 450 Gold to do this. If you think you can get by without taking control of the new Gold Mine, you're sadly mistaken. The Undead base is powerful, so you need the resources from the second mine if you want to ensure victory.

ATTACK THE UNDEAD BASE

The Undead camp directly north of your base is your first major target. It's defended mostly by Ghouls and Acolytes, but there are also some Necromancers and a few Spirit Towers that try to thin your ranks by firing from long-range. As soon as you set foot on the Blighted ground, target the nearest Undead Ghouls and cut them down quickly. Your next target should be the Spirit Towers—the sooner you destroy these structures, the healthier your troops will be! You can topple this structure in a few seconds with a pair of Mortar Teams when all of their firepower is completely focused on it.

Make the Spirit Towers a priority, because they fire on your units relentlessly until they're destroyed.

Andorhal is empty except for a few Ghouls, Kel'Thuzad, and some empty Granaries.

We recommend two attack groups—one for melee combat and the other comprised of just Mortar Units (three or four Mortars)—to bring down the particularly menacing enemy structures like the Spirit Towers and the Crypt.

Next, eliminate all remaining Ghouls and Acolytes, and destroy the Crypt—this is where the Undead create Ghouls. While it's not essential to destroy every last Undead structure, it is still a good idea because of the experience it affords both Arthas and Jaina.

As soon as you pass through the gates out of Andorhal, you'll spot a Goblin Merchant in the northwest area of the map. This is a good time to train additional troops and buy some Scrolls of Protection to buffer your forces before they attack the final Undead base.

You must defeat the last of the Abominations that Kel'Thuzad summons to protect him. These are tough nuts to crack, but you can prevail if you use Jaina's Summon Elemental to add to your ranks, along with a Scroll of Protection or two.

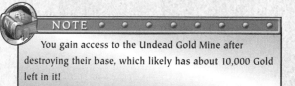

> **NOTE**
>
> You gain access to the Undead Gold Mine after destroying their base, which likely has about 10,000 Gold left in it!

ANDORHAL

Heal up your troops after clearing out the Undead and head into Andorhal (see map). There isn't much going on there, save the smoldering flames and the presence of Kel'Thuzad the Necromancer. Arthas discovers that the Granaries are empty, except for a few persistent Ghouls.

When you reach Kel'Thuzad, he informs you that his death is of little significance, so you kill him and the mission ends!

CHAPTER 5

MARCH OF THE SCOURGE

Early the next morning, Arthas and Jaina move to Hearthglen and warn the town of the coming Undead forces. Arthas learns that the plague is being distributed in the grain when, suddenly, the villagers of Hearthglen become Undead and the battle ensues. You must survive for 30 minutes!

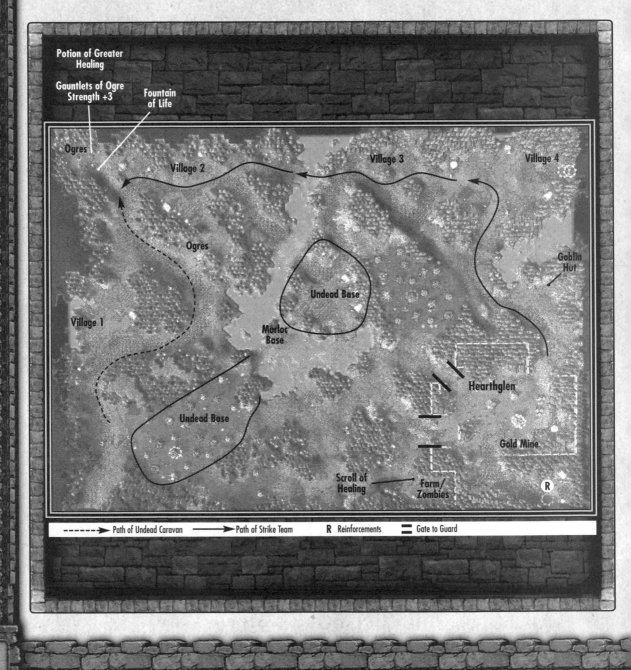

Potion of Greater Healing

Gauntlets of Ogre Strength +3

Fountain of Life

Ogres

Village 2

Village 3

Village 4

Ogres

Goblin Hut

Undead Base

Village 1

Morloc Base

Hearthglen

Undead Base

Gold Mine

Scroll of Healing

Farm/Zombies

R

- - - - - - ▶ Path of Undead Caravan   ───▶ Path of Strike Team   **R** Reinforcements   ▬ Gate to Guard

AVAILABLE STRUCTURES

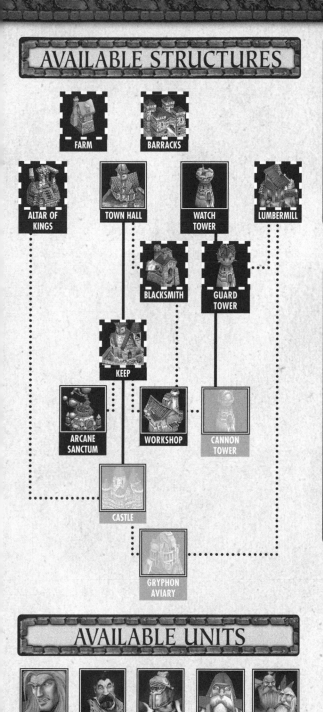

FARM

BARRACKS

ALTAR OF KINGS

TOWN HALL

WATCH TOWER

LUMBERMILL

BLACKSMITH

GUARD TOWER

KEEP

ARCANE SANCTUM

WORKSHOP

CANNON TOWER

CASTLE

GRYPHON AVIARY

AVAILABLE UNITS

ARTHAS

PEASANT

FOOTMAN

RIFLEMAN

MORTAR TEAM

PRIEST

SORCERESS

DEFEND HEARTHGLEN

REQUIRED QUEST

An Undead army has marched against Hearthglen. Arthas must defend the town until Jaina can usher in the help of Lord Uther and his legion of Knights.

REQUIREMENTS

✦ Arthas must survive for 30 minutes.

DESTROY GRAIN CARAVAN

OPTIONAL QUEST

The Undead have constructed a caravan to distribute plagued grain to the four neighboring villages of Hearthglen. Prevent further corruption of the plagued grain by destroying the caravan before it reaches the last village to the north of Hearthglen.

REQUIREMENTS

✦ Destroy Grain Caravan.

Receive on Completion: Medallion of Courage, Scroll of Town Portal

THE PATH TO VICTORY

There are two components to this mission. The first requires you to defend Hearthglen from Undead attack waves that continuously pound the town over a 30-minute period. The second component involves attempting to stop the Undead Caravan from destroying every village on the map. This aspect of the mission is entirely optional, but it's a lot of fun, and we recommend that you try to complete it.

SECURE HEARTHGLEN

As you enter Hearthglen, Arthas is hit with the frightening realization that the tainted grain has already been distributed to the townspeople. Moments later, your troops are thrust into the grasp of the Undead minions. Your first job is to kill off the Zombies in the town center. To do this, quickly click and drag a box around all friendly units and set them as Group 1 by pressing CTRL+1. Move this group from one enemy to the next, wiping them out individually with cooperative attacks. If any of your units become heavily damaged, have Arthas use his Holy Light spell to heal them.

After securing Hearthglen, create a few more Peasants. This helps keep the economy rolling while you build up your forces to defend the town from the imminent onslaught. Have two Peasants collect Lumber while at least five others gather Gold. Also, build a Workshop and an Arcane Sanctum after you train half a dozen Footmen and Riflemen to defend the base.

THE UNDEAD CARAVAN

The Undead launch a Caravan that's hell bent on spreading their plague across every village on the map. The Caravan lurches around the map along a clockwise path, beginning in Village 1, in an attempt to infect each community. Your quest calls upon you to try to save each village from infection and destroy the Caravan.

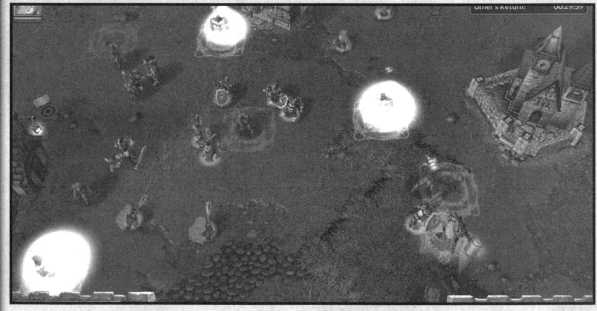

You must first clear Hearthglen of the Undead menace.

Prepare a strike team by taking Arthas and the initial group of soldiers (Footmen, Priest, Riflemen) and immediately follow the road north, then west, through each of the villages. If you move quickly, you can meet up with the Caravan just south of Village 2. Be ready for a significant fight when this happens. Your troops will all become plagued and take damage, but you should be able to defeat the Caravan without losing more than one or two units. The Priest's healing abilities and Arthas' Holy Light are critical to your success.

When the Caravan falls, Arthas is rewarded with a Medallion of Courage and a Scroll of Town Portal. The scroll can transport the entire strike force back to Hearthglen in an instant, but that's not what you're going to do right now. Your troops are plagued and injured, so move up to the northwest corner of the map and replenish their health at the Fountain of Life. Unfortunately, an

Ogre encampment is parked right beside these healing waters, so you may end up in another battle. These Creeps yield Gauntlets of Ogre Strength +3 and a Potion of Greater Healing when you defeat them.

> **TIP**
>
> Avoid the middle of the map when taking the strike team on a path to intercept the Undead Caravan. Cutting through this dangerous area alerts one of the two large Undead bases, spelling certain death for your forces. Instead, move counter-clockwise around the perimeter of the map until you run into the Caravan. As long as just one of the four villages is unaffected by the Caravan, you can still win this optional quest.

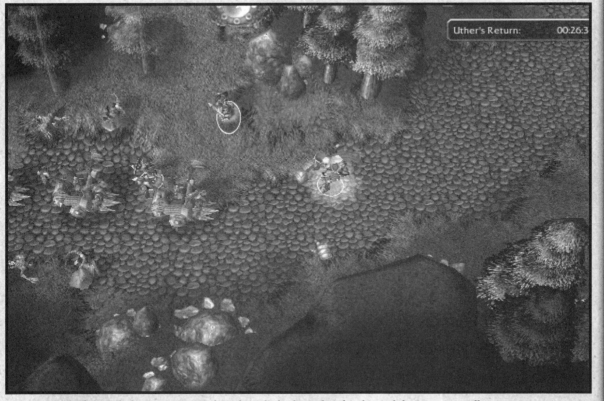

The fight with the Caravan is tough, making the healing roles of Arthas and the Priest especially important.

It's important to stand right beside the Fountain of Life when fighting the Ogres so that your troops recover while they do battle. Even so, Arthas may still have to break out Holy Light more than once to save some of the strike team from death.

The strike team remains plagued for a short time after the Undead Caravan attack and continually loses hit points. Group your wounded soldiers around the Fountain of Life to recover all lost health. Eventually, the Plague leaves their bodies, and you can return them to Hearthglen to defend the town.

The Fountain of Life replenishes lost health in any unit that gets close enough to it.

DEFEND HEARTHGLEN

While the strike team is off taking care of the Caravan, Hearthglen is attacked two or three times by small groups of Ghouls. Two or three Footmen and a pair of Riflemen coupled with the Guard Towers is a sufficient town defense while Arthas is away.

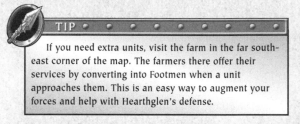

TIP

If you need extra units, visit the farm in the far southeast corner of the map. The farmers there offer their services by converting into Footmen when a unit approaches them. This is an easy way to augment your forces and help with Hearthglen's defense.

Don't forget that Arthas acquired a Scroll of Town Portal in his victory over the Undead Caravan. This item immediately transports him and the units around him back to Hearthglen when invoked, which should make you worry a lot less about getting back to town in time to help thwart a major enemy attack. As long as you have that scroll, Arthas can always be somewhere else on the map.

It's time to pour all of your resources into building up Hearthglen's defense. This includes adding units, including Mortar Teams, Priests, and Sorceresses, as well as upgrading your troops in the Blacksmith and Barracks. Thirty minutes is more than enough time to successfully upgrade everything available in this mission.

Expect a series of minor attacks on the two western gates—mostly four or five Ghouls with a Necromancer in each attack. These attacks are easily turned away, but should still be taken seriously.

There is an Goblin Hut (merchant) just to the North of Hearthglen. It sells Scrolls of Protection, Mana potions, Health potions and numerous other items. We recommend grabbing a few Scrolls of Protection so that when the large assault hits Hearthglen, Arthas can use the scrolls to improve your troop's chances.

FINAL ASSAULT ON HEARTHGLEN

Prepare for a large-scale attack on Hearthglen as the final five minutes begin to tick down on this mission. This assault comes at roughly the two-minute mark, and no matter how well you prepare, it will inevitably be overwhelming. Still, it's important to have a sufficient defensive infrastructure to hold off the onslaught until Uther arrives. It takes a minimum of 20 units to defend Hearthglen from the enemy long enough. When Uther arrives, the mission is over and success will be yours!

When the Undead bring it, you will be overwhelmed.

Build up your force and ensure that all upgrades are in place before the final five minutes of the countdown begin.

> **NOTE**
>
> Don't even consider attacking the Undead base instead of waiting around Hearthglen for them to attack you. If you attempt this, you will unequivocally be crushed. The Undead bases are simply too powerful for you to hit them with a preemptive strike in this mission.

> **NOTE**
>
> There are a few pockets of Zombies and Ogres on the map that you may want to flush out with Arthas and the strike team—it's entirely up to you whether you do this or not, but be warned that you may become overwhelmed by the Undead Scourge if you venture too far into enemy territory.

CHAPTER 6

THE CULLING

The Prophet meets with Arthas to tell him that the land is lost, and nothing Arthas can do will deter it. The Prophet adds that he must also flee across the sea to the west, but Arthas refuses. The Prophet warns that the harder Arthas tries to save his homeland from the Undead, the more successful the Undead will become. The next morning, Uther shows up on the outskirts of Stratholme. Arthas informs him that Stratholme must be purged. Uther challenges him, and then Arthas relieves Uther of his command. Jaina and Uther leave as Arthas begins to kill all of the villagers.

| **M** | Mal'Ganis | ☐ | House with Villagers |

AVAILABLE STRUCTURES

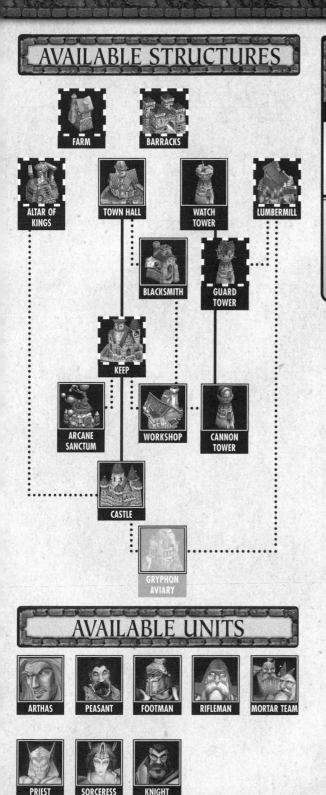

FARM

BARRACKS

ALTAR OF KINGS

TOWN HALL

WATCH TOWER

LUMBERMILL

BLACKSMITH

GUARD TOWER

KEEP

ARCANE SANCTUM

WORKSHOP

CANNON TOWER

CASTLE

GRYPHON AVIARY

AVAILABLE UNITS

ARTHAS

PEASANT

FOOTMAN

RIFLEMAN

MORTAR TEAM

PRIEST

SORCERESS

KNIGHT

THE CULLING OF STRATHOLME

REQUIRED QUEST

Kill 100 villagers to prevent Mal'Ganis from converting them into an army of the Undead with which to overrun Lordaeron. The villagers of Stratholme are hiding inside the city buildings.

REQUIREMENTS

❖ Kill 100 Villagers.

❖ Stop Mal'Ganis from converting 100 Villagers.

THE PATH TO VICTORY

The goal in this chapter of the Human saga is to kill 100 villagers in Stratholme before Mal'Ganis can convert them into Undead Zombies. These pawns in a battle of good versus evil have sequestered themselves inside their homes throughout the map. To get at them, you must specifically attack each house and destroy it. Destroying a house exposes the villagers within.

THE BASE

Although you begin in a substantial base with the resources and ability to assemble a formidable force, Don't lose sight of the quest. Begin the fight with Mal'Ganis and get a head start on killing the villagers. There are a few benefits, however, to improving your base a bit beyond the starting structures.

Even though you can build a significant base in this mission, it's not necessary to do so.

Allocate your Peasants this way—four mining for Gold and two chopping trees with one Peasant set to building a Farm. Upgrade your Town Hall to a Keep, then build a Workshop so that Mortar Teams become available. It's also important to construct a Blacksmith so that you can upgrade your units as the mission progresses. Train an attack force of Riflemen, two Mortar Teams, Arthas, and a few Footmen before going after the villagers.

100 VILLAGERS

The main goal of the mission is to kill 100 villagers before Mal'Ganis converts them into an Undead army. These villagers are hiding in their houses (see map for exact locations). Each house, which must be destroyed to reveal its occupants, contains four villagers. That means 25 houses must be decimated, along with all those inside, to meet the victory conditions for this mission.

Prepare a small attack force consisting of Arthas, two or three Footmen, and a few Riflemen, then venture onto the map and start to target houses right away, killing as many villagers as possible. Mal'Ganis appears and begins destroying houses, too, turning the occupants into Undead Zombies. Go after the Mal'Ganis as soon as he shows up and kill him as quickly as possible.

Mal'Ganis should be eliminated right away to prevent him from turning the villagers into Undead.

Mal'Ganis is resurrected and back in the swing of things about three minutes after he's killed. Continue destroying houses and villagers, but also use this time to build a Workshop so that you can train Mortar Teams. These are important units in this quest because a pair of them can destroy a villager's house in two volleys, vastly improving the effectiveness of your efforts.

> **NOTE**
>
> Two structures can be of great help in this mission. First, there's a Goblin Hut on the north-central edge of the map. This neutral building provides Arthas with Mana potions, Healing Scrolls, and even a Scroll of Protection or two. Another important structure is the Fountain of Life that lies dead center on the eastern edge of the map.

A counter in the top-right corner of the screen tracks the number of villagers Mal'Ganis has converted to Undead compared to the number that you have killed. Keep an eye on this counter—if you're considerably ahead of Mal'Ganis (20 or more villagers up), then you don't have to worry about eliminating him—you can just continue to waste villagers. If his numbers are close to or ahead of your villager count, however, then you should definitely kill him. It's okay to divert Arthas from killing villagers in favor of battling Mal'Ganis; after all, if Mal'Ganis is fighting Arthas, then he can't gain ground by converting villagers. When you've killed 100 villagers, the mission ends in your favor!

Once the 100th villager is dead (not Undead), a cinematic with Mal'Ganis and Arthas ensues.

The Undead Base

The Undead base in the southwest corner of the map produces some units that randomly patrol the map. Its wandering minions may give you a few headaches, but on the whole you shouldn't worry about it. If Mal'Ganis is killed, he's revived at the Altar of Darkness on the western edge of the Undead base. You can head straight for this location and destroy him as soon as he's resurrected.

This base is unbelievably strong, and it's nearly impossible to overcome it with the resources at your disposal. It's best just to leave it alone and focus on killing villagers.

Clever Tactics

There are a few things you can do to make this mission go smoother. First, you can create one attack force that's solely responsible for destroying Mal'Ganis, and a second that concentrates on killing the villagers. This requires more time early in the game to build the force up, but the results are very effective if you can handle the extra management responsibilities of a second attack group.

Another tactic is to build up a series of Guard and Cannon Towers on the few clear areas of grass on the map. In the central area, there's space for *four* towers, and this can really aggravate Mal'Ganis when he wanders by.

Building Cannon or Guard Towers on the few available patches can really be a thorn in the side of Mal'Ganis.

CHAPTER 7

THE SHORES OF NORTHREND

One month later, along the icy coast of Daggercap Bay, Arthas is setting up a base camp to defend against Mal'Ganis and his Undead forces. After a brief exploration, Arthas finds Muradin Bronzebeard. Together with this new ally, there may still be hope.

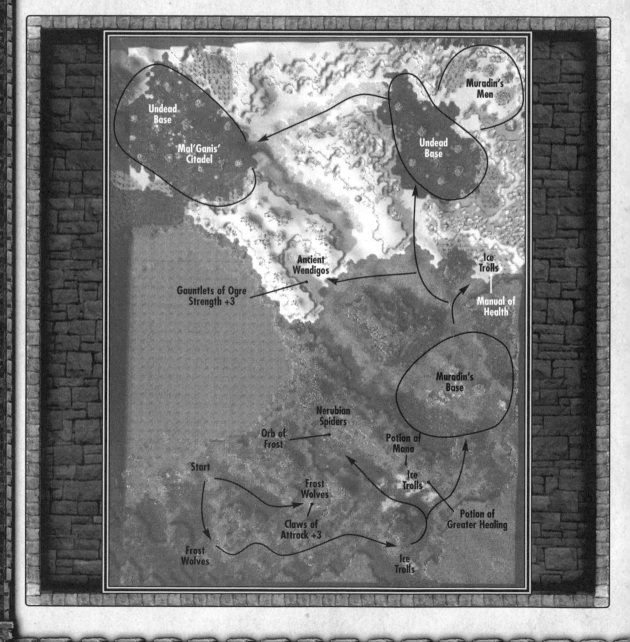

Undead Base

Mal'Ganis' Citadel

Muradin's Men

Undead Base

Ice Trolls

Ancient Wendigos

Gauntlets of Ogre Strength +3

Manual of Health

Muradin's Base

Nerubian Spiders

Orb of Frost

Potion of Mana

Start

Ice Trolls

Frost Wolves

Potion of Greater Healing

Claws of Attack +3

Frost Wolves

Ice Trolls

AVAILABLE STRUCTURES

FARM

BARRACKS

ALTAR OF KINGS

TOWN HALL

WATCH TOWER

LUMBERMILL

BLACKSMITH

GUARD TOWER

KEEP

ARCANE SANCTUM

WORKSHOP

CANNON TOWER

CASTLE

GRYPHON AVIARY

AVAILABLE UNITS

ARTHAS CAPTAIN MURADIN PEASANT FOOTMAN

PRIEST SORCERESS STEAM TANK RIFLEMAN MORTAR TEAM KNIGHT GYROCOPTER

ESTABLISH A BASE CAMP

REQUIRED QUEST

Before you can assault Mal'Ganis, you must first establish a base. Find a Gold Mine in this forsaken land and set up camp there.

REQUIREMENTS

- ✥ Find a Gold Mine.
- ✥ Arthas must survive.

MAL'GANIS

REQUIRED QUEST

Find Mal'Ganis' citadel in Northrend and destroy it.

REQUIREMENTS

- ✥ Destroy Mal'Ganis' Citadel.

RESCUE MURADIN'S MEN

OPTIONAL QUEST

Muradin's Dwarves are being cut off by an Undead base full of Crypt Fiends. Your job is to destroy it and liberate the Dwarves.

REQUIREMENTS

- ✥ Rescue the Dwarven Base.

Receive on Completion: Gain extra base and units.

THE PATH TO VICTORY

This mission has three distinct stages. First, you must find a suitable place to create a base. Stage two involves freeing Muradin's men from the Undead that have them cornered. Finally, you must press forward and demolish Mal'Ganis' Citadel to achieve ultimate victory.

FIND MURADIN BRONZEBEARD

You begin on the shores of Daggercap Bay with Arthas, a Priest, a Captain, and three Footmen. While searching for a suitable base location, you hook up with a new ally, Muradin Bronzebeard, and inherit an already established base. The route to Bronzebeard's camp, however, presents a few obstacles.

The first area beyond the shore is occupied by two groups of vicious Frost Wolves. Keep the Priest in the back of your party, constantly healing, to avoid any casualties when fighting these creatures. One group yields Claws of Attack +3 (see map), so it's worth fighting them.

Defeat the Frost Wolves to get Claws of Attack +3.

Keep moving toward Muradin's base (see map). Fight the Ice Trolls, then decide whether or not you want to tackle the Nerubian Spiders, which yield an Orb of Frost when they perish. Fighting the Spiders is difficult, and requires Arthas to have Holy Light armed and ready to heal very quickly as your units get hit.

TIP

Be sure to destroy the Ice Troll Huts after you dispose of their inhabitants—there's a Potion of Greater Healing in one of these structures.

After clearing out all of the enemies in the maze-like area beyond Daggercap Bay, move into Muradin's base and the friendly Mountain King joins your ranks.

FREE MURADIN'S MEN

Once in Muradin's base, you must build some new facilities, such as a Blacksmith, a Workshop, more Farms, an Altar of Kings, and an Arcane Sanctum. Train an attack force that includes two Steam Tanks, two Priests, as well as some Knights, Footmen, and Riflemen to join Arthas and Muradin. Be prepared for occasional attacks from Mal'Ganis' camp by keeping some troops ready at the northern edge of the base at all times. These modest invasions won't be significant enough to threaten your base. As long as you have a Priest or two with Autocasting enabled for their Heal spell, your troops should be fine.

There are several small attacks on Muradin's base after you arrive, so always have at least a half-dozen units ready (along with the Guard Towers) to deal with them.

Build up the base and be ready for some Undead attacks to come your way.

Once you have a base with multiple upgrades in the Blacksmith, move your attack force north and crush the Ice Trolls and Ancient Wendigos. Eliminating these Creeps is not mandatory, but the Wendigos yield Gauntlets of Ogre Strength +3 and the Ice Trolls cough up a Manual of Health, which permanently raises the hit points of one of your Heroes! The Ice Trolls do not put up much of a fight, but the Wendigos are tough—the chief of this crew is at level 9, so you'll have your work cut out for you. Position your Priests in the back and have Arthas ready to cast his Holy Light spell.

NOTE

You now have two Heroes. Put them into the same group so the experience earned from battles is split between the two rather than one getting all of it. If you want to raise Muradin's experience more quickly, then you can leave Arthas out of the attack group. Note that even when they're together, Muradin still levels up during this mission.

Also be aware that you can switch from Arthas' spells to Muradin's by pressing the TAB key. This is an important skill in battle, so practice using it.

To free Muradin's men, you need only attack the Undead base that's blocking your access to it. Have your attack group hit it hard with the bulk of your group firing at the Crypt Fiends and Ghouls while your Steam Tanks target the Spirit Towers. Again, keep Arthas ready with Holy Light.

The first Undead base won't be much of challenge for you if you've followed our advice on training and upgrading troops.

TAKE THE CITADEL

When Muradin's men are free, you inherit the buildings and units inside the northern base, including a Workshop, a Blacksmith, the Town Hall, some Farms, and several units. If your initial attack force is still intact, you can move directly toward Mal'Ganis' Citadel in the northwest corner of the map. We suggest three attack groups—one with Muradin, another with Arthas, and a third comprised of six Gyrocopters (you inherit two when you liberate Muradin's men).

You need three separate attack groups to crush Mal'Ganis' Citadel.

Move your troops along the road to the Undead base and begin the attack. Your Gyrocopters immediately find some Gargoyles to fight as your ground troops get tied up with Skeletal Warriors and Crypt Fiends. Amidst the chaos, send your Steam Tanks straight for the Spirit Towers one after another until they've all been destroyed. These structures provide a significant amount of fire-power to the Undead, so eliminating them greatly reduces their defenses.

This battle presents an excellent opportunity to use Arthas' Resurrection spell to raise up six fallen warriors from the dead. If you're taking a severe beating and have lost at least half a dozen units, use this spell to bring them all back to life at full health!

This is a bloody battle, but stick with it and use your healing abilities to prevail.

Despite the intensity of the battle, don't give up—even if you're losing. Sometimes it looks very bleak, but your units will ultimately accomplish what you've set out to do. Indeed, even if your troops aren't the last soldiers left standing when the dust clears, the enemy base will still be utterly decimated. Since you have two complete bases (and Gold Mines) running, you can always rebuild (and revive your Heroes) very quickly for a subsequent attack that finishes off the Undead once and for all. The mission is over when the last building in their base has been driven into the Blighted ground.

DISSENSION

An emissary arrives early the next morning at Arthas' new base camp. He informs the Captain that Lord Uther has convinced Arthas' father to recall the troops. Arthas is not happy with this decision and decides that the five ships must be burned down to their frames, thus preventing the troops from following the king's orders to return. Arthas' forces will have no choice but to help him attempt the defeat of Mal'Ganis.

AVAILABLE STRUCTURES

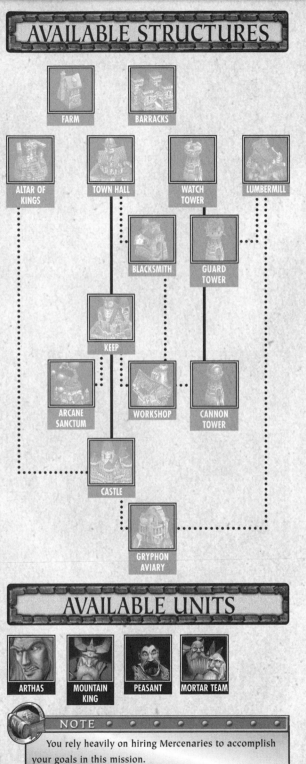

FARM

BARRACKS

ALTAR OF KINGS

TOWN HALL

WATCH TOWER

LUMBERMILL

BLACKSMITH

GUARD TOWER

KEEP

ARCANE SANCTUM

WORKSHOP

CANNON TOWER

CASTLE

GRYPHON AVIARY

BURN THE BOATS

REQUIRED QUEST

Lord Uther has ordered that your expedition be recalled. To prevent your men from abandoning the hunt for Mal'Ganis, you must burn their ships before they reach the frozen shoreline.

REQUIREMENTS

✥ Destroy all five ships.

✥ Timer must not reach 00:00.

AVAILABLE UNITS

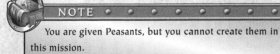

ARTHAS

MOUNTAIN KING

PEASANT

MORTAR TEAM

NOTE
You rely heavily on hiring Mercenaries to accomplish your goals in this mission.

NOTE
You are given Peasants, but you cannot create them in this mission.

You have only 25 minutes to scour the map and destroy all five ships. This may not seem like a lot of time, especially early in the mission, but it is sufficient to comfortably complete the mission with at least five minutes to spare.

ACQUIRE MERCENARIES

You start with just Muradin Bronzebeard and Arthas. Although they both should have significant abilities by this time, you need more than these two powerful Heroes to accomplish your goals. Make your way to the first Mercenary Camp and hire some mercenaries to augment your efforts. Fortunately, the Peasants at your camp are constantly mining Gold and harvesting Lumber, so you have the resources necessary to purchase the fighter's allegiance.

Follow the westward path that leads to a pack of six Ghouls. Quickly waste them with Muradin's Thunder Clap, but don't expect to grab an item for your troubles.

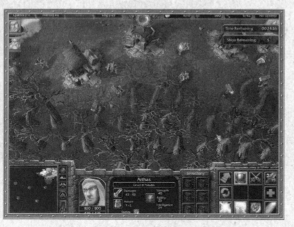
Get started harvesting resources early.

Keep moving west until you reach a small Undead base, complete with a Ziggurat and two Ghouls. Hit the Ghouls first before they have time to get close to you and ravage your troops with their melee attacks. A blast of Muradin's Storm Bolt easily handles these enemies (if the

spell is at Level 3), and the Ziggurat falls quickly when both Heroes pound away at it. Because Holy Light cannot heal Arthas, it's best to let Muradin take the hits in this battle.

After leveling the Undead encampment, continue westward toward the first Mercenary Camp (Camp 1 on the map). You can hire various Creeps here, including an Ice Troll, an Ogre Warrior, and Ice Troll Priest. The latter is an important acquisition because of his ability to heal your units on the fly, including Arthas. The Ice Troll Warlord carries the Trueshot Aura, which increases ranged attacks by 10%. You can afford to purchase all three Ice Troll Mercenaries, and we suggest you do so.

Even if Arthas gets hurt in this battle, the Priest Troll can promptly heal him.

THE FIRST SHIP

After purchasing your Ice Troll mercenaries, move south toward the first ship. If you think you have enough time, head to the northwest corner of the map to fight some Skeletal Marksmen before visiting the ship—eliminating these Creeps yields a Goblin Night Scope.

You must fight a group of Undead en route to the first ship—including Ghouls, a Necromancer, Crypt Fiends, and Ziggurats. These enemies usually target your weakest link first, most likely the Ice Troll Priest. This unit's healing abilities are essential, so monitor his damage carefully and use Holy Light judiciously to keep him (and any other suffering units) from death.

The Undead are tough, so keep a close eye on the battle to heal injured allies in time.

> Once at level 2 or 3, Muradin Bronzebeard's Storm Bolt is a very powerful weapon that can obliterate enemies in a single blow. It's particularly useful in this mission because a level 3 Storm Bolt can destroy a ship in one shot!

Ship 1 is situated right beside an Undead encampment—and the Blighted ground that always conjures that sinking feeling you get whenever you're near the Undead. Fighting the Scourge here may result in the death of one or two of your units; if this happens, simply return to Mercenary Camp 1 and hire replacement Ice Trolls, or just move on without them and pick some up at the next Mercenary Camp.

The ship cannot be destroyed with conventional attacks from Muradin and Arthas—you need a ranged attacker for this task. Ice Trolls are a good choice if you still have them, or have Muradin cast his Storm Bolt.

SHIP 2

Move south along the path, wary of the Nerubian Webspinners, Spiderlings, and Nerubian Warriors. You run into a small Nerubian encampment, complete with Nerubian Ziggurats. Destroy the middle Ziggurat to acquire Claws of Attack +12 and a Potion of Mana. The Claws increase the attack of either Muradin or Arthas, but we suggest that you give the bonus to Arthas. Again, Storm Bolt is a fantastic spell against the Webspinners because it can deal 300 points of damage and the Webspinners have only 340 hit points, expediting their deaths very nicely.

Ship 2 is just past the Nerubian base. Annihilate it with a Level 2 or 3 Storm Bolt. A group of Murloc Nightcrawlers lurks just beyond the ship. These enemies yield a Mana Stone when they are destroyed. Of course, fighting them also adds to your Hero's experience level and, ultimately, helps him to level up.

SHIP 3

Mercenary Camp 2 is just below Ship 2 and sells Ice Troll Berserkers and Ogre Magi. Both of these units are good fighters, and the Ogre Magi can make a significant difference with their magical abilities. The Ice Troll Berserkers are outstanding melee fighters—and a welcome addition to your group.

Move north across the bridge. Look for a path to the east that's blocked by a small forest of dead trees. Take the upper trail to the Goblin Laboratory. There's just one thing for sale there—a Goblin Snapper (three of them). This demolition team of sorts can destroy either buildings or trees. You need three teams of Goblin Snappers to blow open a path through the trees so that your team can pass.

Ship 3 is on the other side of the trees (see map). Destroy it, then hurry up to the next Mercenary Camp.

Nerubian Webspinners possess the dangerous ability to raise Skeletal Warriors.

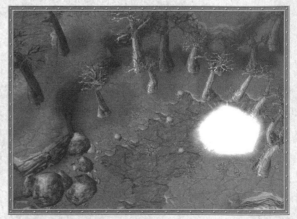

The Goblin Snappers blow a hole through these trees, clearing your path to Ship 3.

Ship 4

The next Mercenary Camp sells Ice Troll Trappers, Ice Troll High Priests, and Ogre Maulers. The Ice Troll Trapper is an excellent land/air fighter, and the High Priest has some superb magic in his arsenal. The Ogre Mauler is a brute-force attacker that helps you in melee situations. As soon as you leave the Mercenary Camp, a group of Dragon Whelps and Drakes attack. Use whatever ranged weaponry you have to bring them down—the Ice Troll High Priests are a good choice for this task. You can also use the Ice Troll Trapper's Ensnare ability to bring the Whelps down to melee level.

Use Web to get the Dragon Whelp on Arthas' terms. Run for your life (literally) through the gauntlet of Spirit Towers. Do not stop for any reason.

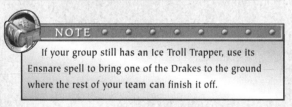

NOTE

If your group still has an Ice Troll Trapper, use its Ensnare spell to bring one of the Drakes to the ground where the rest of your team can finish it off.

There's a Goblin Merchant just past the Dragon Whelp that sells various items, including a Scroll of Healing and an Amulet of Recall—purchase these for use later in the game. When you're done shopping, prepare to run through a very tough Undead Spirit Tower gauntlet. These defensive structures line each side of your path, and they open fire on your group immediately and relentlessly. Sprint through the area as quickly as possible, without stopping even for a split second. If you run, chances are that you will lose only one or two units. If you pause, even to have Arthas cast Holy Light, it will

cost you dearly. The fourth ship is at the end of this treacherous stretch. Destroy it and then head east toward the fifth and final ship.

Run for your life (literally) through the gauntlet of Spirit Towers. Do not stop for any reason.

Ship 5

You've had an arduous journey, but it's not over yet. Ship 5 is beyond three Graveyards. It is surrounded by Necromancers, who (as you know) like to Raise Dead whenever they get a chance. After passing the Graveyards you fight the Necromancers, Ghouls, Abominations, and Crypt Fiends en route to Ship 5. Use all of your magic and hired guns to finish the job and reach the final ship. Once it's destroyed, you move on to the final chapter of the Human Campaign—Frostmourne!

The last two ships are lightly guarded and are positioned in close proximity to each other.

CHAPTER 9

FROSTMOURNE

The next day, Muradin scolds Arthas for betraying of his own men, then Mal'Ganis shows up and announces that the journey is over as he completely surrounds Arthas and his camp. Arthas asks Muradin to help him claim Frostmourne—he feels that this runeblade might be enough to tilt the scales in the Human's favor.

FW   Frost Wolf

AVAILABLE STRUCTURES

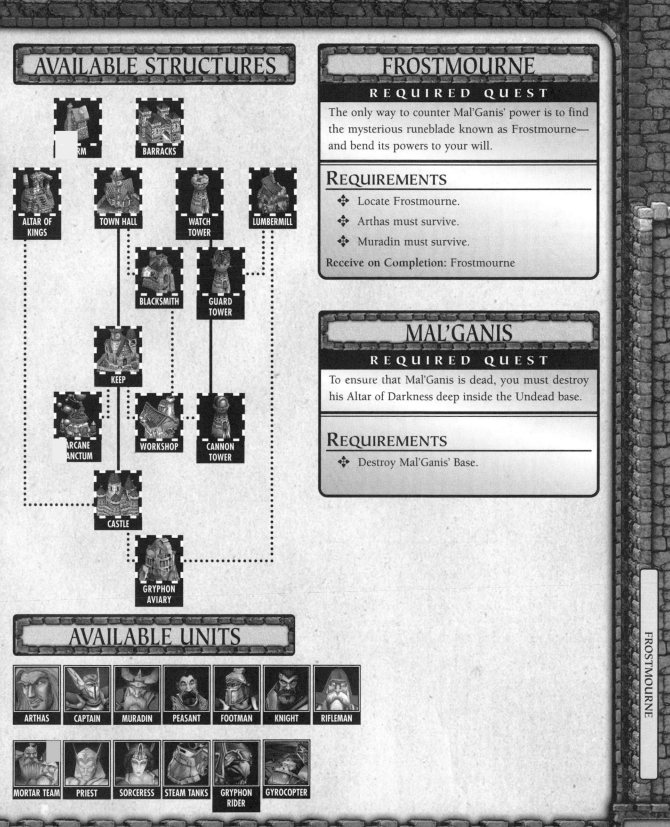

FARM

BARRACKS

ALTAR OF KINGS

TOWN HALL

WATCH TOWER

LUMBERMILL

BLACKSMITH

GUARD TOWER

KEEP

ARCANE SANCTUM

WORKSHOP

CANNON TOWER

CASTLE

GRYPHON AVIARY

FROSTMOURNE

REQUIRED QUEST

The only way to counter Mal'Ganis' power is to find the mysterious runeblade known as Frostmourne— and bend its powers to your will.

REQUIREMENTS

✥ Locate Frostmourne.

✥ Arthas must survive.

✥ Muradin must survive.

Receive on Completion: Frostmourne

MAL'GANIS

REQUIRED QUEST

To ensure that Mal'Ganis is dead, you must destroy his Altar of Darkness deep inside the Undead base.

REQUIREMENTS

✥ Destroy Mal'Ganis' Base.

AVAILABLE UNITS

ARTHAS **CAPTAIN** **MURADIN** **PEASANT** **FOOTMAN** **KNIGHT** **RIFLEMAN**

MORTAR TEAM **PRIEST** **SORCERESS** **STEAM TANKS** **GRYPHON RIDER** **GYROCOPTER**

THE PATH TO VICTORY

There are two distinct objectives in this final mission of the Human campaign. First, Arthas must find the runeblade Frostmourne and return it to his base. A sufficient attack force must also be assembled and brought to Mal'Ganis' base to destroy his means of revival, the Altar of Darkness. Attacks on your base occur throughout entire mission, so you must multitask to be successful, especially when Arthas is out looking for Frostmourne.

FIND FROSTMOURNE

Frostmourne is located in the north-central area of the map. The path that leads you there lacks any tributaries, so it won't be difficult to find. Before Arthas begins moving, group some of the units together at the home base so you can quickly return your screen to this location during an attack (by quickly pressing the group number button twice).

Group Arthas and his companions into a single party and then begin to move north. You almost immediately encounter one Dire Frost Wolf and a pair of Giant Frost Wolves, but they won't pose any problem for your formidable team. You receive a +3 Ring of Protection for slaying these beasts. Give this item to Arthas, not Muradin, because Muradin is about to die.

As soon as you attack the Frost Wolves, two waves of Mal'Ganis attacks hit the main base—one from the north entrance and another from the east entrance. Not to worry, the forces back home can repel this attack on their own if you are not able to shift your attention away from Arthas. Make sure, however, that the Priests survive. If they don't, then train more so that they can heal the injured units.

Keep moving north, claiming a Periapt of Vitality along the way that increases Arthas' hit points by 100. This course then takes you to the Fountain of Mana. A little further up the line, you face a group of Wendigos and Frost Wolves. This is a tough battle, so expect to lose at least one unit in the bloodshed. Use Muradin's Thunder Clap to damage the enemies while your other units attack.

The main base is attacked on two fronts as soon as Arthas engages the Frost Wolves.

Continue along the path until you reach the Skeletal Archers at the top of the map. These enemies give you a run for your money. Use Thunder Clap a couple of times to deal damage by the bushel to these evil incarnates, then head east to confront the final obstacle to Frostmourne—the Guardian and his Frost Revenants. You need only defeat the Guardian to get to Frostmourne, so concentrate your attacks on the big guy rather than wasting your time battling his minions. Use Muradin's Storm Bolt repeatedly to help bring the Guardian down. When he dies, his Frost Revenants perish with him, allowing you to move in and retrieve Frostmourne.

Frostmourne lies just beyond the Guardian. You need only defeat this enemy to get to it, so concentrate on him and not his Revenants.

BUILD AN ATTACK FORCE

Return to the base with Frostmourne in hand. It's time to build an attack force that can penetrate Mal'Ganis' base and destroy his base. Although Mal'Ganis continues to send attack waves on your main base, you can hunker down and defend it while upgrading your units' abilities to the necessary degree for victory. We recommend two attack groups—one with Arthas, the Captain, Knights, Riflemen, Priests, and Footmen; and a second comprised of five Steam Tanks, three Mortar Teams, and two Gryphon Riders. This dual-pronged force should be sufficient to accomplish your goal.

Take the time to build up the proper attack force before you go after Mal'Ganis. Steam Tanks are just the ticket to bring down his buildings quickly.

ACQUIRE SECONDARY RESOURCES (OPTIONAL)

The Gold Mine at your main base is amply stocked, and there should be enough nearby lumber to last for the entire mission. However, you might still consider having a second resource gathering operation on the go to speed up the process of harvesting materials. Perhaps the best location for this is the small Nerubian base just to the northeast of your base. The Gold Mine there has 15,000 Gold in it, and there's plenty of Lumber nearby, as well. If getting your hands on another Gold Mine is a tactic you'd like to embrace, then send an attack force to clear the area out and follow it up with the construction of a Town Hall.

Attacks come frequently, both from Mal'Ganis and the other Undead base on the map, so stand ready to fight as you upgrade your units and build an attack force. Also note that Mal'Ganis pays personal visits during these invasions. You can destroy him, but he'll just keep reviving himself at his Altar of Darkness until you destroy it.

The attacks just keep on coming. Don't get discouraged, just defend yourself and continue to upgrade and build in preparation for an attack of your own.

ATTACK MAL'GANIS AND HIS BASE

When your two attack groups are ready, start moving them north toward Mal'Ganis' base. The attack group with Steam Tanks will be responsible for hastily reducing enemy buildings to rubble, while Arthas' attack group

NOTE

The sole Mercenary Camp in this mission (see map), sells Frost Revenants, Ice Troll Berserkers, and Nerubian Warriors. It is not guarded, but *does* lie near the purple Undead base. There are also a couple of other areas with enemies (see map), one of which contains a Health Stone that increases the wearer's health regeneration rate and can also be consumed for an immediate 500 hit point boost! These areas of the map are entirely optional, but it may be worth going after them if you're looking for some extra action and goodies.

handles the enemy units. Together, they present a powerful force that Mal'Ganis will not be able to handle, especially if they are fully upgraded.

Move into the smaller Mal'Ganis base that's straight up the road from your main base. Have Arthas' attack group hit the Ghoul and the Acolytes while the second attack group destroys the two structures in mere seconds! After you've secured this area, get ready to move into the main base. Follow the route outlined on the map and go directly for the Altar of Darkness. Once his base is completely destroyed, the Human campaign ends victoriously!

Prevailing over Mal'Ganis' base is much more probable when you attack with two fully upgraded attack groups.

The battle against Mal'Ganis is ferocious—your units will take hits from all sides as they move toward the altar. Although your Priests can heal as you go, Arthas' Holy Light is still necessary to further augment these efforts. Keep a Potion of Mana in Arthas' inventory so that he can cast Resurrection followed by Divine Shield. He is invincible with the latter spell, enabling him to single-handedly attack the Altar of Darkness without fear of taking any damage. Resurrection is another critical spell since many of your units will be lost. Cast it to raise six dead units from their graves and give them full hit points! When the Altar of Darkness is finally in ruins, the last chapter in the Human campaign ends victoriously.

UNDEAD CAMPAIGN

PATH OF THE DAMNED

The time has come to take the reigns of another race. Arthas has turned to the Undead and you now control him as a Death Knight, a dark warrior with spectral powers that can heal units and raise the dead. The Undead campaign begins with a pair of manageable missions, but the difficulty ramps up quickly as you progress.

CHAPTER 1

TRUDGING THROUGH THE ASHES

The Lich King's plague of undeath has spread through the Capital City and into the outskirts of Lordaeron. Shocked and disheartened by the loss of their beloved king, the forces of Lordaeron were scattered by the ravenous forces. Now, the Acolytes must be brought to Tichondrius.

AVAILABLE STRUCTURES

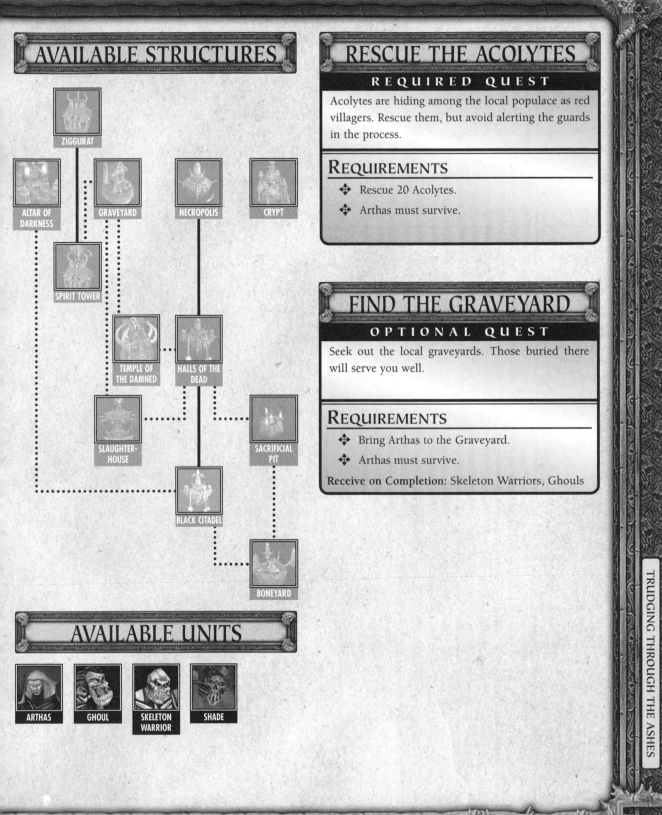

ZIGGURAT

ALTAR OF DARKNESS

GRAVEYARD

NECROPOLIS

CRYPT

SPIRIT TOWER

TEMPLE OF THE DAMNED

HALLS OF THE DEAD

SLAUGHTER-HOUSE

SACRIFICIAL PIT

BLACK CITADEL

BONEYARD

AVAILABLE UNITS

ARTHAS

GHOUL

SKELETON WARRIOR

SHADE

RESCUE THE ACOLYTES

REQUIRED QUEST

Acolytes are hiding among the local populace as red villagers. Rescue them, but avoid alerting the guards in the process.

REQUIREMENTS

- ✤ Rescue 20 Acolytes.
- ✤ Arthas must survive.

FIND THE GRAVEYARD

OPTIONAL QUEST

Seek out the local graveyards. Those buried there will serve you well.

REQUIREMENTS

- ✤ Bring Arthas to the Graveyard.
- ✤ Arthas must survive.

Receive on Completion: Skeleton Warriors, Ghouls

Now that Arthas has turned to the dark side, he has a great deal to learn and a great deal of work to complete before becoming proficient in the ways of the Undead. This mission has you scouring the map for red villagers (hidden Acolytes), who transport themselves to Tichondrius when found. Stealth is not realistic or even practical, so be prepared to do some fighting.

MEET THE SHADE

Move toward the town and cross the bridge (see map). An Acolyte approaches and explains what you must do. Your job is to take Arthas up to all of the red villagers and turn them into Acolytes, who then transport to Tichondrius' position. The first two subjects are visible as you near the end of the bridge. Approach them and release them into Acolytes. One of them tells you to visit the Graveyard to gain extra forces.

Leave the bridge and you are approached by a Shade, an Acolyte that has been sacrificed at a Sacrificial Pit. Shades cannot attack, but are invisible to most units, making them excellent for scouting. Position this unit in front of Arthas to alert your party of what lies ahead.

FREE THE ACOLYTES

Move Arthas through the town, making contact with the red villagers (see map). Your presence attracts the attention of some guards. You can either fight or avoid them. When confronted by a single hostile villager or one or two guards, choose to fight and gain the experience. If a Knight or more than two guards want to rumble, get the heck out of there!

> ### NOTE
> Arthas evolves into a powerful Hero with multiple abilities by the end of the Human campaign. Don't let his former power fool you, however—he is just a newbie in this early Undead mission. Initially, he'll have trouble dealing with a Footman, let alone a Knight, so be careful of how aggressive you are with him.

Move up the map, wary of the reinforced area ahead patrolled by a team of Knights and guards. Avoid this dangerous spot by maneuvering Arthas through the trees to the west (see map), and continue moving from one Acolyte to the next, freeing each one. If the enemy detects you and starts a chase, simply keep moving and you will be able to stay ahead of your pursuers (Arthas is on a horse, after all).

Expect some welcomed company as you approach the graveyard—three Skeleton Warriors and two Ghouls join your cause. Advance your augmented force toward the Bandit Camp in the northwest corner of the map. If you've been scouting ahead with the Shade, you'll know that three Bandits are just waiting for you to step into their trap when you attempt to rescue the Acolyte they have encased in webbing. Charge in with your graveyard buddies and crush the Bandits in one fell swoop. Use Arthas' Death Coil spell to heal any injured Undead units. The vanquished foes leave behind a Potion of Healing and a Spider Ring.

The Graveyard contains some buddies of yours who wake up upon your arrival.

There are two more Acolytes south of the Bandit Camp (and a third being held captive inside the camp). Free them all before leaving this half of the map.

THROUGH THE GATES

A set of gates lies between you and the northeastern portion of the map. An in-game message informs you that the gates may be attacked. Indeed, you must command your forces to attack this barricade in order to gain access to the other half of the map. Target the gate and break on through to the other side. Another Acolyte is activated as soon as you enter this new realm, leaving only seven others to save.

The next area of the map has a circular path. You must grab three Acolytes as you run around this road, but you'll also notice four red villagers (Acolytes) being held captive behind some boxes on the far east side. Keep moving around the ringed road, because Arthas is faster than the Footmen who pursue him. Once you get ahead of them, stop at the prison area and get the last four hidden Acolytes. Be absolutely certain that you have at least 16 Acolytes when you enter the prison—you won't be powerful enough to fight the enemy off here, so use Arthas' speed to get at the prisoners instead.

Don't let this barricade stand in the way of your quest.

If you've saved at least 16 Acolytes, then you can bust into the prison area and complete the mission without worrying about surviving the way out.

> **NOTE**
>
> Arthas will likely level up in this chapter of the Undead campaign, giving you another discretionary point to put into a new spell. We recommend spending it on Unholy Aura to increases his hit point regeneration rate by 50% and movement rate by 10%.

> **NOTE**
>
> The 'Hard' version of this level requires you to save 24 Acolytes.

CHAPTER 2

DIGGING UP THE DEAD

The next morning on the outskirts of Andorhal, Arthas learns that he must kill the Paladin guard protecting Kel'Thuzad's tomb, then use a Meat Wagon to gather up the remains of the deceased Necromancer and bring them back to be reanimated.

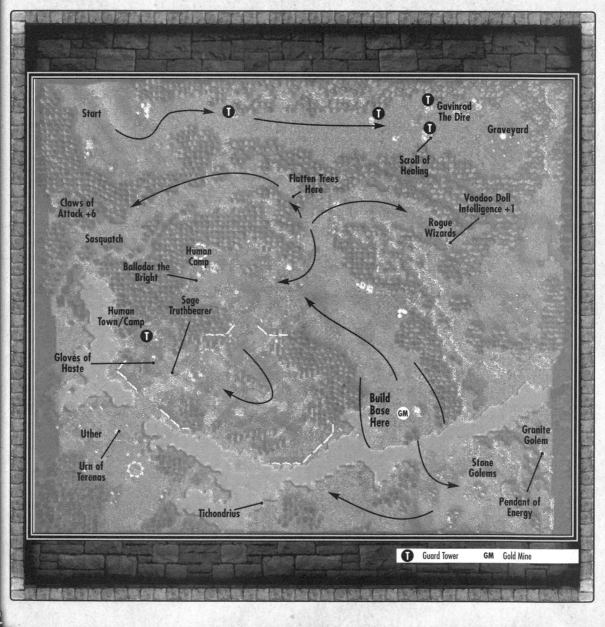

Start

T Gavinrod The Dire

Graveyard

Scroll of Healing

Flatten Trees Here

Voodoo Doll Intelligence +1

Claws of Attack +6

Rogue Wizards

Sasquatch

Human Camp

Ballador the Bright

Sage Truthbearer

Human Town/Camp **T**

Gloves of Haste

Build Base Here **GM**

Granite Golem

Uther

Stone Golems

Urn of Terenas

Pendant of Energy

Tichondrius

| **T** | Guard Tower | **GM** | Gold Mine |

AVAILABLE STRUCTURES

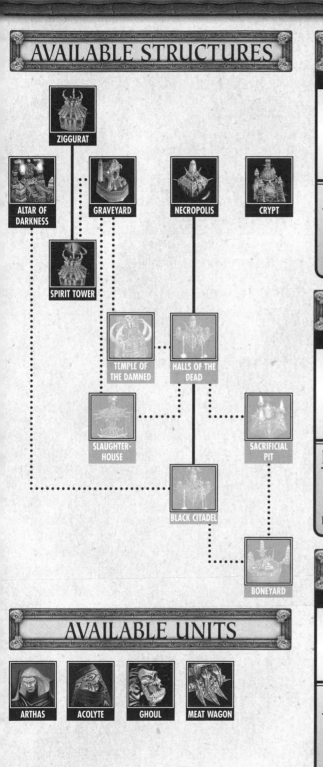

ZIGGURAT

ALTAR OF DARKNESS

GRAVEYARD

NECROPOLIS

CRYPT

SPIRIT TOWER

TEMPLE OF THE DAMNED

HALLS OF THE DEAD

SLAUGHTER-HOUSE

SACRIFICIAL PIT

BLACK CITADEL

BONEYARD

AVAILABLE UNITS

ARTHAS

ACOLYTE

GHOUL

MEAT WAGON

RECOVER REMAINS

REQUIRED QUEST

You must recover the horribly decayed remains of Kel'Thuzad. The Necromancer's remains lie within a cemetery guarded by the stoic Paladins of the Silver Hand. Deal with these holy knights before the remains can be exhumed.

REQUIREMENTS

- ✥ Kill the Paladins.
- ✥ Bring Arthas to Kel'Thuzad's grave.

Receive on Completion: Kel'Thuzad's remains

CLAIM THE URN

REQUIRED QUEST

The special urn required to hold Kel'Thuzad's remains is also guarded by Paladins of the Silver Hand. You must slay the remaining Paladins and recover the urn before your journey to Quel'Thalas can begin.

REQUIREMENTS

- ✥ Kill the Paladins.
- ✥ Recover the Urn.

Receive on Completion: Urn of King Terenas

ESTABLISH A BASE

REQUIRED QUEST

The Paladins maintain a strong hold over the surrounding area. You must establish a base and bolster your forces. Aided only by Ghouls and Meat Wagons, your challenge is to break through the Paladin's defenses.

REQUIREMENTS

- ✥ Build a Necropolis.
- ✥ Haunt a Gold Mine.
- ✥ Build a Crypt.
- ✥ Build three Ziggurats.

THE PATH TO VICTORY

This mission has two parts. First, you must move your troops across the northern portion of the map and find the Graveyard with Kel'Thuzad's remains, killing the Paladin, Gavinrad the Dire, along the way. The second portion of the mission involves building up an Undead base and then flushing the map of the three remaining Paladins, thus capturing the urn required to transport Kel'Thuzad.

RETRIEVING KEL'THUZAD'S BONES

This chapter begins with Arthas (now a Death Knight) and a group of Ghouls and Meat Wagons in the northwest corner of the map. Arthas must move these troops along a narrow path on the northern edge of the map to the graveyard that houses the dead Necromancer Kel'Thuzad. Organize your troops into two groups, with the Meat Wagons in one pack and the Ghouls and Arthas in the other. Follow the path that leads east, destroying any Human buildings along the way.

> **NOTE**
>
> Beware that the Meat Wagon's attacks *will* damage your other troops if their projectiles land on or near your units. This is why it's important not to group Meat Wagons together with melee units. You must be careful to have either one of these units attack the enemy units, but not both at the same time.

Destroy the Human buildings along the path to the east.

You eventually meet Gavinrad the Dire, one of the Paladins aligned firmly against your Undead plans. Be careful when fighting him and his Footmen, because a mass attack can quickly kill Arthas. Try to battle these troops two or three at a time.

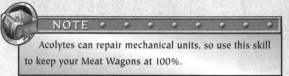

> **NOTE**
>
> Acolytes can repair mechanical units, so use this skill to keep your Meat Wagons at 100%.

Once Gavinrad the Dire is dead, enter the Graveyard in the northeast corner of the map. Inside, you meet the ghost of Kel'Thuzad. Collect his bones and you trigger the second half of this mission. Don't bother destroying all of the Human buildings in the area unless you have a strong desire to do so—they don't contain any valuable items.

BONUS MATERIAL

This map contains several Creep areas that yield some decent items, including a Voodoo Doll Intelligence +1, +6 Claws of Attack, and a Pendant of Energy. All of these areas are in remote sectors, set apart from the main action in this mission, so you don't have to worry about becoming overwhelmed. The Stone and Granite Golems in the southeast portion of the map are the Creeps closest to your base. The Granite Golem is hidden behind some trees, but quickly destroys this natural barrier and comes after you when you approach.

There are some great items to be had if you're willing to fight against nasty creatures like these Sasquatch!

The second bunch of Creeps is a group of Rogue Wizards, north of your base, that protects a +3 Mantle of Intelligence. The third bonus lies down a long forested path that leads to the western edge of the map. To access this area, you must use your Meat Wagons to flatten the trees that block your path (see map). Get ready to battle three ferocious Sasquatch, who can also summon Treants to fight in their name. Don't go after the Golem or the Sasquatch if Arthas has anything less than a full complement of Ghouls at his side or the results will be catastrophic.

TICHONDRIUS

Tichondrius does his bidding in the south-central portion of the map. He sucks the souls out of a row of sleeping villagers and rants impatiently at you. Other than the entertainment value of his morbid theatrics, traveling to his realm is of no value toward the completing the mission. Skip this area, if you wish, and you will not compromise your success in this chapter of the Undead campaign.

BALLADOR THE BRIGHT

The first Paladin is in town near a Human Barracks. He fights with Footmen at his side, and the Town Hall summons Militia to supplement the Human cause against your forces. Don't go into this fight until you've upgraded your Ghouls as much as you can—otherwise, you risk getting decimated. Use Meat Wagons (as a separate group) to level the Human Farms and Barracks as quickly as possible. Destroying Ballador yields a Potion of Healing.

SAGE TRUTHBEARER

Sage Truthbearer guards a Barracks further within the town. Slaying him nets you a set of Gloves of Haste, but again the fight is difficult because the Barracks (which is tucked away in an alcove of buildings) continually produces Footmen. Use your Meat Wagons to destroy this unit-generating structure while your ground troops deal with Sage Truthbearer.

Ballador summons Militia, which makes killing him that much harder.

UTHER LIGHTBRINGER

Once Sage and his troops have been eliminated, cross the land bridge that leads you to Uther Lightbringer. After exchanging a few harsh words, fight and kill Arthas' former mentor. Don't expect the leader of the Paladins to go down without a fight—he uses Holy Light against you and your forces. Use Death Coil on him to reduce his hit points as much as possible. When he dies, he leaves the Urn of Terenas behind. Claim this artifact to end the mission.

The Urn of Terenas appears once Uther is dead.

CHAPTER 3

INTO THE REALM ETERNAL

Six days later, near the forested borderlands of Quel'Thalas, Kel'Thuzad warns Arthas of certain Elven attacks. He suggests using great caution in this area.

AVAILABLE STRUCTURES

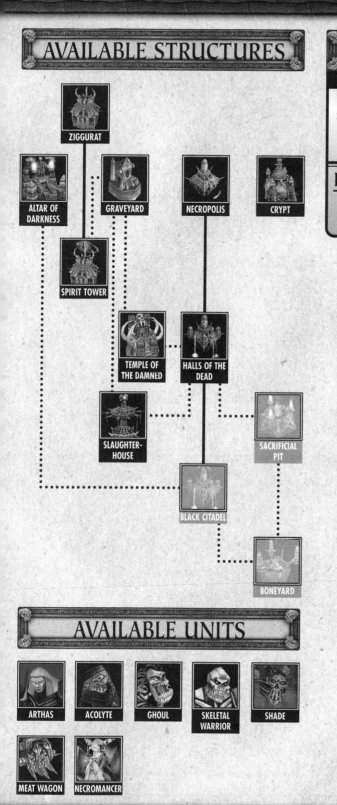

ZIGGURAT

ALTAR OF DARKNESS

GRAVEYARD

NECROPOLIS

CRYPT

SPIRIT TOWER

TEMPLE OF THE DAMNED

HALLS OF THE DEAD

SLAUGHTER-HOUSE

SACRIFICIAL PIT

BLACK CITADEL

BONEYARD

AVAILABLE UNITS

ARTHAS

ACOLYTE

GHOUL

SKELETAL WARRIOR

SHADE

MEAT WAGON

NECROMANCER

THE ELF GATE

REQUIRED QUEST

In order to march upon the High Elve's capital, Silvermoon, you must destroy the High Elf capital base (blue) guarding the Elf gate.

REQUIREMENTS

❖ Destroy the Elf base.

THE PATH TO VICTORY

Your ultimate goal is to capture and destroy the Elf Gate, but this map is a complex one with many hidden areas and blocked paths. Your melee units and Meat Wagons must be working in concert to access all that this map has to offer.

ESTABLISH A BASE

The area initially occupied by the High Elves is the ideal location for your base. The Gold Mine has 13,000 Gold, and there's enough nearby Lumber to get the ball rolling quickly. Destroy their base, then make it your own. Construct all the essential structures, then create an attack force of Ghouls and Necromancers.

CAPTURE NORTHEAST ELF BASE

Move your Meat Wagons and your main attack group (complete with Arthas) toward the northeast corner of the map. There are a couple of areas that are blocked by trees along the way. One such location in the north blocks off a group of Gnolls that yield a Potion of Healing when killed. The other forest blockade separates your

troops from a lightly defended High Elf base, complete with a Gold Mine. Destroy this base and establish a secondary base of your own here, thereby affording you two areas from which to harvest resources and create attack units. Use your Meat Wagons to clear a path to the enemy base, then set them loose on the Elf structures.

Use your Meat Wagons to get into this base, then level it quickly.

Get your base rolling quickly; of course, you'll have to get rid of the Elves first.

THE UNDEAD CAMPAIGN

Capture Eastern Elf Base

After securing the second base and Haunting its Gold Mine, visit the Goblin Merchant just to the west. The Archers guarding this Neutral building don't delay your shopping trip too long. Kill them, then stock up on some Scrolls of Protection, Potions of Healing, or even Potions of Mana—take your pick.

Yet another Elf base lies south of the Goblin Merchant. Once again, place Arthas and the melee attack units in one group, and your Meat Wagons in another squad that focuses on destroying buildings. Attack the enemy in this manner to crush their structures and units quickly and with minimal casualties.

Keep moving through the map, capturing and destroying Elf bases.

> **TIP**
>
> Have an Acolyte tag along with your Meat Wagons to repair these mechanical units when they take damage.

Capture Southwestern Elf Base

The next step toward total domination is the destruction of the High Elf base in the southwest corner of the map. A nearby Fountain of Mana is guarded by some Mud and Rock Golems. Clobber these Creeps for some Gloves of Haste, not to mention free use of the healing waters.

What makes this Elven base so difficult to overcome is its two defensive towers and substantial defensive force. To reduce Militia resistance, storm the base with your melee units while your Meat Wagons head straight for the Town Hall. Once this structure is gone, Militia can no longer be summoned. Next up on your list of things to reduce to rubble should be the defensive towers.

You're getting closer to the Elf Gate, so expect fierce opposition. By this time, you may even have to Haunt another Gold Mine. If your Gold coffers are drying up, then claim one of the many mines you've left behind in your continuing conquests.

The Elven bases are getting tougher. Use Scrolls of Protection and Death Coil to keep your units alive during the attack.

THE GNOLLS

There are four groups of Gnolls on the map, each hidden by a forest. Use Meat Wagons to target the trees and gain access to the Gnolls. There are several valuable items to be gained in these areas, including the Health Stone and Book of the Dead, located in the central region of the map.

The various Gnoll groups around the map control some important items.

MOVE ON THE ELF BASE

Before making your final move on the Elf base, head south and waste the Golems guarding the Fountain of Mana. This allows Arthas and your Necromancers to top off their spell-casting fuel before the big fight. Also, make sure you have one group of at least three Meat Wagons and four or five Necromancers with *full* Mana. Finally, assemble Arthas among a team of Ghouls to fight as melee units.

The key to defeating the Elves in this mission lies in the Necromancers and their ability to raise dead. Make absolutely *sure* that their Raise Dead spell is set to Autocast so that they automatically raise up Skeleton Warriors by the pair. With the attack group we've described, you will initially appear to be losing the battle at the Elf base; however, the tides turn in your favor once the Necromancers start summoning Skeleton Warriors from both your Ghouls and the enemy units that fall in battle.

A group of Necromancers can raise a sea of Skeleton Warriors in the heat of battle and bring victory to your side.

With mobs of Undead skeletons supporting your troops, the enemy will be unable to keep up. Use the Meat Wagons to obliterate the Town Hall, defensive Towers, and Barracks (in that order), then continue to destroy the base.

Destroy the base and the mission is over!

CHAPTER 4

KEY OF THE THREE MOONS

Moments later, just beyond the shattered Elf Gate, Sylvanas Windrunner informs Arthas that he will never get through the second Elf Gate on account of a special key that is required to do so. Sylvanas then destroys the bridge that Arthas was about to cross.

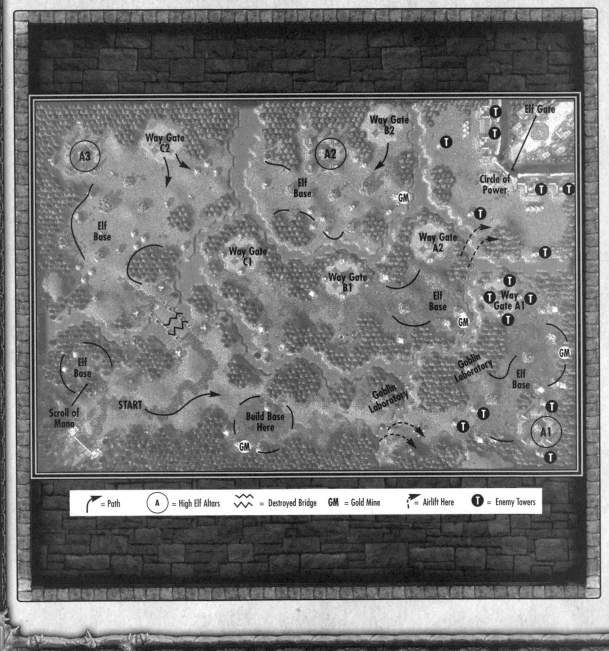

= Path   (A) = High Elf Altars   〜〜 = Destroyed Bridge   **GM** = Gold Mine   = Airlift Here   **T** = Enemy Towers

AVAILABLE STRUCTURES

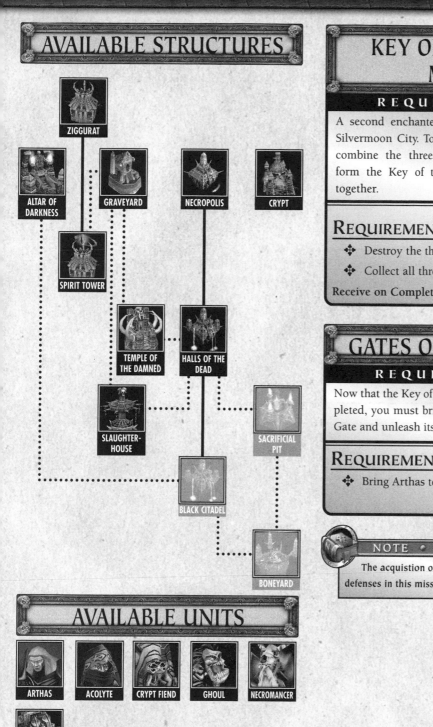

ZIGGURAT

ALTAR OF DARKNESS

GRAVEYARD

NECROPOLIS

CRYPT

SPIRIT TOWER

TEMPLE OF THE DAMNED

HALLS OF THE DEAD

SLAUGHTER-HOUSE

SACRIFICIAL PIT

BLACK CITADEL

BONEYARD

KEY OF THE THREE MOONS

REQUIRED QUEST

A second enchanted Elf Gate blocks the path to Silvermoon City. To bypass it, you must locate and combine the three separate Mooncrystals, which form the Key of the Three Moons when pieced together.

REQUIREMENTS

- ❖ Destroy the three High Elf Altars.
- ❖ Collect all three Mooncrystals.

Receive on Completion: Key of the Three Moons

GATES OF SILVERMOON

REQUIRED QUEST

Now that the Key of the Three Moons has been completed, you must bring it to the heavily guarded Elf Gate and unleash its ancient power.

REQUIREMENTS

- ❖ Bring Arthas to Elf Gate.

NOTE

The acquistion of Goblin Zeppelins is key to your defenses in this mission.

AVAILABLE UNITS

ARTHAS

ACOLYTE

CRYPT FIEND

GHOUL

NECROMANCER

MEAT WAGON

The mission begins with your troops stranded on the wrong side of an Elven river. Not to worry, though, as you eventually gain control of Goblin Zeppelins to transport your troops to the enemy. Your goal is to destroy the three High Elf Altars, but the path to do so involves the destruction of several Elf bases and plenty of hard work on your part.

SECURING THE BASE AND ZEPPELIN

Move to the nearby Elf base and destroy it quickly. Use the Crypt Fiend's Web ability to snare airborne units and bring them down to the ground where your melee forces can get to them.

> **TIP**
>
> Set the Crypt Fiend's Web spell to Autocast to automatically capture enemy air units.

The Gold Mine in this new location provides sufficient resources to create a solid base from which to strike the enemy. Haunt the Gold Mine, then summon a Necropolis, Crypt, Ziggurats, and the rest of your available structures. Beware of the Elf attacks from above! The enemy loads into Goblin Zeppelins, then drops units into your base for surprise attacks!

Upgrade your units' abilities in the Graveyard before striking the next Elf base (in the east). You should also convert your Ziggurats to Spirit Towers to help defend against the repeated Elf attacks via Zeppelins. Move your troops east to the Goblin Laboratory—you'll gain control of two Goblin Zeppelins and have the opportunity to purchase Goblin Sappers, which are powerful demolition teams.

Build your base here, but eradicate the Elves first.

ATTACK THE EAST (ALTAR 1)

Your next goal is to attack to the eastern sector of the map and destroy Altar 1 (see map). This area is heavily defended by a number of Elf units and structures, including some tough Towers. Build up a force of Crypt Fiends, Necromancers, and Meat Wagons in one group, with Arthas and Ghouls in a second group. Load these forces into your Goblin Zeppelins (you are initially given two Zeppelins, but can purchase more if necessary), then fly the short distance to the Elf base to the east and unload your troops.

Drop your troops on the edge of the river so that they're not immediately in danger.

Move your troops due east, with your Crypt Fiend/Meat Wagon group concentrating on the defensive Towers, and your Necromancer/Arthas/Ghoul group targeting the Elf units. Make sure your Crypt Fiends' Web skill is set to Autocast so they can reel in airborne enemies for your melee troops to destroy.

The High Elf Altar is not heavily defended, but don't rush in. Wait until the base is secured before destroying the Altar, then claim the Mooncrystal. After fully exploring the Elf base you discover a Way Gate (Way Gate A1 on map). This gate allows your troops to automatically appear somewhere else on the map (Way Gate A2).

You get a Mooncrystal after destroying the Altar.

Before entering Way Gate A1, repair and replace any lost units, and bring an Acolyte over to Haunt the Gold Mine you just captured. If your units are not fully upgraded, continue to work on this in your Graveyard.

ALTAR 2

Once you've upgraded/repaired/replaced your troops, head through Way Gate A1. Your troops appear nearby in the northwest, surrounded by both enemy Towers and plenty of hostile units. The same tactics apply—use your Meat Wagon/Crypt Fiend group to topple the Towers while Arthas and the Necromancers and Ghouls deal with the enemy units.

Use the Way Gates to move to the Altars where the Moon Crystals are kept.

Use Death Coil to repair any damaged units during the frenzy of the attack on this Elf base. Another Way Gate (Way Gate B1 on map) takes your troops to an area near the second High Elf Altar. Again, rest your forces and be sure that your attack groups are ready before you enter the Way Gate—take your time, there's no rush.

> **NOTE**
>
> Your original base will take an occasional beating from the Elven enemy. The attacks come in the form of aerial bombardments or as assaults from Goblin Zeppelins dropping troops into your base. As long as you have a Crypt Fiend, a couple Ghouls, and some Spirit Towers, your base should be safe, but be aware that these attacks continue to come.

Once you're ready for the next fight, move through Way Gate B1 to Way Gate B2 (see map). Your troops appear in a firmly established Elf base, complete with Towers, a Castle, and some mean units. The Elf Towers can do a lot of damage in a short period of time, so keep your forces out of their reach and unleash your siege group on them.

THE UNDEAD CAMPAIGN

Expect repeated attacks on your base. Spirit Towers help deal with this problem.

In this battle, it's imperative that your Necromancers have their Raise Dead skill set to Autocast. Just when you think you may lose the battle, your Necromancers will raise a veritable army of Skeleton Warriors that turn the tide and grant you victory.

The battle for the second Mooncrystal is tough, but attainable, when your Necromancers raise the dead.

> ### NOTE
>
> Don't worry if Arthas' inventory is full when you go to the second Mooncrystal. Just drop one of your items and pick up the Crystal. When you do this claim, it joins together with the first to become a single, unified item, thus allowing you to reaquire the discarded item.

ALTAR 3

After capturing the second Mooncrystal, re-enter Way Gate B2 and transport to Way Gate B1. You must again replenish your forces and prepare to attack. This time it's also a good idea to get a few Goblin Sappers to demolish Elf Towers very quickly. Move west toward Way Gate C1 en route to Way Gate C2 (see map), which puts you very close to the final High Elf Altar. The Elf base near the third Altar is formidable. There's a Castle right beside the Way Gate, so be prepared for a tough fight. Again, make sure your Necromancers have Raise Dead set to Autocast. Bludgeon your way to the third Altar and destroy it. If your inventory is full, you'll have to drop an item to pick up the third Mooncrystal, but can then reclaim the discarded item once the Mooncrystal links up with the previous two.

THE ELF GATE

Once the third Mooncrystal is yours, enter the Circle of Power by the Elf Gate to finish the mission. The Elf Gate is secured with Elf units and several Towers. Still, you can load up your two attack groups onto Goblin Zeppelins and drop your troops by the Circle of Power before either of your Zeppelins is destroyed.

You need only get Arthas into the Circle of Power to end the mission. Once he's in, the gates fly open and you are victorious.

The Elf Gate is reasonably well defended, but a mass-attack drop from a pair of Zeppelins will overcome them.

CHAPTER 5

THE FALL OF SILVERMOON

Moments later, on the outskirts of the Elves' capital of Silvermoon, Tichondrius appears and advises Arthas that the Sunwell is a difficult prize. Arthas argues that he can still achieve it.

AVAILABLE STRUCTURES

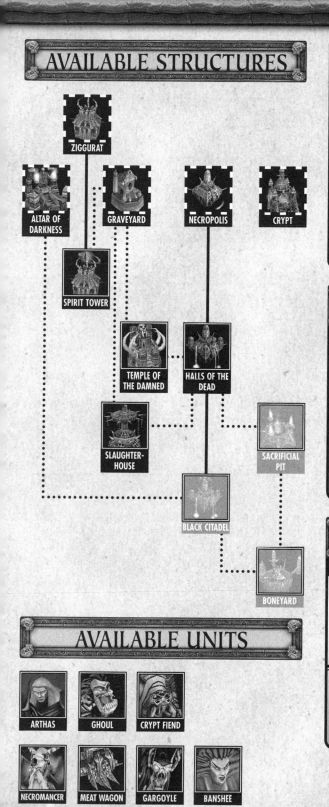

ZIGGURAT

ALTAR OF DARKNESS

GRAVEYARD

NECROPOLIS

CRYPT

SPIRIT TOWER

TEMPLE OF THE DAMNED

HALLS OF THE DEAD

SLAUGHTER-HOUSE

SACRIFICIAL PIT

BLACK CITADEL

BONEYARD

AVAILABLE UNITS

ARTHAS

GHOUL

CRYPT FIEND

NECROMANCER

MEAT WAGON

GARGOYLE

BANSHEE

THE SUNWELL

REQUIRED QUEST

The time for Kel'Thuzad's rebirth is at hand! You must place the urn containing the Necromancer's remains within the Sunwell's sacred waters. Only then will Kel'Thuzad live again to serve the Lich King.

REQUIREMENTS

✥ Defeat the Sunwell's Guardians.

SYLVANAS WINDRUNNER

OPTIONAL QUEST

Sylvanas Windrunner, the Elves' Ranger-General, has harried your efforts long enough. The time has come to deal with the Elf-woman in the manner she deserves. Hunt her down and put an end to her defiance!

REQUIREMENTS

✥ Destroy Sylvanas' Base.

Receive on Completion: Hood of Cunning

SILVERMOON

OPTIONAL QUEST

Sylvanas intends to warn Silvermoon of your approach. If just one of her runners reaches the city, the Elves will be alerted to your presence and attack. Use your Gargoyles to intercept her runners before they reach the capital.

REQUIREMENTS

✥ Eliminate every runner Sylvanas sends.

✥ Do not alert Silvermoon to your presence.

While this mission begins with just one quest, you soon learn of two optional quests—one to destroy Sylvanas' base and another to stop the runners Sylvanas dispatches to alert Silvermoon. You must work quickly to upgrade your units and have an attack group ready to counter the troops Sylvanas sends after you.

BUILD BASE

Although your base starts out largely intact, you need to add a Slaughterhouse and a Temple of the Damned to round out your structures. It's also important to create enough Ziggurats to support your attack force. Build up an attack force of Necromancers, Ghouls, and Crypt Fiends to travel with Arthas, and a group of Meat Wagons to back them up. You should also have three or four extra Gargoyles as a fast-strike team to eliminate Sylvanas' runners if your other defenses fail.

Sylvanas Windrunner attacks your base from the north early in the mission.

Sylvanas attacks the northern entrance of your base—this is when you receive the optional quests. Soon thereafter, the first runner embarks on his journey to Silvermoon and you gain control of four Gargoyles that allow you to kill anyone that attempts to pass.

> **NOTE**
>
> The runners attempt to reach Silvermoon via two different routes, so be prepared to move your Gargoyles quickly depending on which route they choose.

As the runners are released, use your Gargoyles to destroy them as quickly as possible. Sylvanas also sends attack groups at your base, so upgrade your Ziggurats to Spirit Towers and have a small defensive force standing by.

ELIMINATE SYLVANAS' BASE

One way to eliminate the runners that Sylvanas is sending to Silvermoon is to destroy Sylvanas' base altogether. Move your attack toward his base in the northwest (see map). You can purchase items at a Goblin Merchant along the way, but your inventory may already be full.

> **NOTE**
>
> All is not lost if a runner makes it to Silvermoon. You are attacked repeatedly from this location, and although your task may be more difficult, it is not impossible.

Before tackling Sylvanas, you may want to kill the Stone Golems to the north of your base—there are Gloves of Haste to be had there. When you're ready to attack, hit

If you come well prepared, you can defeat Sylvanas' base in one effort, although you'll likely lose a fair number of units.

Sylvanas' base using the same tactics you used to attack the Elf bases in the last mission—Arthas with his Ghouls and Necromancers fight ground units (and raise dead), while your Meat Wagons punish enemy structures.

As the base nears destruction, a showdown takes place between Arthas and Sylvanas. Arthas uses Frostmourne to convert Sylvanas into a Banshee to fight by his side! With Sylvanas' base in ruins and a new unit available (Banshee), you can prepare for the assault on Silvermoon.

ASSAULT ON SILVERMOON

Before you attack Silvermoon, it behooves you to fully explore the rest of the map, which includes a Mercenary Camp, Fountain of Health, Fountain of Mana, Goblin Merchant, and a group of Gnolls hiding a Scroll of the Beast. The troops within Silvermoon leave you alone as long as you don't penetrate their perimeter, so take your time to properly refine and improve your forces.

Use some of the extras on this map, such as the Mercenary Camp, to ensure your attack force is everything it can be.

Once you are ready to attack Silvermoon, use the same plan as we've professed before—two attack groups, one for melee attack and another for destroying buildings. This time, however, add in a group of Gargoyles to increase your chances of success. No matter which bridge you cross to enter Silvermoon, several High Elf Guard Towers await. These defensive structures have such a fast rate of fire that they can single-handedly decimate a pack of your units if you don't concentrate Meat Wagon fire

on them. Meat Wagons (as a rule) have a greater range than the High Elf Guard Towers, so use these Mechanical units to destroy the Towers as soon as possible.

Your goal in this mission is to get Arthas into the Sunwell. Unfortunately, it's defended by four High Elf Guard Towers and just as many Granite Golems! Don't waste any time—get your melee group into the area while your Meat Wagons work on the Towers. As long as Arthas survives and gets into the Circle of Power near the Sunwell, the mission is a success, so concentrate on running him into that area rather than destroying Silvermoon in its entirety.

Focus on getting Arthas into the Circle of Power near the Sunwell to ensure victory.

The area near the Sunwell is defended by Kelen the Seeker and his troops. Kelen is an Archmage capable of summoning Water Elementals, which presents some interesting challenges for you during your attempt to capture the Sunwell. If your first attack falls short of its goal to reach the Sunwell, then Kelen counter-attacks at your base. This is why you should always have at least one small defensive force in place to defend your home turf.

ALTERNATIVE STRATEGY

Another method of approaching this battle involves having two equal forces attack Silvermoon from either side simultaneously (this area has only two entrances). While this can be a very effective tactic, it tends to be difficult to manage two battles at the same time without losing units unnecessarily. Still, for experts of the Warcraft universe, this alternative tactic may be worth a try.

CHAPTER 6

BLACKROCK & ROLL, TOO!

On the outskirts of the Blackrock camp, Arthas meets with Kel'Thuzad. He learns that the Blackrock Orcs maintain a functional Demon Gate. They must be destroyed.

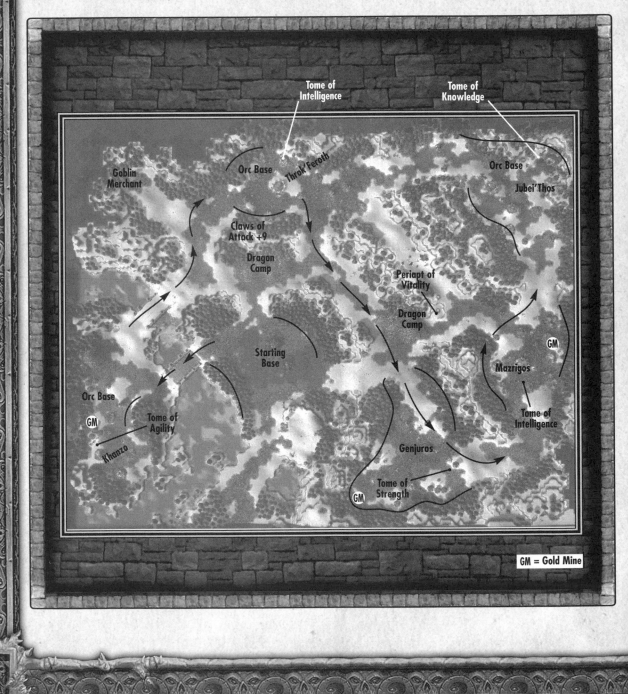

Tome of Intelligence

Tome of Knowledge

Goblin Merchant

Orc Base

Throk'Feroth

Orc Base

Jubei'Thos

Claws of Attack +9

Dragon Camp

Periapt of Vitality

Dragon Camp

GM

Starting Base

Mazrigos

Orc Base

GM

Tome of Agility

Tome of Intelligence

Khanzo

Genjuros

Tome of Strength

GM

GM = Gold Mine

AVAILABLE STRUCTURES

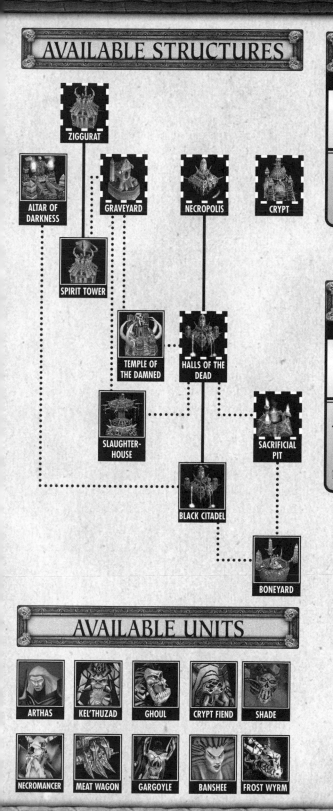

ZIGGURAT

ALTAR OF DARKNESS

GRAVEYARD

NECROPOLIS

CRYPT

SPIRIT TOWER

TEMPLE OF THE DAMNED

HALLS OF THE DEAD

SLAUGHTER-HOUSE

SACRIFICIAL PIT

BLACK CITADEL

BONEYARD

DEMON GATE

REQUIRED QUEST

Kel'Thuzad must reach the Demon Gate to commune with the mysterious Demon Lord, but the adjacent Orc village must be destroyed first.

REQUIREMENTS

❖ Red Orc base must be destroyed.

ORC HEROES

OPTIONAL QUEST

Defeat the Orc Heroes from every Blackrock village to reach the Demon Gate. Each vile Hero carries a magical tome that aids you in your dire mission.

REQUIREMENTS

❖ Kill Throk'Feroth, Mazrigos, Khanzo, Genjuros, and Jubei'Thos.

Receive on Completion: Various Tomes

AVAILABLE UNITS

ARTHAS

KEL'THUZAD

GHOUL

CRYPT FIEND

SHADE

NECROMANCER

MEAT WAGON

GARGOYLE

BANSHEE

FROST WYRM

THE PATH TO VICTORY

Kel'Thuzad, now a Lich, aids you in your quests. A Lich is also a Hero, which means that he can pick up and use Items, and also has access to Lich spells. Your goal is to wipe out six Orc Heroes, then crush their bases to allow Kel'Thuzad to access the Demon Gate.

STABILIZE BASE

A raging mob of Orcs attacks almost immediately after the mission begins. For this reason, you should upgrade the two eastern Ziggurats to Spirit Towers immediately, and create a couple more Ghouls to shore up your melee forces. By this time, Arthas should also have the Raise Dead spell, which is very useful as you stave off the Orc attack.

Once the first wave of Orc attacks is over, Kel'Thuzad presents you with an optional quest to destroy five more Orc Heroes. Each Hero has a Tome of some kind that improves your Hero, so it's a good idea to defeat these Orcs. Before you go after them, however, there's a Dragon Camp just to the east of your base that deserves some attention. Have your Gargoyles attack the Dragons one at a time (four Gargoyles against one Dragon). You may have a couple of casualties in the fight, but you'll get a Periapt of Vitality out of it. This item increases the hit points of the Hero.

KHANZO

Prepare an attack force—including Kel'Thuzad, Arthas, Ghouls, and Necromancers—to go after the Orcs. Also, amass the obligatory trio of Meat Wagons in a second group for destroying the Orc buildings. Khanzo's camp contains a Gold Mine that you can subsequently Haunt after securing the area. Move west and sweep Khanzo from the map. As soon as some units have been killed in action (yours or theirs), have Arthas use his Animate Dead spell to change the odds in your favor. Instantly, six dead units will rise up to fight for your side!

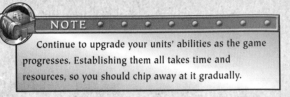

NOTE

Continue to upgrade your units' abilities as the game progresses. Establishing them all takes time and resources, so you should chip away at it gradually.

When Khanzo is dead, you get a Tome of Agility for Arthas or Kel'Thuzad (it's up to you who should use it). Take the time to heal your wounds, replenish your army, and Haunt the new Gold Mine while you're there, then get ready to move on Throk'Feroth.

Khanzo's base isn't very well defended, so it should be a breeze for you to sweep through.

THROK'FEROTH

Throk'Feroth's base is located in the north-central section of the map. Another Dragon Camp lies between your base and Throk'Feroth's. It holds Claws of Attack +9. Go after this valuable item if you can.

The same tactics apply when attacking Throk'Feroth's camp—use your Meat Wagons to quickly destroy the Guard Towers and Barracks while Arthas and Kel'Thuzad lead the Necromancers and Ghouls against the Orc units. When Throk'Feroth dies, he yields a Tome of Intelligence that increases the Mana of the Hero using it. Slaying this Orcish Hero will have likely depleted your troops, so hunker down, continue your upgrades, and rebuild your attack force.

GENJUROS

The next Orc target is Genjuros' base in the southeast corner of the map. Guide your troops through your base (taking time to recover if necessary), then move down and hit Genjuros' base hard with your melee units and Meat Wagons. Again, have your Necromancers Raise Dead automatically and go straight for the Hero.

Genjuros' death earns you a Tome of Strength. You can finish off the entire base if you like, but it's not necessary to complete the quest.

Concentrate on keeping your units alive and healthy as you continue your crusade.

Genjuros has a robust base with plenty of Peons and defensive units.

MAZRIGOS

The next Hero on your list of Orcs to kill is found on the eastern edge of the map, just south of the final Hero that guards the Demon Gate, Jubei'Thos. Mazrigos' camp is less heavily defended than Genjuros' so your primary task is made easier if you attack Mazrigos from the south since he tends to loiter near the southern entrance. By now, the attacks on your main base will be few and far between (because you've already eliminated most of the Orcs on the map), enabling you to concentrate on resupplying your main attack force.

NOTE

Each Orc base has a Gold Mine that you can Haunt and exploit. The catch is that Haunting *all* of the available mines requires so many Acolytes that you put your forces into a High Upkeep situation. For this reason, it's best to avoid harvesting Gold from more than two mines at a time.

JUBEI'THOS

Jubei'Thos' camp is in the northeast corner of the map, and it defends the Demon Gate! He is well defended with both Towers and units, so don't go into battle until your attack groups are healed and fully replenished. To ensure victory, the *entire* base of Jubei'Thos must be destroyed before Kel'Thuzad proceeds to the Demon Gate.

A good tactic for hitting this base is to send Arthas, along with his melee troops and some Gargoyles, into the center of the base while two groups of three Meat Wagons approach from opposite sides, taking down the buildings in their paths. Combined with Necromancers' and Arthas' ability to raise the dead, this tactic completely overwhelms Jubei'Thos and his forces. When the Orc Hero falls, you get a Tome of Knowledge! The mission ends as the last of Jubei'Thos' structures collapses into ruins.

You must destroy every structure in Jubei'Thos' camp to finish the mission.

CHAPTER 7

THE SIEGE OF DALARAN

The next morning, at the gates of Dalaran, Arthas and Kel'Thuzad demand that the Wizards open the doors before them. Antonidas informs Arthas that they have prepared Auras that will kill the Undead if they try to pass.

Book of Summoning

Antonidas

Blue Drakes (2)
Black Spiders (5)

Kirin Tor

Fountain of Health

Cages

Khadgar's Pipe of Insight

Pendant of Mana

Tome of Intelligence

Boots of Elvenkind

Magic Vault

Sorceress League

Shai Lightbinder

Fountain of Health

Peril Spellbinder

Caged Rock Golems

Kelen the Seeker

Mantle of Intelligence

Mage's Guild

Conjurus Rex

Health Stone

Anti-magic Potion

Goblin Merchant

Ruined Elf Base

Your Base

T = Tower   GM = Gold Mine

AVAILABLE STRUCTURES

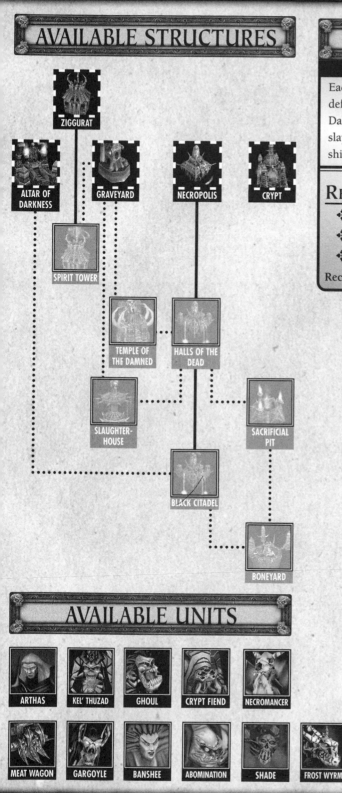

ZIGGURAT

ALTAR OF DARKNESS

GRAVEYARD

NECROPOLIS

CRYPT

SPIRIT TOWER

TEMPLE OF THE DAMNED

HALLS OF THE DEAD

SLAUGHTER-HOUSE

SACRIFICIAL PIT

BLACK CITADEL

BONEYARD

AVAILABLE UNITS

ARTHAS

KEL' THUZAD

GHOUL

CRYPT FIEND

NECROMANCER

MEAT WAGON

GARGOYLE

BANSHEE

ABOMINATION

SHADE

FROST WYRM

THREE ARCHMAGI

REQUIRED QUEST

Each of the three Archmagi who power the city's defensive shield have hidden somewhere within Dalaran's streets. You must charge into the city and slay each Archmage to bring down the crippling shield.

REQUIREMENTS

- ❖ Slay the First Archmage.
- ❖ Slay the Second Archmage.
- ❖ Slay Antonidas.

Receive on Completion: Destruction of the Auras

THE PATH TO VICTORY

Kel'Thuzad informs Arthas that three separate wizards are maintaining these Auras. Kill them all and the Auras collapse, clearing your path. Before you begin to search out the Archmagi in earnest, you need to upgrade your troops as much as possible—don't rush into this mission before you're ready.

STABILIZE AND UPGRADE BASE

The first thing you need to do is build a Temple of the Damned and begin to upgrade every unit. Start with the upgrades in the Graveyard, then augment the damage Abominations and Meat Wagons inflict with Plague Cloud, as well as improving your Ghouls, Necromancers, and Banshees. Your starting forces are sufficient to defend your base once you upgrade a couple of Ziggurats to Spirit Towers, but take your time to grow strong before you venture forth.

A couple of bonuses lie to the south that Arthas and Kel'Thuzad can use. There's an Archmage with a Health Stone in the southwestern portion of the map—target the tent and you'll also find an Anti-magic Potion! A Goblin Merchant provides some additional goodies in the southeast.

Upgrade your troops before you get into the thick of this mission.

Conjurus Rex

Although we don't recommend *fully* upgrading before you venture forth, you should attain at least the first level of upgrades. Once this is done, use your Meat Wagons to topple the High Elf Towers that guard the entrance, then rush one Ghoul into the Aura (north)—it's time to reel in some victims with your ghoulish bait. When the Ghoul gets close to the group of Footmen, quickly run him back to your base and the Footmen will follow! Annihilate the unsuspecting soldiers as they pass through the Aura. Use Arthas' Animate Dead to raise up the fresh kill, then send them back into the Aura to attack the next group of enemies!

When your melee group is ready (Arthas, Kel'Thuzad, Ghouls, and Necromancers) send them into the Aura and attack the Archmage, Conjurus Rex. Your units take a constant beating while within the Aura, so it's imperative that you waste no time killing Conjurus. The Aura disappears from this area when the Archmage dies, relieving your units of its damaging effects.

The first Aura collapses with the death of Conjurus Rex.

Kill the first group of enemies, use Animate Dead to resurrect them, then send them back to fight against their kin.

MAGE'S GUILD

Next, you must neutralize the Mage's Guild to the west of Conjurus Rex's location. This Human base is well defended with both units and Towers. Command your Meat Wagons and Crypt Fiends to attack the Towers, Town Hall, and Barracks, while your other units deal with the Human warriors. Expect the Town Hall to ring the Militia bell, and use your Necromancer's Raise Dead spell to match the Human's extra fighters.

Free the Rock Golems to gain some valuable allies.

The Mage's Guild is a strong and entrenched base.

If you need some help, there's a pair of caged Rock Golems not far from the Mage's Guild (see map). Attack the cages to release these monsters and they join your side! The Golems are tough and can fight in the Aura to deflect damage from your core units.

> **NOTE**
>
> The Mage Guild base's mine contains over 20,000 Gold, so Haunt it as soon as you take control of the area. After all, your own mine will soon be exhausted.

KELEN THE SEEKER

There's another Archmage (although not one of the three that you're after) to the east of the Mage's Guild. His name is Kelen the Seeker and he coughs up Mantle of Intelligence +3 if you kill him. There's also a Workshop nearby that produces rather pesky Mortar Teams. These units always attack your warriors by targeting the weakest in your flock first. Destroy a pack of Riflemen and a Tower, too, if you want to be thorough in your destruction.

SHAL LIGHTBINDER

You are inside the Aura as you approach Shal Lightbinder Spellbinder, and take constant damage as a result. At first, it looks as though you might be able to take a direct route to Shal Lightbinder, but unfortunately, you must follow a circuitous route east, then north, to reach him from above his position. There's a Fountain of Health along the way that you may be tempted to huddle near and heal the wounds inflicted by Water Elementals and the Aura. However, the Aura is *more powerful* than the healing properties of the Fountain of Health, so ignore it and just move as quickly as you can toward Shal Lightbinder! Not until he falls will the Aura relinquish its attack on your men. Expect heavy casualties.

Kill Shal Lightbinder quickly, ignoring momentarily the nearby Orb of Lightning and caged Ogre Magi. Again, you can pick those things up later. For now, just concentrate on Shal Lightbinder. Once he's dead, the Aura ceases its damaging force and you are free to claim your items and creature unimpeded!

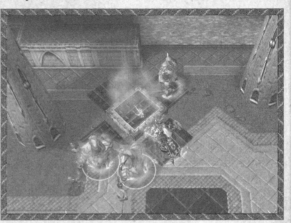

Release the Ogre Magi from its cage and it fights for you.

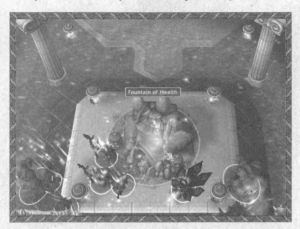

Don't delay—go straight to Shal Lightbinder. This Fountain of Health can't help you now.

Peril Spellbinder, The Sorceress League, and the Magic Vault

A substantial base of the Sorceress League lies to the east. It defends a Magic Vault that yields Khadgar's Pipe of Insight, a Pendant of Mana, and a Tome of Intelligence when opened! Don't worry about the vault initially, however, because you'll have your hands full dealing with the Sorceress League and their structures. This base is guarded with Cannon Towers that tend to target your Necromancers, who are not at all prepared to take that kind of a beating.

This battle is arduous. It may require multiple attempts before you finally defeat the Sorceress League.

Hit the base with the usual tactics, except this time you may want to consider two groups of two Meat Wagons that work separately on the numerous enemy structures giving you problems, including the different Barracks and Cannon Towers, and the Town Square that continuously converts Peasants into Militia until you destroy it! The Archmage in this area is Peril Spellbinder. He's not difficult to destroy, but unfortunately, he does not control one of the Auras.

Once the base assault is under control, send Kel'Thuzad and Arthas to the Magic Vault and extract its treasures. Divide these items between the two Heroes however you like, but we recommend giving at least the Khadgar's Pipe of Insight to Arthas.

Antonidas

The final Archmage is Antonidas and, believe us, he is well protected. Augment your forces with plenty of melee attack units like Ghouls and Abominations, but don't worry too much about Meat Wagons at this point. The path to Antonidas is long, and most of it is under an Aura that quickly destroys your troops. You must rush up to Antonidas to destroy him. Arthas may be able to slay him on his own if you can rush your Hero up toward this foe. Even if Arthas dies, the Ankh of Reincarnation brings him back to life to finish Antonidas off.

Don't worry about Kirin Tor. Just rush Antonidas with Arthas and any other units that you can bring.

There are two cages along the way to Antonidas (see map). Open them to get two Blue Drakes and five Black Spiders! These units are *not* affected by the Aura, so you can send them in to attack Antonidas, as well. The Blue Drakes are airborne, enabling them to assist Arthas within a matter of seconds.

Kirin Tor is a huge base that you may be tempted to defeat in its entirety; however, this is a most perilous endeavor with the Aura hanging over your head. Once the Aura has been disabled, the mission ends with Kel'Thuzad obtaining the Book of Summoning. For these reasons, it's best, perhaps essential, to just leave Kirin Tor alone unless you simply must exact total vengeance on the Archmages. If you decide to take on this challenge, expect to also spend a huge amount of resources on repairing and rebuilding your units, who will take a heavy beating from the Aura.

When Antonidas is dead, the mission is yours!

CHAPTER 8

UNDER THE BURNING SKY

An hour later, on a hill overlooking Dalaran, Arthas has readied the Circle of Power for Kel'Thuzad to perform the Summoning. Tichondrius arrives and the ritual commences. Kel'Thuzad must survive for 30 minutes during the summoning of Archimonde.

GM = Gold Mine   T = Towers

AVAILABLE STRUCTURES

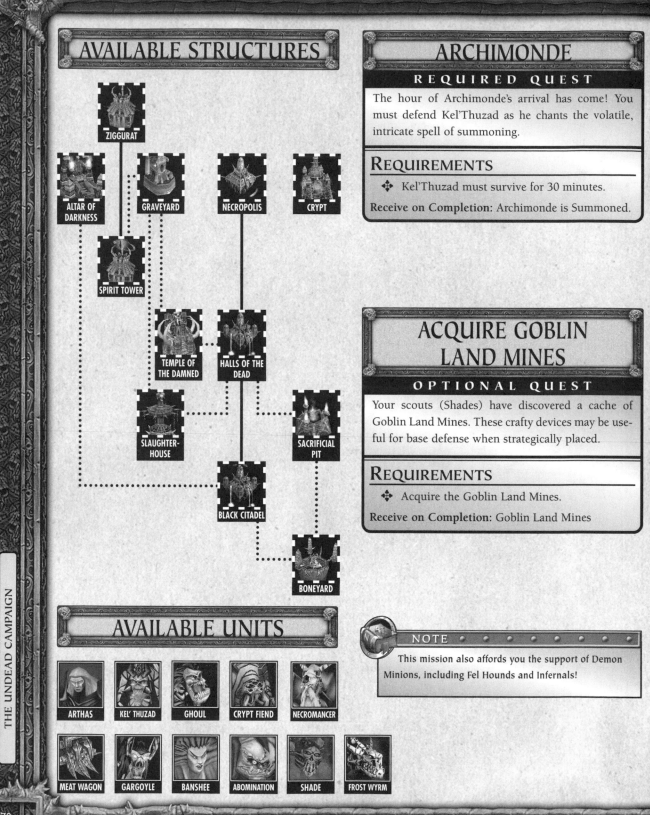

ZIGGURAT

ALTAR OF DARKNESS

GRAVEYARD

NECROPOLIS

CRYPT

SPIRIT TOWER

TEMPLE OF THE DAMNED

HALLS OF THE DEAD

SLAUGHTER-HOUSE

SACRIFICIAL PIT

BLACK CITADEL

BONEYARD

ARCHIMONDE

REQUIRED QUEST

The hour of Archimonde's arrival has come! You must defend Kel'Thuzad as he chants the volatile, intricate spell of summoning.

REQUIREMENTS

❖ Kel'Thuzad must survive for 30 minutes.

Receive on Completion: Archimonde is Summoned.

ACQUIRE GOBLIN LAND MINES

OPTIONAL QUEST

Your scouts (Shades) have discovered a cache of Goblin Land Mines. These crafty devices may be useful for base defense when strategically placed.

REQUIREMENTS

❖ Acquire the Goblin Land Mines.

Receive on Completion: Goblin Land Mines

AVAILABLE UNITS

ARTHAS

KEL' THUZAD

GHOUL

CRYPT FIEND

NECROMANCER

MEAT WAGON

GARGOYLE

BANSHEE

ABOMINATION

SHADE

FROST WYRM

NOTE

This mission also affords you the support of Demon Minions, including Fel Hounds and Infernals!

THE UNDEAD CAMPAIGN

THE PATH TO VICTORY

The basic mission is to defend Kel'Thuzad from attack for 30 minutes while he summons Archimonde. You need only upgrade your units and build a substantial defensive force that can obliterate any enemy attacks. Although that doesn't sound too difficult, there is another layer to this mission that you can attempt to conquer—if you believe you're good enough to overcome the obstacles set before you. In short, there are a few juicy items hidden around the map that greatly improve Arthas' ability to defend Kel'Thuzad.

HUNKER DOWN

The area of Archimonde's summoning is flanked on three sides by areas controlled by your forces. Your base is on the west flank, while Area 1 and Area 2 (see map) sit on the north and east flanks respectively. You are constantly attacked in each direction from all three enemy groups on the map—Kirin Tor, The Mage's Guild, and The Sorceress League—so you must maintain your defenses at all times.

Start by converting existing Ziggurats to Spirit Towers, and then build new Ziggurats in Areas 1 & 2. You must also send an Acolyte to Haunt the Gold Mine in the southeast corner of the map (you need that Gold). Be sure to upgrade the Crypt Fiends so that they can use their Web ability, because the enemy sends plenty of Gryphon Riders your way.

THE GOBLIN LAND MINES

There are four crates of Goblin Land Mines on the western edge of the map (12 mines total). Send Arthas over to pick the mines up—he must specifically target each crate in order to destroy them and reveal the mines. You may have to clear out one or two items from Arthas' inventory to carry them all.

These mines are useful for establishing a final defensive perimeter around Kel'Thuzad. Avoid placing them too far out or the enemy's Gyrocopters will drop bombs on the mines and destroy them before they do you any good.

Plant them close to Kel'Thuzad, and they'll do their work in the final minute of the mission when the enemy attempts to rush in to halt the summoning.

The Goblin Land Mines are best placed closer to Kel'Thuzad. If you plant them out this far, then enemy Gyrocopters might destroy them from the air.

GET THE GOODIES

There are several extra goodies on this map, but getting them is a great challenge. There's a lightly defended Goblin Laboratory just below the Goblin Mines. You can purchase a Goblin Zeppelin here to airlift your troops over to the Gnoll camp in the southeast corner of the map. Crush these Creeps and their huts to get a Scroll of Healing.

Marn Magesinger makes his home in the center of the map. This Archmage guards a hut that yields both a Tome of Strength +2 and a Ring of Protection +5 (a *very* nice item!).

> **TIP**
>
> If you click on a critter 25 consecutive times, it explodes into a giant ball of fire! No joke! Try it on the sheep in the middle of this map and watch them go BOOM!

There is also a Magic Vault at the Kirin Tor camp in the far northeast corner of the map. This area heavily defended area has Towers and plenty of enemy units. If you can get inside the vault, however, there is a Scepter of Mastery and a Medallion of Courage to be had! Both of these are excellent items, but the sacrifice you must endure to get them is significant. Perhaps the greatest challenge to attaining these extras is the fact that you must control your attacking force while still defending Kel'Thuzad. To access the Magic Vault, you may want to purchase Goblin Sappers to help destroy some of the particularly nasty enemy structures you pass along the way.

Click on a critter 25 times and it explodes, causing area of effect damage!

![NOTE]
> If you're scouring the map trying for bonus items, be mindful of the two Fountains of Health where you can regenerate (see map).

DEFEND KEL'THUZAD

Your ultimate goal is to keep Kel'Thuzad safe for 30 minutes, and if you concentrate on this task you should be able to succeed without much difficulty. To accomplish this, *never* leave *any* of the three flanks undefended. The base is under constant attack from Steam Tanks and other enemy units, while Area 1 gets repeatedly attacked by Gryphon Riders and Area 2 is besieged with ground-unit assaults throughout the mission.

Use the Fountains of Health and Mana behind Kel'Thuzad to replenish your units. Also make sure you're mining enough Gold to keep your unit construction flowing. A nearby Goblin Merchant sells Scrolls of Protection and Wands of Negation to help deal with the enemy when the attacks occur (the Archmagi use Blizzard on your Ziggurats).

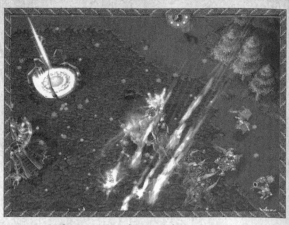

The enemy attacks in unrelenting waves.

Position Crypt Fiends with Web and Necromancers with Raise Dead (both set to Autocast) near Kel'Thuzad. We also suggest keeping a couple of Acolytes near the Ziggurats to repair any damage they incur. As the mission continues, you acquire nine Felhounds to help aid in the defense of Kel'Thuzad. Near the end of the mission, a group of four Infernals appear, as well, to aid in the cause.

As the mission winds to a close, the enemy throws everything they've got at Kel'Thuzad—this is when those Goblin Land Mines really come in handy! Use the Goblin Merchant to purchase Scrolls of Protection and Scrolls of Healing, and save up Arthas' Animate Dead spell for the final minute of action.

The final push on Kel'Thuzad is harrowing. Even if the enemy gets to him, you will still be victorious as long as he doesn't perish before the clock reaches zero!

ORC CAMPAIGN

THE INVASION OF KALIMDOR

The time has come to revisit the 'other' familiar Warcraft race: the Orcs. The Horde has some new units and their Heroes have some of the best spells in the game, so prepare for some exciting battles!

CHAPTER 1

LANDFALL

Following the mysterious Prophet's instructions, Thrall led the Horde across the Great Sea. After weeks of traversing the raging seas, the Orcish Horde arrived on the savage shores of Kalimdor. With their stolen ships broken and drowned, the Orcs cautiously venture inland, wary of the unseen dangers lurking within the crags of the desolate land.

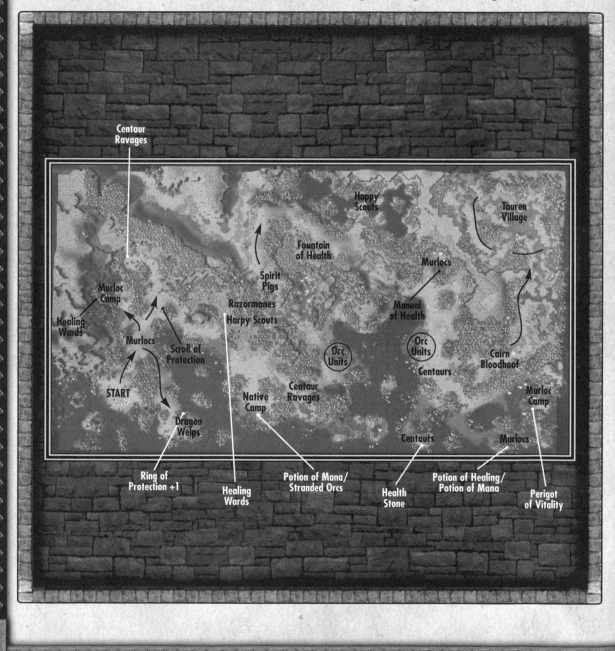

AVAILABLE STRUCTURES

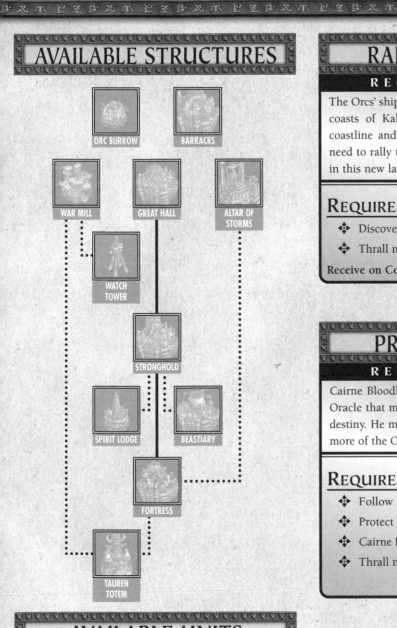

ORC BURROW

BARRACKS

WAR MILL

GREAT HALL

ALTAR OF STORMS

WATCH TOWER

STRONGHOLD

SPIRIT LODGE

BEASTIARY

FORTRESS

TAUREN TOTEM

AVAILABLE UNITS

THRALL

GRUNT

HEADHUNTER

RALLY THE HORDE

REQUIRED QUEST

The Orcs' ships were separated and broken along the coasts of Kalimdor. You must explore the rocky coastline and reunite your scattered warriors. You need to rally the Horde before it can find its destiny in this new land.

REQUIREMENTS

✦ Discover where the other ships have landed.

✦ Thrall must survive.

Receive on Completion: More Orc Troops.

PROTECT CAIRNE

REQUIRED QUEST

Cairne Bloodhoof possesses knowledge of a distant Oracle that might be able to help the Horde find its destiny. He must be protected so that you can learn more of the Oracle.

REQUIREMENTS

✦ Follow Cairne to the Tauren village.

✦ Protect Cairne from his enemies.

✦ Cairne Bloodhoof must survive.

✦ Thrall must survive.

THE PATH TO VICTORY

This mission is your re-introduction to the Orcish ways. The Orc Hero is Thrall, who is a Farseer. Farseers have a number of abilities and our favorite spell: Chain Lightning! The goal in this mission is to find the other Orc landing parties and reunite the Horde.

Time to get the ball rolling for the Orcs.

GETTING THE LAY OF THE LAND

First, get a feel for the land and your Hero, Thrall. Move north from the starting position and eliminate the Murlocs, then turn right back down to the south to fight some Dragon Welps. After the fight, look for some crates in the water to the right. Target and destroy them for a Ring of Protection +1!

Use Chain Lightning to teach these Dragon Welps a lesson!

Move up to the northwest and take out the Murloc camp. Search for a set of three Healing Wards, too. These are posts that you can place in the ground that heal nearby friendly units. Continue to move through the map, picking up items along the way.

NATIVE CAMP

When you reach the camp of Native Huts and enemies, destroy them to obtain a Potion of Mana. This is a good time to set down a Healing Ward to ensure that all of your units survive the battle. After disposing of the Natives, look for two Troll Headhunters stranded in an area in the southern portion of the camp. Free them and they join your cause.

Healing Wards keep your Orcs alive.

FOUNTAIN OF HEALTH

Although you have more than one choice as to where you can lead your troops, move them back to the northwest to the area where they find Spirit Pigs (see map). After the battle, some Centaurs move in the valley below, but their path doesn't intersect with the Centaurs right now. Move to the Fountain of Health and destroy the Razormanes guarding it. Replenish your troops before moving onward.

There are some Harpy Scouts further up the trail. Instead of using Chain Lightning to defeat them, conserve your Mana and coax them closer to your troops. After doing so, bring them into range of your Trolls.

The Fountain of Health is a welcome site.

THE MURLOC CAMPS

There is a huge Murloc camp in the far southeast corner of the map, plus several other smaller Murloc congregations spread throughout the watery portions of the map. Take your troops down and get some items from the Murlocs, like a Periapt of Vitality, as well as Mana and Healing Potions. Venturing to the Murloc camps is an entirely voluntary endeavor, so not going won't affect the course of the game.

CAIRNE BLOODHOOF

Move to the next group of Orc units to complete your rallying of the Horde. When you arrive, the Centaurs attack and you meet with Cairne Bloodhoof, who learns that his village is in danger. You must now follow him to save it.

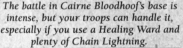

> **NOTE**
>
> You don't have to follow Cairne right away. If you want to scour the rest of the map for items, then this is the time to do it because once you help Cairne defend his base, the mission ends.

When you reach Cairne's base, three waves of Centaurs attack. Included in the final wave of the attack is a Centaur Champion. This is an excellent time to use another Healing Ward to keep your troops alive. Use Thrall's Chain Lightning and, if you have a Potion of Mana, use it to hit the enemy with multiple blasts of Chain Lightning! After defeating the Centaurs, the mission ends.

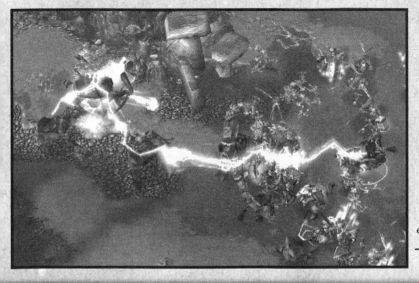

The battle in Cairne Bloodhoof's base is intense, but your troops can handle it, especially if you use a Healing Ward and plenty of Chain Lightning.

LANDFALL

CHAPTER 2

THE LONG MARCH

Two days later, while on the desolate planes of the Barrens, Thrall tells Cairne that he appreciates his surroundings. Thrall agrees to help Cairne make it to the three Oases in the Barrens.

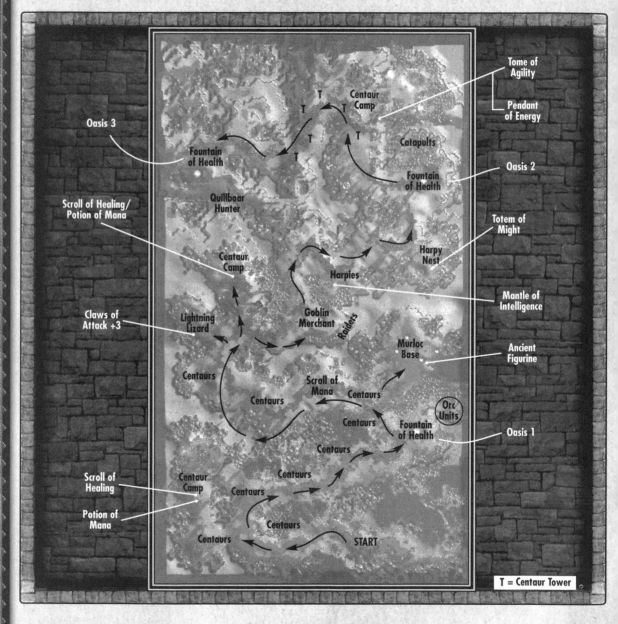

Tome of Agility

Pendant of Energy

Oasis 3

Fountain of Health

Centaur Camp

Catapults

Oasis 2

Fountain of Health

Scroll of Healing/ Potion of Mana

Quillboar Hunter

Totem of Might

Harpy Nest

Centaur Camp

Harpies

Mantle of Intelligence

Claws of Attack +3

Lightning Lizard

Goblin Merchant

Raiders

Murloc Base

Ancient Figurine

Centaurs

Scroll of Mana

Centaurs

Centaurs

Orc Units

Oasis 1

Centaurs

Fountain of Health

Scroll of Healing

Potion of Mana

Centaur Camp

Centaurs

Centaurs

Centaurs

Centaurs

Centaurs

Centaurs

START

T = Centaur Tower

AVAILABLE STRUCTURES

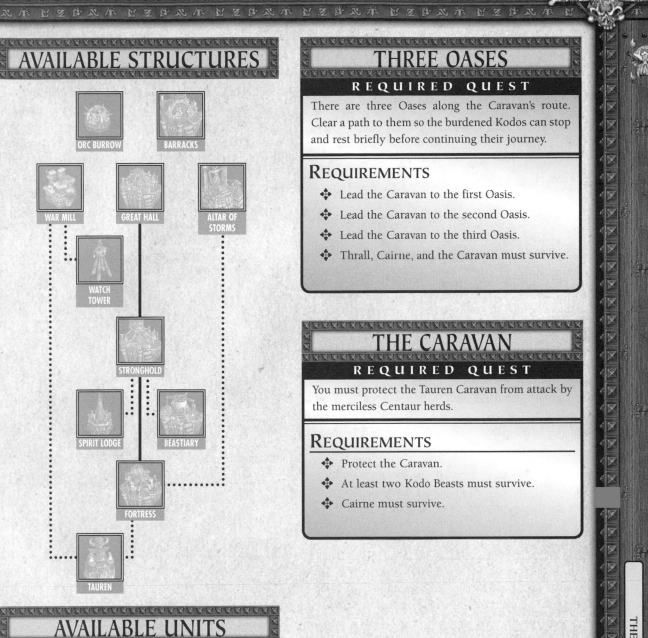

ORC BURROW

BARRACKS

WAR MILL

GREAT HALL

ALTAR OF STORMS

WATCH TOWER

STRONGHOLD

SPIRIT LODGE

BEASTIARY

FORTRESS

TAUREN

AVAILABLE UNITS

THRALL

GRUNT

TROLL HEADHUNTER

TAUREN

RAIDER

CATAPULT

KODO BEAST

THREE OASES

REQUIRED QUEST

There are three Oases along the Caravan's route. Clear a path to them so the burdened Kodos can stop and rest briefly before continuing their journey.

REQUIREMENTS

- ✥ Lead the Caravan to the first Oasis.
- ✥ Lead the Caravan to the second Oasis.
- ✥ Lead the Caravan to the third Oasis.
- ✥ Thrall, Cairne, and the Caravan must survive.

THE CARAVAN

REQUIRED QUEST

You must protect the Tauren Caravan from attack by the merciless Centaur herds.

REQUIREMENTS

- ✥ Protect the Caravan.
- ✥ At least two Kodo Beasts must survive.
- ✥ Cairne must survive.

You can move off the Caravan path and attack the Centaurs if you're feeling adventurous.

This mission provides you with a set number of troops. Use them to help guard the four Kodo Beasts as you move them through the map in Caravan form to the three Oases. The path is long and there are lots of Centaurs to battle along the way. You can stray from the Caravan and attack Centaurs that fall outside of the path (see map). Follow this tactic and you will find some stray items.

As a rule, the Tauren stay at the back of the Caravan and do an admirable job of protecting the Kodo Beasts from the rear. It is your job to blaze the trail.

THE FIRST OASIS

The first Oasis isn't far from the start, but there are plenty of Centaurs to fight along the way. You don't have to destroy the Centaur Camp in the southwest corner, but you can pick up a pair of items if you choose to do so.

> **TIP**
>
> If you wander off the path, the Caravan will stop until you return to it. When it ceases to move, you'll know you're offtrack. Remember, though, that most of the areas off the Caravan path have items if you destroy the creatures in the area.

The Tauren and Cairne do a good job of attacking the rear-charging Centaurs as you move toward the first Oasis. Although you shouldn't have to help them, you can lend a hand to speed things up. When you reach the Oasis (Fountain of Health), you receive three new Grunts to add to your forces. Take the time to heal your troops, then continue onward. When the Caravan reaches the first Oasis, it rests for one minute, giving you time to venture out if you choose.

Get the new Grunts at the first Oasis and then heal up.

THE SECOND OASIS

Now, it's time to head to the second Oasis. Right away, take note of the Murloc Base to the north of the first Oasis. You can destroy the Murloc Huts to acquire a Ancient Figurine.

As you proceed to the second Oasis, destroy a pack of Lightning Lizards to get Claws of Attack +3. Continue along the Caravan path toward the second Oasis. When you reach the Goblin Merchant, you gain access to three Raiders—a new unit to supplement your forces.

Gather your new units and purchase anything you want/need from the Goblin Merchant.

The Centaur Camp houses a beast that reincarnates after the first time you kill it.

Destroy the Harpy Nest along the way to get a Mantle of Intelligence +3. Stay close to the Kodo Beasts in this area, because they can be quickly overcome by Centaurs approaching from the rear. The second Harpy Nest is tougher to handle, so use your Raiders to Ensnare the Harpies, then bring them to the ground and hack them to pieces with your Grunts. A +1 Ring of Protection is your reward.

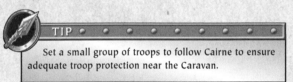

TIP

Set a small group of troops to follow Cairne to ensure adequate troop protection near the Caravan.

Upon arriving at the second Oasis, you receive three Catapults. Group them separately and prepare to use each on a series of Centaur Towers you encounter en route to the third Oasis.

THE THIRD OASIS

Move the new Catapults down the Caravan route to dispose of the Centaur Towers lining the path. There is also a Centaur Camp and Centaur Champion off the path. The beast carries an Ankh of Reincarnation, which means he can come back to life at full health! Defeat him to receive a Tome of Agility and a Pendant of Energy.

Continue toward the final Oasis. A group of Centaurs greets you and numerous others are in the valley to the north. Don't worry—they're *not* part of this mission! When the Caravan reaches the Fountain of Health (the third Oasis), the mission ends (provided that you still have *at least* two Kodo Beasts).

The Catapults make short work of the Centaur Towers.

CRY OF THE WARSONG

Five days later, near the foothills of the Stonetalon Mountains, Thrall's troops complain of boredom. Just then, they run into the Warsong Clan fighting the Humans.

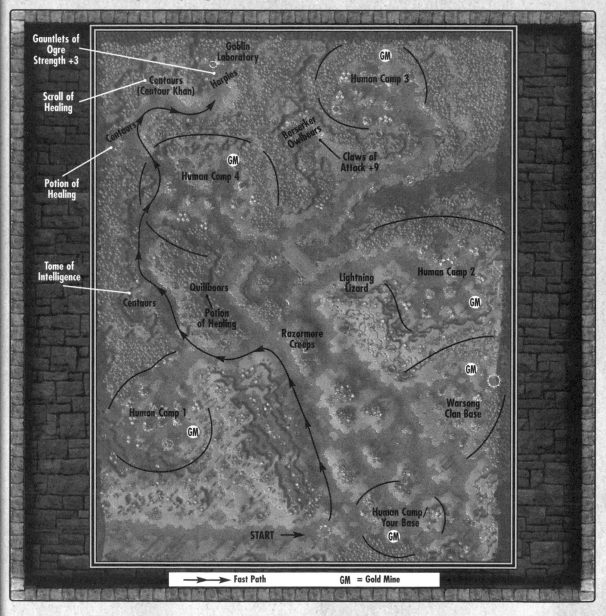

Gauntlets of Ogre Strength +3

Goblin Laboratory

Harpies

Centaurs (Centaur Khan)

Scroll of Healing

Centaurs

Potion of Healing

Human Camp 4

Tome of Intelligence

Centaurs

Quillboars

Potion of Healing

Razormore Creeps

GM

Human Camp 3

Berserker Owlbears

Claws of Attack +9

Lightning Lizard

Human Camp 2

GM

GM

Warsong Clan Base

Human Camp 1

GM

START →

Human Camp/ Your Base

GM

→ Fast Path   GM = Gold Mine

AVAILABLE STRUCTURES

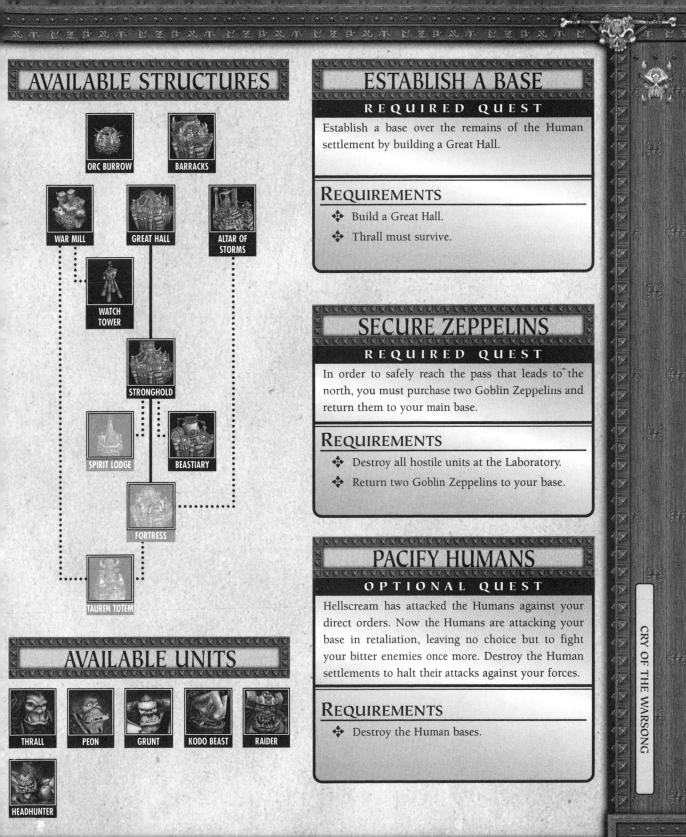

ORC BURROW

BARRACKS

WAR MILL

GREAT HALL

ALTAR OF STORMS

WATCH TOWER

STRONGHOLD

SPIRIT LODGE

BEASTIARY

FORTRESS

TAUREN TOTEM

AVAILABLE UNITS

THRALL

PEON

GRUNT

KODO BEAST

RAIDER

HEADHUNTER

ESTABLISH A BASE

R E Q U I R E D   Q U E S T

Establish a base over the remains of the Human settlement by building a Great Hall.

REQUIREMENTS

- ❖ Build a Great Hall.
- ❖ Thrall must survive.

SECURE ZEPPELINS

R E Q U I R E D   Q U E S T

In order to safely reach the pass that leads to the north, you must purchase two Goblin Zeppelins and return them to your main base.

REQUIREMENTS

- ❖ Destroy all hostile units at the Laboratory.
- ❖ Return two Goblin Zeppelins to your base.

PACIFY HUMANS

O P T I O N A L   Q U E S T

Hellscream has attacked the Humans against your direct orders. Now the Humans are attacking your base in retaliation, leaving no choice but to fight your bitter enemies once more. Destroy the Human settlements to halt their attacks against your forces.

REQUIREMENTS

- ❖ Destroy the Human bases.

THE PATH TO VICTORY

Now it's time to build an Orc base. As the mission begins, the Warsong Clan starts to attack a small Human encampment. Despite Thrall's reluctance to fight, he helps destroy the Humans so that he can build his own base there. Indeed, your task is to eliminate all four Human bases each time the Warsong Clan provokes them against Thrall's wishes.

That said, there is another way to victory. If you follow the path on the west side of the map, you can reach the Goblin Laboratory and finish the mission without fighting the main Human forces on the map.

It's time for some old school battle—Orcs versus Humans!

BUILD YOUR BASE

Begin constructing your base to the fullest extent allowed in this mission. Create a Great Hall to satisfy the first quest, and then augment your town with structures that can supply a war effort. Build Orc Burrows, a War Mill, a Barracks, and a new structure—the Beastiary. You need to increase your food capacity to at least 70, and upgrade everything as much as possible in the War Mill.

The various Human groups occasionally attack, but your starting troops can repel them. As was the case with the Undead and their Meat Wagons, build two attack forces—one for melee combat and another force (comprised of three or four Catapults) to destroy Human structures.

HUMAN CAMP #1

With an attack group of Thrall, several Grunts and Headhunters, three Raiders, and a pair of Kodo Beasts, move toward Camp #1 (see map). Group three Catapults together to attack the Human buildings. During this journey, eliminate a group of Razormane Creeps for a Potion of Mana. Use it later to help replenish the Chain Lightning and Feral Spirit during battle.

THE ORC CAMPAIGN

> **NOTE**
>
> The Warsong Clan constantly attacks the various Human camps throughout the mission. Therefore, time your attacks with your battle-hungry comrades to increase your chances of victory.

Move your melee units into Human Camp #1 and start fighting. The Town Hall summons a Call to Arms to convert Peasants to Militia, so use Chain Lightning (preferably Level 2) to eliminate them with two bolts. Have the Catapults destroy the Guard Tower, Barracks, and Town Hall. With the main structures destroyed, the Human camp will be history in short order. Don't be afraid to use Chain Lightning and Feral Spirit, which summons two Wolf companion fighters for Thrall. Once the camp is in your possession, build a Great Hall by the Gold Mine and harvest this precious metal.

Decimating Human Camp #1 is a breeze with Chain Lightning in your arsenal.

HUMAN CAMP #2

Human Camp #2 is located on the eastern edge of the map and is defended much like Camp #1, except that this one has some Lightning Lizards near its entrance. You must eliminate them on your way past. Move your Catapults in and destroy the two Guard Towers, then attack with Thrall and your melee attack force. Human Camp #2 should fall fairly quickly, but you can expect some casualties.

Human Camp #2 is guarded by two Guard Towers, but three Catapults will quickly dispose of them.

HUMAN CAMP #3

Human Camp #3 is the most difficult area to reach. It's in the northeast corner of the map, but remember that you have to destroy it to complete the mission. If you choose the violent approach, use the same tactics as we discussed for Camps #1 and #2. A group of Berserker Owlbears roams near this third camp; destroy them to get Claws of Attack +9!

Defeat the Owlbears for some Claws of Attack +9.

HUMAN CAMP #4

Human Camp #4 is the big one. If you want to destroy it (and all the other camps), use a group of Catapults to eliminate the key buildings while Thrall and the melee troops attack the Human units.

THE FAST TRACK

There is a fast track to the Goblin Laboratory that essentially bypasses the Human settlements and exposes your troops only to Creeps along the way. Follow the path on the map that runs north along the west side if you'd rather avoid confrontation (although it does skim the western edge of Camp #4) and your troops will reach the Goblin Laboratory with minimal fuss.

Look out for a group of Centaurs, including Centaur Khan. This tough beast has the ability to reappear after it dies! The Centaur Khan uses stun attacks and other punishing methods to cut through your units in a hurry.

Centaur Khan can reincarnate, so prepare for round two!

GOBLIN LABORATORY

A group of Harpies may attempt to put Thrall to sleep near the Goblin Laboratory. To prevent this use a few Raiders with the Ensnare ability to bring the Harpies to the ground where your Grunts can make quick work of them. Thrall's Chain Lightning spell is also effective. Defeat the main Harpy for Gauntlets of Ogre Strength +3.

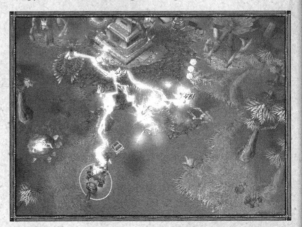

Use Chain Lightning on the Harpies. This, along with the Raider's Ensnare ability, should do the trick.

CHAPTER 4

THE SPIRITS OF ASHENVALE

Two days later, along the borderlands of Ashenvale forest, Grom Hellscream is upset that he has been set to the task of clearing the forest for Lumber. Grom's Grunts feel that the forest is Haunted, but Grom pushes them to clear the forest all the quicker.

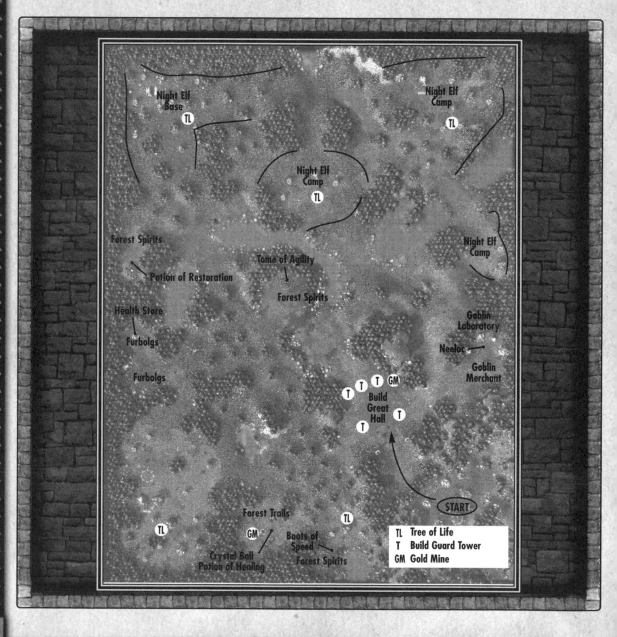

Night Elf Base — TL
Night Elf Camp — TL
Night Elf Camp — TL
Night Elf Camp

Forest Spirits
Potion of Restoration
Tome of Agility
Forest Spirits

Health Store
Furbolgs
Furbolgs

Goblin Laboratory
Neeloc
Goblin Merchant

T T T GM
Build Great Hall
T
T

START

Forest Trails
TL
TL
GM
Crystal Ball
Potion of Healing
Boots of Speed
Forest Spirits

TL	Tree of Life
T	Build Guard Tower
GM	Gold Mine

AVAILABLE STRUCTURES

ORC BURROW

BARRACKS

WAR MILL

GREAT HALL

ALTAR OF STORMS

WATCH TOWER

STRONGHOLD

SPIRIT LODGE

BEASTIARY

FORTRESS

TAUREN TOTEM

AVAILABLE UNITS

GROM HELLSCREAM

PEON

GRUNT

KODO BEAST

TROLL HEADHUNTER

RAIDER

SHAMAN

SLASH AND BURN

REQUIRED QUEST

Before Thrall can attain his vision of a new Orc settlement, a massive amount of Lumber must be harvested. Luckily, the dense forests of Ashenvale prove to be an abundant source of Lumber.

REQUIREMENTS

✦ Amass 15,000 units of Lumber.

FURBOLG CHIEFTAIN

OPTIONAL QUEST

A nearby tribe of Furbolgs has begun to harass the Goblin Merchant, scaring away potential customers. If you can slay the beast's Chieftain, the tribe may disperse and improve the Goblin Town's commercial viability.

REQUIREMENTS

✦ Slay the Furbolg Chieftain.

Receive on Completion: Shredders

TREES OF LIFE

OPTIONAL QUEST

The enchanted Trees of Life provide your forces with vast amounts of high-quality Lumber. Seek out the sacred trees and rip them down! Beware, though, of the warrior women protecting the forests—they're sure to take offense at the despoiling of their lands.

REQUIREMENTS

✦ Destroy the Trees of Life.

Receive on Completion: 3000 Lumber for each Tree of Life.

THE PATH TO VICTORY

This is a difficult and somewhat complex mission. The main goal is to amass 15,000 Lumber. Once accomplished, the mission ends. However, this enormous quanity of Lumber is difficult to obtain with a group of Peons amassing 10 Lumber at a time. If you proceed at this pace, it will take 1500 complete trips. Fortunately, there are alternate ways to accomplish this mission's goals.

The first tactic is to complete the Optional Quest for the Goblin Neeloc Greedyfingers. Do this and you gain access to the Goblin Shredders, which can harvest Lumber *very* quickly. The other way to complete the mission is to destroy the five Trees of Life. You receive 3000 Lumber for destroying each one; destroy all five to gain the required total.

Setting up several Guard Towers early on goes a long way in defending your base.

SET UP YOUR BASE

Secure the Gold Mine to the north of the starting position. If you fail to do so, you won't have an immediate source of Gold (other than from Pillaging). Train some extra Headhunters, secure the Gold Mine, then immediately build a Great Hall. As you amass more Gold, build at *least* three Guard Towers on the northwest side of the Great Hall. The enemy attacks in several waves, including some with archer-mounted Hippogryphs. This is why you need the ground-to-air attack capabilities of the Guard Towers.

NEELOC GREEDYFINGERS

There is a Goblin Laboratory and a Goblin Merchant to the north of the starting location (see map). Move your Hero to this area to receive a quest from Neeloc Greedyfingers. He says that if you defeat the Furbolg Chieftain, then he will grant you access to the Shredders. These machines are giant mechanized Lumber collectors that gather Lumber at 200 units at a time!

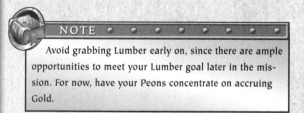

> **NOTE**
>
> Avoid grabbing Lumber early on, since there are ample opportunities to meet your Lumber goal later in the mission. For now, have your Peons concentrate on accruing Gold.

After establishing another Great Hall, upgrade your units in the War Mills and supplement your troops with more Grunts and Headhunters.

The Shredders collect Lumber quickly.

Take your attack force over to the Furbolg camp and attack. Use Mirror Image to confuse the Furbolgs and avoid attacks against your Hero. Destroy them all to get a Health Stone. When you return to Neeloc, you get two Shredders and access to buy more if you want. You can complete the main mission with just the Shredders, so buy some extras to gather the Lumber more quickly.

TREES OF LIFE

The Night Elf bases are difficult to destroy–they rebuild with great haste after an attack.

There are a number of Trees of Life located throughout the map (Night Elf bases). Each one provides 3000 Lumber when you destroy it, not to mention the resources you can pillage from it as you attack it. This is another way to gather the 15,000 Lumber necessary for victory.

Our map shows the locations of each Tree of Life. However, following this approach is particularly difficult for a number of reasons. Because of the numerous Night Elf installations, you'll need lots of additional resources. Still, if you want to complete both quests simultaneously, destroy the five Trees of Life. This enables you to gather the necessary Lumber and satisfy the Trees of Life quest.

YOUR CHOICE

There are several ways to win this mission. You can use Peons to slowly collect the Lumber, but this method is somewhat flawed because the Night Elves will target your Peons and slow down the process. Alternatively, you can kill the Furbolg Chieftain and gain access to the Goblin Shredders. With the Shredders working (two pairs will do), hunker down and defend them and your base while the Lumber piles up. Lastly, you can go after the five Trees of Life to attain the Lumber.

You can always use a combination of these tactics. For example, you can clear out the two Trees of Life in the southern portion of the map (6000+ Lumber), and then you can finish the job with the Shredders.

BONUSES

There are a few bonus items in plain view on the map. However, Forest Spirits attack as you attempt to grab them. The items include the Boots of Speed (see map), which are worth the effort.

The items out in the open are protected by Forest Spirits that appear only when you try to grab the item.

CHAPTER 5

THE HUNTER OF SHADOWS

The next morning in the shadowed woods of Ashenvale, the trees in the forest come to life and attack the Orc settlements. Cenarius, the Keeper of the Grove (a Night Elf Hero), is attempting to disrupt Orc efforts and it's up to Grom Hellscream's troops to stop him.

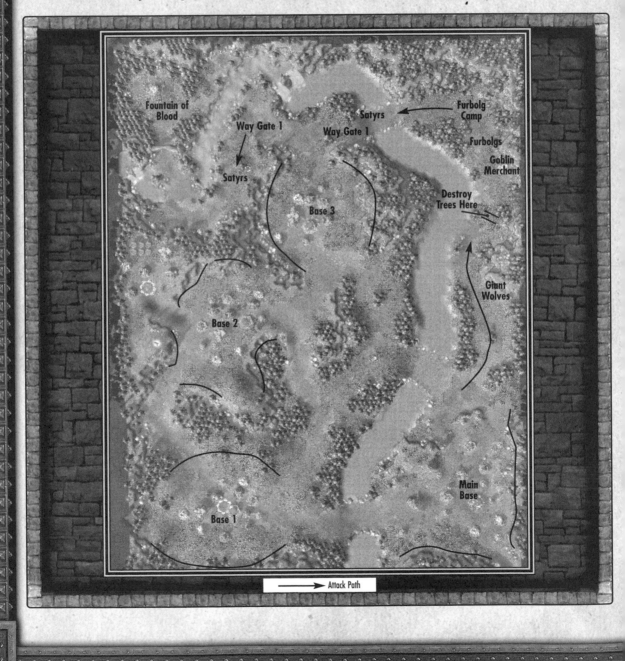

Fountain of Blood

Way Gate 1

Satyrs

Base 3

Base 2

Base 1

Satyrs

Way Gate 1

Furbolg Camp

Furbolgs

Goblin Merchant

Destroy Trees Here

Giant Wolves

Main Base

→ Attack Path

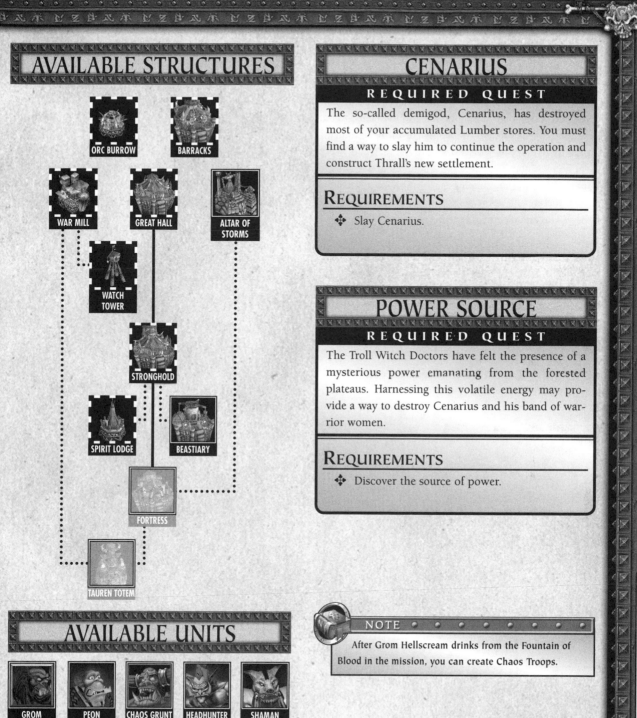

AVAILABLE STRUCTURES

- ORC BURROW
- BARRACKS
- WAR MILL
- GREAT HALL
- ALTAR OF STORMS
- WATCH TOWER
- STRONGHOLD
- SPIRIT LODGE
- BEASTIARY
- FORTRESS
- TAUREN TOTEM

CENARIUS

REQUIRED QUEST

The so-called demigod, Cenarius, has destroyed most of your accumulated Lumber stores. You must find a way to slay him to continue the operation and construct Thrall's new settlement.

REQUIREMENTS

❖ Slay Cenarius.

POWER SOURCE

REQUIRED QUEST

The Troll Witch Doctors have felt the presence of a mysterious power emanating from the forested plateaus. Harnessing this volatile energy may provide a way to destroy Cenarius and his band of warrior women.

REQUIREMENTS

❖ Discover the source of power.

AVAILABLE UNITS

- GROM HELLSCREAM
- PEON
- CHAOS GRUNT
- HEADHUNTER
- SHAMAN
- WITCH DOCTOR
- KODO BEAST
- RAIDER
- CHAOS WARLOCK

> **NOTE**
> After Grom Hellscream drinks from the Fountain of Blood in the mission, you can create Chaos Troops.

THE PATH TO VICTORY

As the mission begins, your Orc troops have four considerable bases on the map. All of them are well established but not especially well defended. The Night Elf forces quickly hit the three bases on the west side of the map and sweep them from existence in a few short minutes. Your goal is to hunker down in your main base (southeast) and defend against the attack. Upon doing so, you must regain your fighting legs and destroy Cenarius!

DEFENDING HOME BASE

Don't think for a second that you can hold off the Night Elves on the west side of the river—it just can't be done. You can, however, take advantage of the infrastructure of the base in the southwest corner of the map. Set the War Mills to upgrade right away. By the time the Night Elves reach this camp and destroy the structures, the upgrades will be ready! Also, move some Peons and Witch Doctors from the other bases back to the home base in the southeast corner of the map.

Get everyone back to your base as soon as possible, then start building more Guard Towers immediately!

To fend off the attack, you can use one of two strategies. First, train as many new units as possible in the time before the Night Elf army hits your base. Second, build five more Guard Towers in your base to fend off the attack. It may not seem like the best option at the start, but the only way to effectively stop the enemy is to erect these defensive structures on the west and north entrances to your base. Although you already have Guard

Towers in your base, the Night Elf attack contains Hippogryphs, Chimaeras, Huntresses, a Dyrad, and Archers. You need the Towers to deal with the Chimaeras and Hippogryphs while your melee troops handle the other enemies. The key to a successful defense is to have the Guard Towers arranged so that their cross fire ensures the enemy gets hit by multiple Towers at once.

Set up the Guard Towers and prepare for some real fun!

The Night Elf attack comes from the north and west sides of your base. Keep your troops together and use the Raiders' Ensnare (if you've researched it) to bring down the Chimaeras and continue to produce units as the attack unfolds. You can also place some Peons in the Orc Burrows for added defense, but *don't* create extra Peons for this purpose.

After the attack, build your defenses back to their pre-attack condition and continue to upgrade your units. Don't venture away from your base until all of the upgrades are in place! You have only a finite amount of Gold in this mission, so wasting resources on early skirmishes isn't an option. It is important to research Pillage right away, though, since the Furbolg camps you discover later will help you replenish your coffers a bit.

THE FOUNTAIN OF BLOOD

After upgrading your units, move your troops directly north up the east side of the map. This leads to a cave with Giant Wolves. You can't get any items from slaying them, but Grom can gain some experience. The Giant Wolves attack when your units pass by the area, so don't allow a small group to venture through or they'll get thrashed!

The Giant Wolves appear as your troops move past!

When you move as far north along the path as possible, the Troll Witch Doctors inform you that they sense a source of power in the wilderness. This triggers the Power Source quest. If you look closely, you'll notice that there *is* a path to the north, but you need a Catapult to destroy the trees blocking the way. Blast open a hole using Catapults, and move your troops north to the Goblin Merchant. Be advised this area is guarded by some fierce Furbolgs.

Purchase Scrolls of Protection and Health from the Goblin Merchant, then move north to the Furbolg Camp. Use a Scroll of Protection in this battle (if needed), because you don't want to deplete your troops too much! You should also purchase a Scroll of Town Portal to zap your forces back to town after you complete this quest.

Follow the path through the Furbolg camp (across the river) to the Way Gate, which is guarded by some Satyrs. Defeat them and pass through the Way Gate, which deposits you close to another Way Gate. Keep heading west toward the northwest corner of the map.

The Goblin Merchant is a welcome sight, but it's guarded by vicious Furbolgs.

Move through the archway to reach the Fountain of Blood, which is guarded by more Satyrs, and use Grom's Bladestorm and a Scroll of Protection to help defeat them. Grom can now drink from the Fountain of Blood to create Chaos troops!

CENARIUS

Now that you have Chaos troops, it's time to go after Cenarius. Build a balanced attack force that includes two Kodo Beasts, six Raiders, six Grunts, six Headhunters, along with any other troops you desire. Take this force west toward Base 1 (see map) and attack it to make Cenarius appear. At some point during the battle, Cenarius shows up. When this occurs, target him with *everything* you have!

Hit Night Elf Base 1 hard, and then wait for Cenarius to appear.

Cenarius uses plenty of magic on your troops. The key is to get Grom close and use Bladestorm on him. Doing so takes down his hit points enough to enable the rest of your troops (Grom included) to defeat him. When Cenarius falls, the mission ends in victory!

When Cenarius shows up, forget about Base 1 and concentrate on attacking only him.

CHAPTER 6

WHERE WYVERNS DARE

In the base at Stonetalon Peak, an Orc scout informs Thrall that the Humans have increased their defenses. Cairne Bloodhoof shows up to repay their debt to you with blood. They want to help you reach the Oracle.

Human Camp 1

Human Camp 2

(Wyverns) Harpies

Potion of Mana

Centaurs

Glyph of Purification

Centaur Kahn

Razormare Brutes

Periapt of Vitality

Harpies

Centaurs

Goblin Laboratory

Centaurs

Razormare Hunters

Quillboar Hunters

Goblin Merchant

Lightning Lizards

Starting Base

Health Stone

Defiled Fountain

→ Attack Path   **GM** Gold Mine

AVAILABLE STRUCTURES

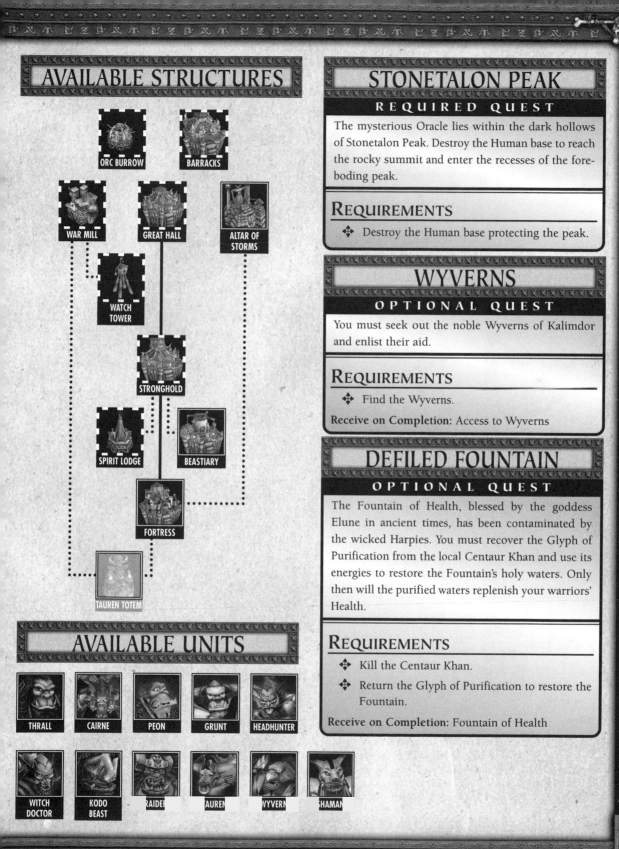

ORC BURROW   BARRACKS

WAR MILL   GREAT HALL   ALTAR OF STORMS

WATCH TOWER

STRONGHOLD

SPIRIT LODGE   BEASTIARY

FORTRESS

TAUREN TOTEM

AVAILABLE UNITS

THRALL   CAIRNE   PEON   GRUNT   HEADHUNTER

WITCH DOCTOR   KODO BEAST   RAIDER   TAUREN   WYVERN   SHAMAN

STONETALON PEAK

REQUIRED QUEST

The mysterious Oracle lies within the dark hollows of Stonetalon Peak. Destroy the Human base to reach the rocky summit and enter the recesses of the foreboding peak.

REQUIREMENTS

❖ Destroy the Human base protecting the peak.

WYVERNS

OPTIONAL QUEST

You must seek out the noble Wyverns of Kalimdor and enlist their aid.

REQUIREMENTS

❖ Find the Wyverns.

Receive on Completion: Access to Wyverns

DEFILED FOUNTAIN

OPTIONAL QUEST

The Fountain of Health, blessed by the goddess Elune in ancient times, has been contaminated by the wicked Harpies. You must recover the Glyph of Purification from the local Centaur Khan and use its energies to restore the Fountain's holy waters. Only then will the purified waters replenish your warriors' Health.

REQUIREMENTS

❖ Kill the Centaur Khan.

❖ Return the Glyph of Purification to restore the Fountain.

Receive on Completion: Fountain of Health

THE PATH TO VICTORY

There is one ultimate goal in this mission: To clear out the Human Camp in the northern section of the map. There are, however, two other optional quests. First, rescue the Wyverns to gain some extra firepower. Second, kill the Centaur Kahn to reverse the defiling of the Fountain of Health near your base.

SECURE BASE

Although you begin with some decent forces, it's important to build your base and upgrade your units before venturing out. This is primarily because the enemy attacks in waves, so you need adequate defenses to stave them off. Thrall's Chain Lightning is effective against the early attacks.

Set up your base with defensive measures so that your main attack group won't have to return to save the day.

Create a self-sufficient base by building several Guard Towers around it as a defense from land and air (Gryphon Rider) attacks. Also, keep a small group of Grunts and Headhunters back home to quickly respond to a major invasion.

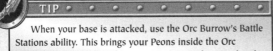

> **TIP**
>
> When your base is attacked, use the Orc Burrow's Battle Stations ability. This brings your Peons inside the Orc Burrows, thus enabling this structure to attack ground and air units! It's also important to upgrade to Spiked Barricades to deter the enemy from attacking your buildings.

THE DEFILED FOUNTAIN AND CENTAUR KAHN

Just to the west of your base (see map) is a Defiled Fountain protected by Lightning Lizards. Simply approach the fountain to receive the Defiled Fountain quest. This one involves finding the Centaur Kahn so that you can retrieve the Glyph that restores the fountain. Move up the map to the Gold Mine and Goblin Laboratory. Eliminate the pesky Centaurs and build a Great Hall if you're in need of more Gold.

> **NOTE**
>
> The Goblin Laboratory sells Goblin Shredders, which greatly increase the harvesting of Lumber. Therefore, if you're short on Lumber, you may want to take this area early.

The entrance to Centaur Khan's lair is just past the Gold Mine and Goblin Laboratory. Move in and attack him, but remember that he can reincarnate so you'll have your hands full. Use all of your spells and abilities in this battle.

A group of Human Gryphon Riders may also attack just after you defeat Centaur Khan; if this happens, use your Raiders' Ensnare ability to bring them down to your level, or attack with your Wyverns. With the Glyph in your possession, use the Fountain of Health by your base to regenerate your magical units.

The Centaur Khan is one tough enemy, doubly so because he reincarnates after his first death!

THE WYVERNS

The Wyverns are guarded by some Harpies, while the rest of the path to their lair is full of various Creeps. Move to the west to find some Quillboar Hunters guarding a Goblin Merchant. Destroy the Razormane Hunters just past the Goblin Merchant to yield a Health Stone.

When you reach the Harpy base, use Chain Lightning (hopefully at Level 3) to thin them out. You may also want to have your Troll Witch Doctors put down a Healing Ward during the battle to keep your units healthy. The Harpies are *very* powerful and use spells like Cyclone, Faerie Fire, Curse, and Sleep against your units, thus making the valuable Chain Lightning spell temporarily useless. Use the Raiders' Ensnare ability to bring the Harpies closer to the ground so your melee troops can fight them. With the Harpies defeated, you gain access to a new unit—the Wyvern. It's important to note that you get six of them right away!

HUMAN CAMP 1

There are two Human camps on the map, but you need to destroy only one of them. However, if you don't destroy them both, then the tenants from Camp 1 will constantly harass your troops as you attempt to pummel Camp 2. Camp 1 is in the northwest corner of the map and is easily toppled by using Catapults and a melee attack force. There are two Guard Towers near the camp's entrance, in addition to the unit-producing structures, Town Hall, and the units inside the base. Even if you don't completely destroy the base, eliminating the Barracks and the Town Hall will suffice.

Human Camp 1 isn't the primary target, but it's fun to crush it, especially after all the nagging attacks they've sent on your home base.

HUMAN CAMP 2

You may have to hit Human Camp 2 in several waves, because their defenses are strong.

This camp is accessible only via an airlift with Goblin Zeppelins or Wyverns. Ideally, a combination attack involving Catapults and melee attack units (dropped by Zeppelins) and a large group of Wyverns is the best approach. The plateau serves as a perfect landing spot; it's on the southern edge of this base. Note, however, that it is extremely well defended! Make sure you load up with Scrolls of Protection and healing items before attempting to take over Human Camp 2.

The Human resistance is substantial, so you may need to attack several times before wearing them down. To get your Goblin Zeppelins in safely, first run six to eight Wyverns into the area to keep the Gryphon Riders busy. After doing so, immediately follow up with the Zeppelins and drop your troops near their base!

Be prepared to take over the central Gold Mine (if you haven't done so already) and use Goblin Shredders to quickly gather the Lumber needed to finance your attacks.

With a firm foothold in Human Camp 2, you will most likely finish off the base. Thrall probably has the Earthquake spell at this point in the game, so use it to dispose of groups of enemy buildings. After eliminating the principle structures in Human Camp 2, victory is yours.

CHAPTER 7

THE ORACLE

The path splits inside the caverns of Stonetalon Peak. Cairne goes in one direction while Thrall goes in another—in search for the Oracle.

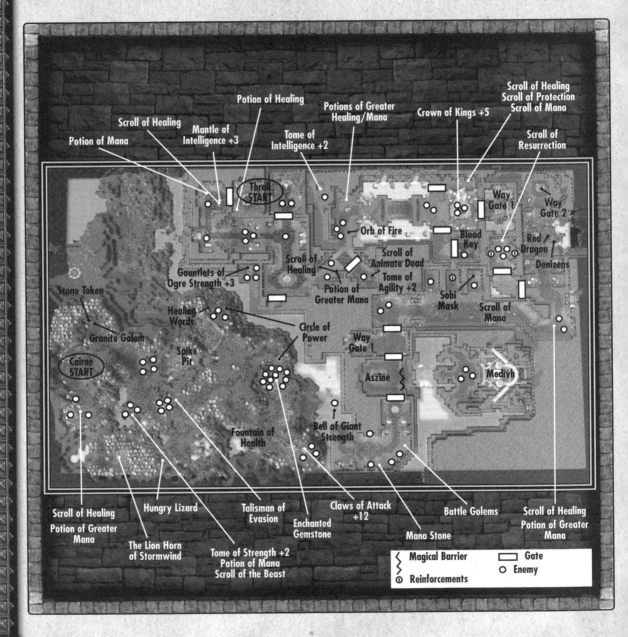

Labels within the map:

Potion of Mana
Scroll of Healing
Mantle of Intelligence +3
Potion of Healing
Tome of Intelligence +2
Potions of Greater Healing/Mana
Crown of Kings +5
Scroll of Healing
Scroll of Protection
Scroll of Mana
Scroll of Resurrection

Thrall START

Orb of Fire
Blood Key
Way Gate 1
Way Gate 2
Red Dragon
Denizens

Gauntlets of Ogre Strength +3
Scroll of Healing
Scroll of Animate Dead
Tome of Agility +2
Sobi Mask
Scroll of Mana

Stone Token
Potion of Greater Mana

Granite Golem

Cairne START

Healing Words
Spike Pit
Circle of Power
Way Gate 1
Aszine
Mediyh

Fountain of Health
Bell of Giant Strength

Scroll of Healing
Potion of Greater Mana
Hungry Lizard
The Lion Horn of Stormwind
Talisman of Evasion
Tome of Strength +2
Potion of Mana
Scroll of the Beast
Enchanted Gemstone
Claws of Attack +12
Mana Stone
Battle Golems
Scroll of Healing
Potion of Greater Mana

Magical Barrier
Reinforcements
Gate
Enemy

AVAILABLE STRUCTURES

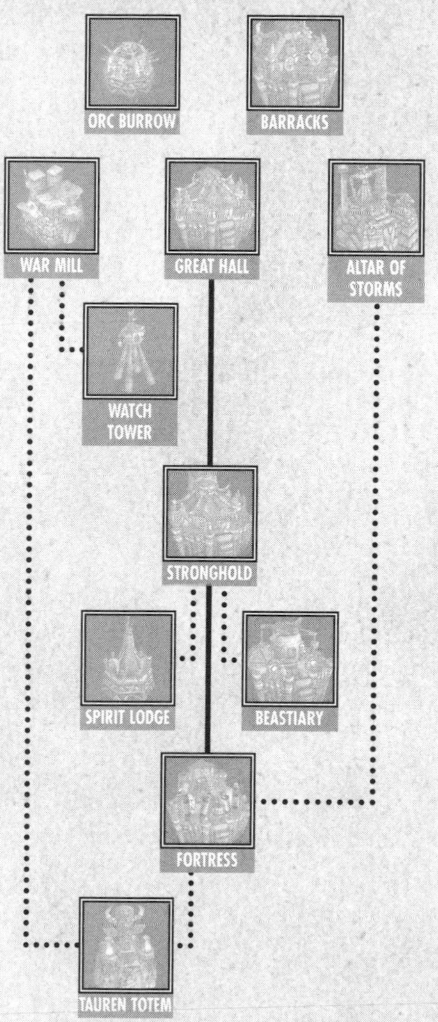

ORC BURROW

BARRACKS

WAR MILL

GREAT HALL

ALTAR OF STORMS

WATCH TOWER

STRONGHOLD

SPIRIT LODGE

BEASTIARY

FORTRESS

TAUREN TOTEM

AVAILABLE UNITS

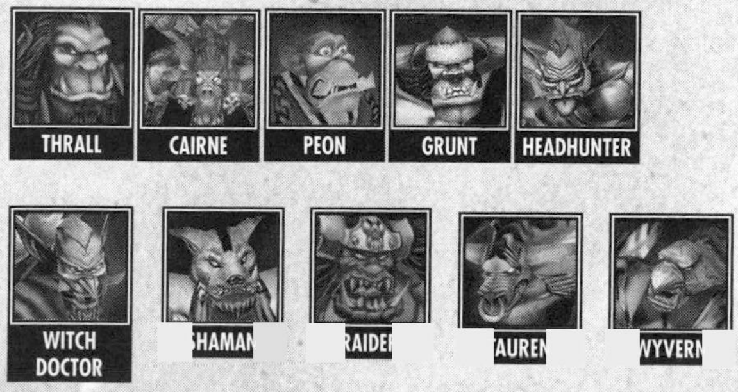

THRALL

CAIRNE

PEON

GRUNT

HEADHUNTER

WITCH DOCTOR

SHAMAN

RAIDER

TAUREN

WYVERN

THE ORACLE

REQUIRED QUEST

Legends state that the ancient Oracle of central Kalimdor lived within the caverns of Stonetalon Peak. You must seek out the Oracle's domicile and request that it shows the Horde the path to its true destiny.

REQUIREMENTS

- ✛ Seek out the Oracle.
- ✛ Thrall must survive.

HEART OF ASZUNE

REQUIRED QUEST

Long ago, the Night Elf princess, Aszune, mocked the Oracle's wisdom. As punishment, she was transformed into living stone. Now, only the retrieval of her gemstone heart can end the curse and allow passage to the Oracle's domicile.

REQUIREMENTS

- ✛ Find the Heart of Aszune.
- ✛ Return the Heart of Aszune.

Receive on Completion: Access past magical barrier

THE ENCHANTED GEMSTONE

REQUIRED QUEST

The spectral bridge leading to the Oracle's domicile is powered by an enchanted gemstone. You must recover the enchanted stone to activate the bridge's magic.

REQUIREMENTS

- ✛ Find the Enchanted Gemstone.
- ✛ Bring the Enchanted Gemstone to the Spectral Bridge.
- ✛ Cairne Bloodhoof must survive.

Receive on Completion: Spectral Bridge appears.

THE PATH TO VICTORY

The main goal is to find the Oracle. The first portion of the mission centers around Thrall, while the second half revolves around Cairn. There are some extra goodies to pick up as you move through the maze of Stonetalon's caverns.

THRALL

There are some nice items in the first few chambers.

The area where Thrall begins contains three items. Destroy the crates in the first two chambers to get a Potion of Mana, a Potion of Healing, and a Scroll of Healing. You must specifically target the gate to the west to get through it. There are some enemies on the other side, but nothing you can't handle.

There are several areas tucked off to the sides that you could easily miss.

Your troops take some damage as you fight the various enemies. There is no rush to finish this mission, so take your time and use the Troll Witch Doctor's Healing Ward to stay healthy.

Behind the gate to the north (see map) is a room full of enemies protecting a Mantle of Intelligence +3. This item increases Thrall's Mana capacity by 45 points. As noted earlier, target the gate to open it. Look around to find another small gate to the south of the second gate (see map). This one opens to a narrow passage that leads to three Creeps (some Sludge Monstrosities) and some Gauntlets of Ogre Strength +3.

CROWN OF KINGS AND BLOOD KEY

To reach the Crown of Command, you must first pass through the king's door, and you need the Blood Key to unlock it. This essential item is located in a room due south of the king's door. Be careful, though—you must slay two Salamanders to get the key.

Defeat the Creeps and get a Crown of Kings +5.

WAY GATE

When you're ready, attack the gate to the east, then pass through to the next room with a Way Gate and enter it.

Walk your remaining troops into the Way Gate.

HEART OF ASZUNE

You appear in a room with a north and south gate blocking your path. You need to travel both paths. To the north is the Heart of Aszune, which you *must* have. However, you first need to go south to get the quest. Attack the south gate and move into the room. Inside is a Moon Priestess statue that speaks to you. It says that you must find her heart before she will grant you passage beyond the magical barrier.

Now that you have the quest, move north through the corridors until you find an area with three closed gates on the upper side of the corridor. The central gate conceals three Troll Headhunters (which you probably need), while the other two contain enemies. The third gate has a very nasty Creep (a Salamander Lord) that summons fire against your troops. If you defeat it, though, you receive a Sobi Mask, which grants Thrall 50% faster Mana regeneration. Use your Shadow Wolves to attack the Salamander Lord, since they're disposable fighters.

As you move to the east, target the crates on the ground to gain more items (see map). When you reach the area full of Sheep, quickly kill them. If you don't, they will turn into Footmen and attack you. Don't forget to destroy the Sorceresses, too.

The statue of Aszune asks you to help her return her heart.

Move up the corridor to the north to find a group of flying Denizens fighting a Red Dragon. Let the fight unfold and then move in and use Chain Lightning to finish things off. The Red Dragon is immune to Magic, so throw down a Healing Ward and use your Troll Headhunters to defeat him. You receive the the Heart of Aszune for defeating this creature.

The Heart of Aszune is held by the Red Dragon.

The Way Gate directly to the north transports you back to the area near the Statue of Aszune. Return the Heart of Aszune to the statue and the magical barrier drops, granting you access to the east. However, you need an Enchanted Gem to create a Spectral Bridge that will lead to the Oracle. The job of finding this Gem falls to Cairne and his troops.

When the Barrier falls, the mission moves to Cairne and his men.

CAIRNE

Cairne, accompanied by three Tauren, starts in the rocky area on the western portion of the map. Move to the north of the starting location to find a Stone Token tucked in amongst some rocks. Attack the rocks to free the token. Note that doing so also releases a Granite Golem, which attacks. The Stone Token gives you a Rock Golem to control, so save it for later. Head south to the mine entrance and pick up the Scroll of Healing for battling the Creeps in the area.

The Stone Token is hidden among some rocks.

FIND THE GEMSTONE

Move to the east along the only path. This takes you to a group of Jaina's men, who perish in a Spike Pit. Don't follow them or your troops will take considerable damage. Continue to the south to discover more of Jaina's expedition, along with some fierce Kobolds. Eliminate the Creeps and destroy the crates to reveal more items (see map).

Follow the path to a Spiked Pit filled with Creeps. It seems that these creatures are protecting the Enchanted Gemstone. The gate to the area is indestructible, so follow the path to the northern edge of the Spiked Pit, then make Cairne step on the Circle of Power to kill the enemies in the pit.

Follow the path to the north, disposing of Creeps along the way. This is probably a good time to use the Stone Token to gain another fighting unit. Pick up any Healing Wards and use them if your Tauren are in need. When you reach the most northern point (the cliff overlooking the other side of the map), the gate to the Enchanted Gemstone opens. Return to collect it.

Move to the east to find the Salamander Lord and destroy this Creep for a Belt of Giant Strength +6. After doing so, return to the western portion of the map to fight the Creeps protecting a Tome of Strength +2, Claws of Attack +12, and even a Cloak of Flames. Whether or not you go after these is entirely up to you. See the map for their exact locations.

RETURN THE GEMSTONE

With the Gemstone in Cairne's possession, move toward the Southern Gate that leads to the Statue of Aszune. You must fight Battle Golems along the way, but the fight should be easy to win. When the Siege Golem drops the Ghost Key required to open the gate, Cairne meets Thrall and the Spectral Bridge appears. You then learn that the Humans and Orcs must work together in the next mission.

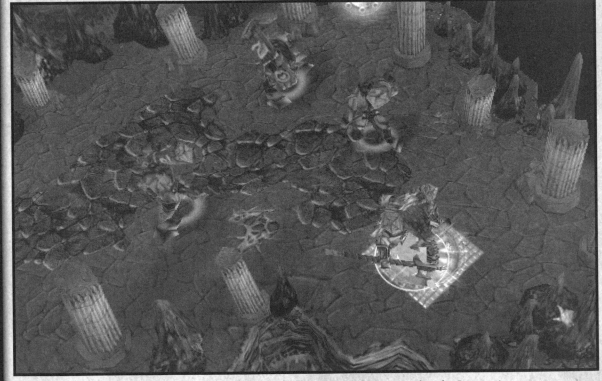

Have Cairne step on the Circle of Power to eliminate the Creeps guarding the Gemstone!

CHAPTER 8

BY DEMONS BE DRIVEN

Three days later near the edge of the Barrens, Cairne Bloodhoof meets Jaina and Thrall. It becomes clear that they need to capture Grom Hellscream's soul inside a Soul Gem and return it to Jaina's Ritual Circle.

→ Attack Path	
⊙ Reinforcements	
T Build Guard Tower	
GM Gold Mine	
O Enemy	

AVAILABLE STRUCTURES

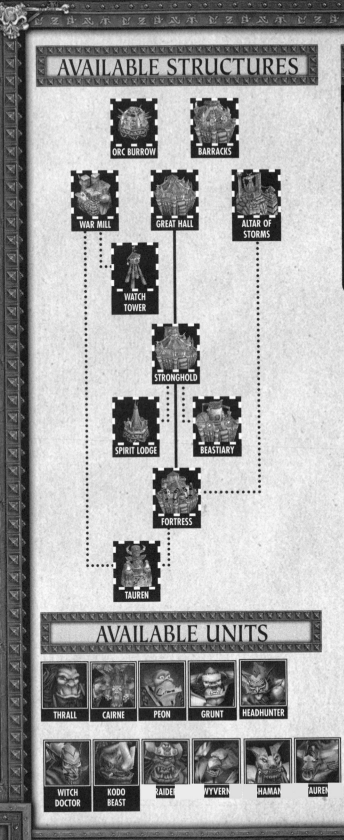

ORC BURROW

BARRACKS

WAR MILL

GREAT HALL

ALTAR OF STORMS

WATCH TOWER

STRONGHOLD

SPIRIT LODGE

BEASTIARY

FORTRESS

TAUREN

HELLSCREAM

REQUIRED QUEST

Hellscream has given himself over to the Legion's control. You must find him and trap his spirit within Jaina's Soul Gem. Bring the Gem to Jaina's ritual circle, where a combined effort might save Grom from the Demon's influence.

REQUIREMENTS

❖ Capture Grom in the Soul Gem.

❖ Bring Grom to Jaina's Ritual Circle.

AVAILABLE UNITS

THRALL | CAIRNE | PEON | GRUNT | HEADHUNTER

WITCH DOCTOR | KODO BEAST | RAIDER | WYVERN | SHAMAN | TAUREN

THE PATH TO VICTORY

This is the final—and toughest—Orc mission. The goal is to encase Grom inside the Soul Gem and bring him to Jaina's Ritual Circle in the southwest portion of the map. The Humans are your allies, while the Warsong Clan of the Orcs is your enemy.

SECURE BASE

First, secure your base with a thick, albeit costly, perimeter of Guard Towers. (Ensure they have the Spiked Barricades upgrade.) The Demons will send some tough Infernals, which constantly attack your base. Therefore, you need some backup units and two Peons to help repair damage to the Guard Towers. Concentrate on upgrading your units and buildings immediately, because the enemy will fiercely attack.

TIP

The Goblin Laboratory sells Goblin Shredders. These units collect 200 Lumber at a time and are very efficient and fast. Purchase at least one of them.

WARSONG DANCE

The Warsong Clan is the dominant force on this map, meaning you must cut through them to reach Grom and his Doom Guards (which are also flanked by Felhounds). Since the entire map is covered with Warsong Clan troops and bases, you need to carve a path up to Grom's area in the northeast. To do so, go up the east (right) side of the map, taking out enemies (both Creeps and Warsong Clan). This is only one significant Warsong Base to flatten, then you can go after Grom's Doom Guards and Felhounds.

Move to the east, secure the Goblin Laboratory, and move up to capture the Gold Mine defended by the Warsong Clan. This is the mine on the far eastern edge of the map.

You'll encounter some battles with the Warsong Clan, but nothing significant—yet!

After capturing the Gold Mine, you can set up a Great Hall to harvest the Gold but it's not necessary for the mission's success. Now, you need to secure the Fountain of Health to the northwest of the Gold Mine. Some tough Creeps roam this area, and unfortunately the Warsong Clan may also send some troops to hinder your progress. Still, a Fountain of Health is valuable, so it's important to take it. You also receive a Scroll of Protection for your effort.

For obvious reasons, control over the Fountain of Health is worth the effort.

NOTE

The Demons drop Infernals from the sky throughout the mission, so be prepared for them to appear at any time. This is, in part, why we suggest bolstering your base's defenses.

213

Infernals appear from time to time. Watch out—they're tough!

The Doom Guards are tough, but with Chain Lightning and a group of Tauren, you can defeat them.

WARSONG BASE ELIMINATION

There is one base that stands between you and Grom, and it's labeled as Warsong Clan Base 1 on the map. Move an attack group of Thrall, Cairne, three Taurens, three Raiders, one Grunt, one Headhunter, and two Troll Witchdoctors toward this location. Also, send a secondary group of three Catapults to focus on the Warsong buildings. Move up to the base and have Cairne hit it with Warstomp, while Thrall uses Chain Lightning. Lastly, use Thrall's Feral Spirit. With your units engaged in action, have a Witch Doctor drop a Healing Ward near your troops to keep them healthy.

While your melee troops are fighting, use the Catapults to destroy each structure with two rounds. Topple the Guard Towers, followed by the Barracks, then the other unit-producing structures. After eliminating the enemy, set up a base of your own (this is not required to succeed).

GET GROM

After clearing a path, heal your troops and send them to fight the Doom Guards and Felhounds guarding Grom. There are two levels of sentries to fight. The Doom Guards are tough, but they're weak against a group of four Tauren with additional help from Thrall and Cairn. For added security, bring a pack of Wyverns to hit the Doom Guards simultaneously from the air.

After the second round of Doom Guards, you'll see Grom! Use the Soul Gem (click on the gem and then Grom) to capture his soul and encase it inside the Soul Gem. Your job is now simple: Take the Soul Gem down to the Ritual Circle in the southwest corner of the map to end the mission.

Get the Soul Gem to this location.

MAP EXTRAS

This map has many Warsong Clan Bases, lots of Creeps, and areas such as Fountains of Health and Goblin Merchants. See the map for locations and items you may want to pursue. Of course, the path to reach the Doom Guards is just a suggestion. Indeed, passing through Jaina's camp may enable you to access the Doom Guards and Grom with somewhat less difficulty.

NIGHT ELF CAMPAIGN

ETERNITY'S END

The Night Elves are the other new race to set foot in the realm of Warcraft. Their unique symbiotic relationship with nature means they have many unique abilities, not the least of which is an unlimited supply of Lumber. This is the final segment in the single-player saga.

CHAPTER 1
ENEMIES AT THE GATE

With the heroic sacrifice of Grom Hellscream, the pit lord Mannoroth was slain and the Demon curse that had plagued the Orcs was put to rest. However, the combined Human and Orc forces have moved deeper into Ashenvale Forest to ascertain whether a demonic threat still lingers in the land. Tyrande Whisperwind, the leader of the Night Elf Sentinels, believes that the outlanders will only bring doom to her enchanted homeland.

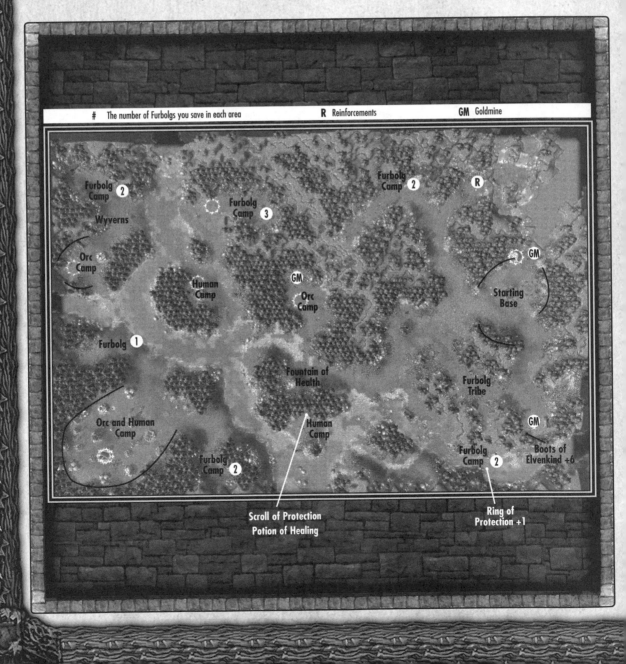

#	The number of Furbolgs you save in each area	**R** Reinforcements	**GM** Goldmine

Furbolg Camp 2

Furbolg Camp 3

Furbolg Camp 2

R

Wyverns

GM

Orc Camp

Human Camp

GM

Orc Camp

Starting Base

Furbolg 1

Fountain of Health

Furbolg Tribe

GM

Orc and Human Camp

Human Camp

Furbolg Camp 2

Furbolg Camp 2

Boots of Elvenkind +6

Scroll of Protection
Potion of Healing

Ring of Protection +1

AVAILABLE STRUCTURES

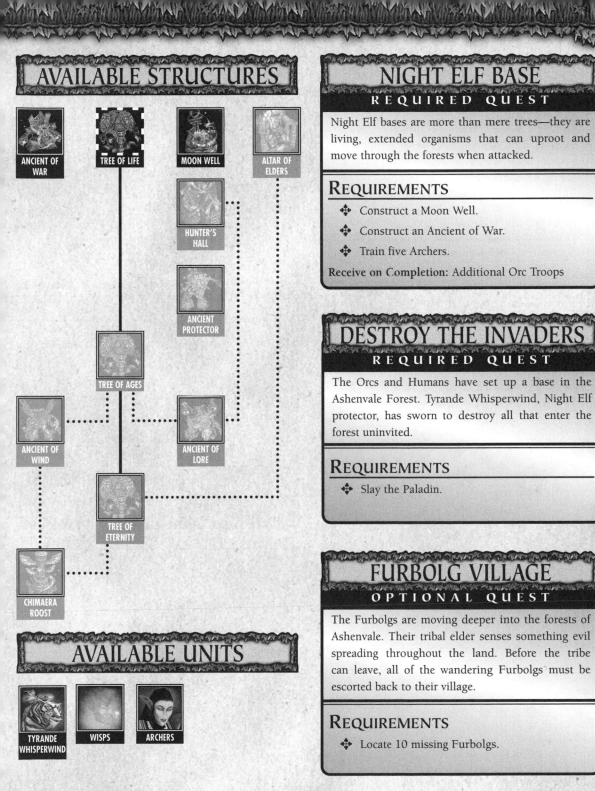

ANCIENT OF WAR

TREE OF LIFE

MOON WELL

ALTAR OF ELDERS

HUNTER'S HALL

ANCIENT PROTECTOR

TREE OF AGES

ANCIENT OF WIND

ANCIENT OF LORE

TREE OF ETERNITY

CHIMAERA ROOST

AVAILABLE UNITS

TYRANDE WHISPERWIND

WISPS

ARCHERS

NIGHT ELF BASE
REQUIRED QUEST

Night Elf bases are more than mere trees—they are living, extended organisms that can uproot and move through the forests when attacked.

REQUIREMENTS

- Construct a Moon Well.
- Construct an Ancient of War.
- Train five Archers.

Receive on Completion: Additional Orc Troops

DESTROY THE INVADERS
REQUIRED QUEST

The Orcs and Humans have set up a base in the Ashenvale Forest. Tyrande Whisperwind, Night Elf protector, has sworn to destroy all that enter the forest uninvited.

REQUIREMENTS

- Slay the Paladin.

FURBOLG VILLAGE
OPTIONAL QUEST

The Furbolgs are moving deeper into the forests of Ashenvale. Their tribal elder senses something evil spreading throughout the land. Before the tribe can leave, all of the wandering Furbolgs must be escorted back to their village.

REQUIREMENTS

- Locate 10 missing Furbolgs.

THE PATH TO VICTORY

This mission serves as your introduction to the Night Elf race. While some of their structures are familiar, the way in which the Night Elves harvest resources and create structures is somewhat different. The main quest of building a small base is simple to achieve, but the other quests will keep you on your toes.

BUILD BASE

Follow the built-in instructions to build your base. Place your Tree of Life next to the Gold Mine and Entangle it. This enables you to mine it later. Send two of your Wisps to harvest Lumber in the nearby trees; note that they harvest Lumber without damaging any of the trees! Build a Moon Well and an Ancient of War, then prepare to build the requisite five Archers. When an attack group is ready to move out, leave at least three or four Archers behind to defend your base. This is important because both the Humans and Orcs will send small groups to attack it.

Build up your Night Elf base.

> **TIP**
>
> Moon Wells can automatically regenerate Mana and hit points to your units. This can work manually as well, but it's best to set them to Autocast for replenishing Mana and Health. This way, your units will be replenished when they are close to the Mana Wells.

FURBOLGS

After creating a base and 5-10 Archers, head south to find the Furbolg Tribe village. They give you the quest to return 10 of their missing Furbolgs to their village in return for a gift.

Move your troops to the south to find a Furbolg camp and save the two Furbolgs. After doing so, the Humans attack from the west. Eliminate them and move to the west to destroy the small Human camp. Make sure you destroy the two tents in the camp, because they yield a Scroll of Protection and a Potion of Healing.

The Humans attack after you rescue the first two Furbolgs.

Instead of heading to the west, send your forces north to find a Fountain of Health. Take the time to build more Moon Wells and construct a second attack group of Archers. To the north of the Fountain of Health is a small Orc Camp protecting the Gold Mine—destroy it and secure the mine.

For the most part, the only camp you can't destroy is the large Human/Orc camp in the southwest corner of the map.

> ### NOTE
>
> Once you secure the Gold Mine in the central portion of the map, it's not necessary to build a new Tree of Life. Instead, simply uproot the Tree of Life and move it to the new Gold Mine! This is the best tactic if you want to save resources. Also, if your Tree of Life takes any hits, you can have it Eat Trees to replenish its life!

There are four more Furbolg camps (see map)—one with three Furbolgs, two with two, and one camp with a lone Furbolg. Showing up at these camps is all you need to do to succeed in the quest. The quest ends after you've located all 10 Furbolgs.

Keep moving through the map. There are extra Furbolg camps, so you don't have to get them all.

There are reinforcements to the north of your base, as well as a group of Orcs to the north of the central Gold Mine that are holding some Furbolgs captive. You must destroy the Orcs to free the Furbolgs. After freeing them, return to the Furbolg Village to the south of your base to receive two Level 4 Furbolgs and a Level 7 Furbolg Champion.

THE PALADIN (DUKE LION HEART)

The main goal of this mission is to kill the Paladin. Although you may be tempted to eliminate the Human base in the southwest corner of the map, you will have a difficult time doing so with only standard (not upgraded) Archers. Move two groups of Archers (perhaps 25-30 total) into the main Orc/Human camp in the southwest corner of the map and aim *all* of your attacks on the Paladin, Duke Lion Heart. Kill him, claim the Circlet of Nobility and Healing Wards, and the mission ends in victory!

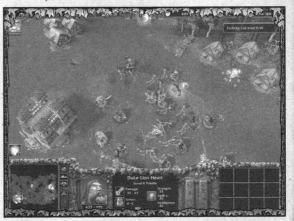

When attacking the major Human/Orc encampment, concentrate on Duke Lion Heart. He is your primary target.

CHAPTER 2
DAUGHTERS OF THE MOON

Three hours later, somewhere in the foothills of Mount Hyjal, Tichondrius and Archimonde meet Tyrande Whisperwind and attempt to kill her. She hides, forcing them to believe she has disappeared. This gives Tyrande a chance to warn her kin.

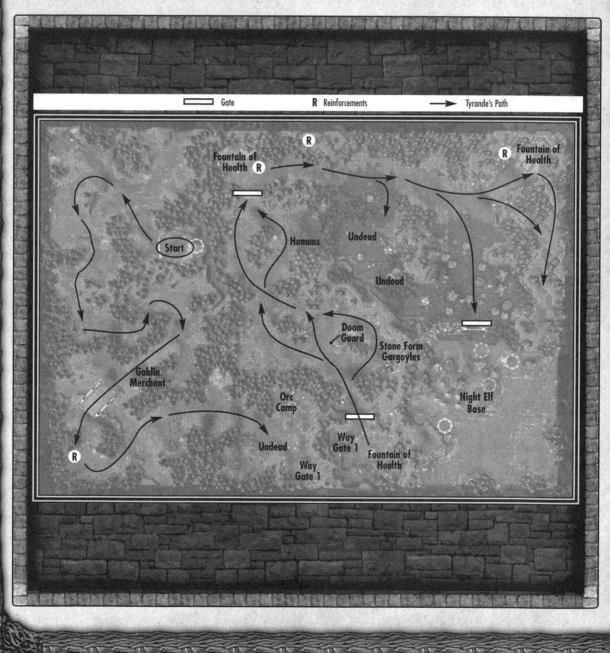

AVAILABLE STRUCTURES

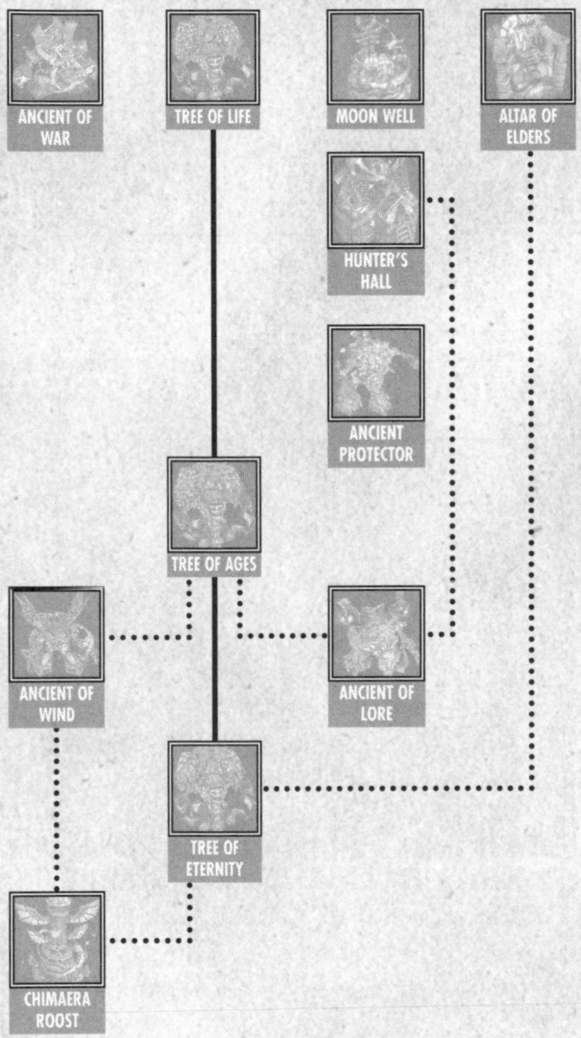

ANCIENT OF WAR

TREE OF LIFE

MOON WELL

ALTAR OF ELDERS

HUNTER'S HALL

ANCIENT PROTECTOR

TREE OF AGES

ANCIENT OF WIND

ANCIENT OF LORE

TREE OF ETERNITY

CHIMAERA ROOST

AVAILABLE UNITS

TYRANDE WHISPERWIND

ARCHERS

BALLISTAE

ESCAPE INTO SHADOW

REQUIRED QUEST

The Burning Legion has invaded Ashenvale and placed the land under a terrible pall. You must make your way, undetected, through the demon patrols and reach the distant Night Elf village where Shandris and the rest of the Sentinels await.

REQUIREMENTS

❖ Bring Tyrande to the Nigh Elf town.

❖ Tyrande must survive.

THE PATH TO VICTORY

The goal in this mission is to get Tyrande to the Night Elf base in one piece—alive! Follow the map to see exactly how to get from the starting location to the gate that leads to the Night Elf base.

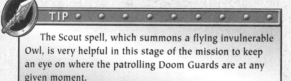

> ### NOTE
> Although you may be told to wait in certain instances, it's important to not delay too long. Remember that the Night Elves' ability to Hide occurs only in the dark and the night won't last forever!

STAGE 1

The first stage of the mission is a twisting area filled with patrolling Doom Guards. The ground is soiled with Blight as Tyrande progresses through the mission. In this initial area, there are six patrolling Doom Guards, and their patrol routes tend to overlap. When the Doom Guards see you, they can cast Cripple on you, which lowers your ability to cause damage and makes it very difficult for Tyrande to move.

You must use Tyrande's Hide ability to make it through this area this area alive, you should not attempt to kill the Doom Guards—they are simply too tough. Instead of fighting, Tyrande can use Hide to let the Doom Guards slip past her, then when they have moved on, you can move her again.

> ### TIP
> The Scout spell, which summons a flying invulnerable Owl, is very helpful in this stage of the mission to keep an eye on where the patrolling Doom Guards are at any given moment.

There is a cage in the area patrolled by the fourth Doom Guard. When this cage is destroyed, a Furbolg will pop out and fight for you. Unfortunately, the Furbolg is doomed to die a short time later, but for now you'll take all you can get!

STAGE 2

The second stage begins when you cross the bridge in the southwest corner of the map. Tyrande comes to a barrier of crates guarded by a Footman. Fortunately at this point, five Archers appear and help Tyrande destroy the Footman. They also act as reinforcements for you battles.

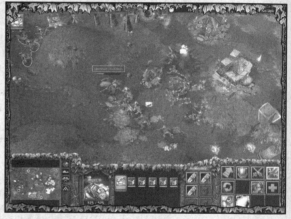

Let the battle unfold while Tyrande and her Archers hide nearby.

> ### TIP
> If you destroy one of the tents in this camp, another Footman will pop out that you can kill.

When you move down the path to the northeast, you'll run into a camp of Footmen fighting Ghouls. You can run by this, or take part in the slaughter—we suggest that you watch the battle sort itself out, thus preventing your precious troops from taking any unnecessary damage. There's a Goblin Merchant just beyond this point, so stock up on Scrolls of Protection and Potions of Healing.

You will then come to a large Orc camp that is getting pounded by a group of Undead Crypt Fiends and Meat Wagons. Use the Hide ability and sit back and watch the action. When the battle is almost over, run your troops through the base to the Way Gate beyond. If you want, there is a Mantle of Intelligence +3 in the Orc base, but you'll have to do some fighting to get it, and it's probably not worth the risk of damaging your troops.

STAGE 3

When your troops move through the Way Gate, you enter the third stage of this mission. Three Huntresses appear and cast Sentinel Owls on the trees. A Shade appears and the Huntresses kills it, then warns you of Shades ahead; there are five Shades positioned in the next region. The three Huntresses join your cause, giving you even more reinforcements.

On the other side of the Way Gate is a Fountain of Health, along with a gate that you must destroy in order to keep moving. There are two Doom Guards patrolling the Shade area, and you must kill the Shades or the Doom Guards will be able to attack your troops even if they're hiding! You'll approach five Gargoyles in Stone form, clustered around a pair of Gloves of Haste, sitting on the ground. If Tyrande picks up the item, the Gargoyles will leave Stone form and attack your troops, but if you leave the gloves alone, they won't disturb you.

The Infernal won't give up, so get to the Fountain of Health where some reinforcements await.

Now move northwest to the next gate; right before you reach the gate you'll see Footmen fleeing the scene. If you pursue the Footmen, you will find more Footmen, battling a Doom Guard. When the Doom Guard dies, he drops a Tome of Strength!

STAGE 4: BREAKING THROUGH

There are two groups of reinforcements left—a group of Ballistae in a small clearing just north of the path you're currently on, as well as some Archers and more Ballistae at the Fountain of Health in the northeast corner of the map. Gather up the reinforcements and prepare for an assault on the Undead base.

With six Ballistae, you can punch through the Undead's Spirit Towers. Mass your forces into two groups—Ballistae in one squad and everything else in the other. Move south toward the gate, but destroy as many Spirit Towers as possible before doing so. You can topple several of them before the full might of the Undead base is thrust upon you. Send everything at the gate, because you must destroy it to pass through.

Make a push to get through the Undead base, and break down the gate to end the mission.

> **TIP**
>
> Remember that only Tyrande must survive and pass through the gate. Make a run for the gate that blocks your path to victory. This is an excellent time to use Scrolls of Protection or Potions of Healing. When you break through, you meet Shandris Feathermoon and victory is yours.

CHAPTER 3

THE AWAKENING OF STORMRAGE

The next day, near the outskirts of the sacred Moonglade, Tyrande advises that the Night Elves must recover the sacred Horn. She also tells of Furion Stormrage, a Druid that must be awakened by his people before being destroyed by the Undead.

Map Labels:
- Antimagic Potion
- Horn of Cenarius
- Fountain of Mana
- Jade Ring
- Undead Base
- Healing Wards
- Goblin Merchant
- Orc Base
- Tree Barrier
- Furion Storm Rage
- Fountain of Health
- Orcs
- Pendant of Energy
- Start Base

Legend:
- A — Ancient Protector
- → — Path to Merchant
- ↓↓↓ — Undead Assault on Trees
- GM — Gold Mine

AVAILABLE STRUCTURES

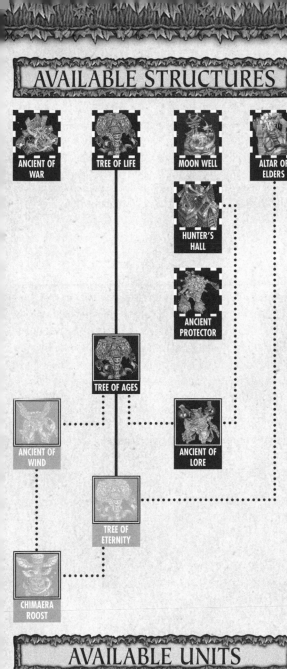

ANCIENT OF WAR

TREE OF LIFE

MOON WELL

ALTAR OF ELDERS

HUNTER'S HALL

ANCIENT PROTECTOR

TREE OF AGES

ANCIENT OF WIND

ANCIENT OF LORE

TREE OF ETERNITY

CHIMAERA ROOST

AVAILABLE UNITS

TYRANDE WHISPERWIND

WISPS

ARCHERS

HUNTRESS

BALLISTA

DRYAD

FURION STORMRAGE

REQUIRED QUEST

Furion Stormrage has slept within his Barrow Den for a thousand years, and only the Horn of Cenarius can awaken him. The Undead draw closer to defiling his Den, so you must retrieve the Horn from the three Ancient Protectors to allow him to arise from his slumber.

REQUIREMENTS

❖ Slay the three Ancient Protectors.

❖ Retrieve the Horn of Cenarius.

❖ Slumbering Furion Stormrage must survive.

THE PATH TO VICTORY

There are two main enemy bases on this map—an Undead base on the western edge and an Orc base that blocks your access to the three Ancient Protectors. Focus only on the Orc base and the Ancient Protectors.

BUILD ATTACK FORCES

First, build your attack force and upgrade in the Hunter's Hall. Although you start with an adequate force, you need to augment it and upgrade everything as far as it will go. Also, build the Ancient of Lore, which creates access to Dryads. The Undead constantly hack away at the trees that separate them from Furion Stormrage, but there's plenty of time to work on these upgrades.

> ### NOTE
>
> Soon after the mission starts, you gain access to a new unit: the Dryad. Later, three Dryads join your forces. This unit is immune to magic and adds poison to its attacks.

The Orc base eventually sends small waves of attackers at your main camp, so set your Moon Wells to Autocast to repair the troops standing in defense. If you want some items like Scroll of Protection, Healing, or even Potions of Anti-Magic, there is a Goblin Merchant near the central area of the map.

Your base gets attacked a few times, but it's nothing your starting forces can't handle.

SECONDARY BASE

If you have the time and the resources, build a second Tree of Life to the east of your base at the undefended Gold Mine. While you can build a second functional base in this area, the amount of time available is limited, so only do this if you're in dire need of extra Gold.

ORC BASE

Build an attack force of Huntresses, Archers, Dryads, and Ballistae. Place a group of three or four Ballistae in one group with Tyrande leading a second group that includes all of your other units. Send your troops up to the Fountain of Health in the east (see map) and eliminate the Orc Raiders in the area. Use the Fountain of Health to repair your units, then move your Ballistae to the north and destroy the Guard Towers and Barracks.

The Ballistae make quick work of the Guard Towers in the Orc base.

Once the Ballistae engage the Orc base, the Horde throw everything they have at these Mechanical units. When this occurs, bring up the nearby attack group to engage the Orcs. If you have any Scrolls of Protection, use them! As your attack group fights with the Orc units, concentrate the Ballistae attack on destroying the buildings one at a time. Expect to take some losses in this fight. Even if the Orcs defeat the first wave of attackers, you will damage them enough that your second wave of attackers will have better luck.

The Orc base fights back hard, but you must secure this area.

THE ANCIENT PROTECTORS

With the Orc base under control, regroup your attack team and pursue the Ancient Protectors to the north. All three Ancient Protectors are guarded by rather nasty Owlbears. You can acquire some good items here, and there's also a Fountain of Mana that replenishes your magical units.

With three Archers, four Huntresses, four Dryads, and Tyrande, move north to meet the first Ancient Protector and his Owlbears. Attack the Ancient Protector first, then worry about the Owlbears.

You face the Ancient Protectors one at a time, each protected by an Owlbear.

Continue through the northern portion of the map. The only enemies in this area are the Ancient Protectors. If one of them heavily damages your party, or if they kill Tyrande, rebuild at your base and send a new attack force to finish them off.

The Horn of Cenarius rests on a pedestal near the last Ancient Protector, but you can't take it until you destroy the last Guardian. Furion Stormrage is freed when the last Guardian falls and the mission ends.

The Ancient Protectors are tough, but manageable, if you focus all your firepower on them.

> **TIP**
>
> There are a few bonuses on the map that are worth going after if you have the time. Refer to the map for these locations.

CHAPTER 4
THE DRUIDS ARISE

Two days later, deep in the Winterspring Valley, Tyrande meets Furion Stormrage. Tyrande informs Furion that his awakening occurred because there are urgent matters. Tyrande further explains that the Burning Legion has returned, and Archimonde will attempt to attack the World Tree.

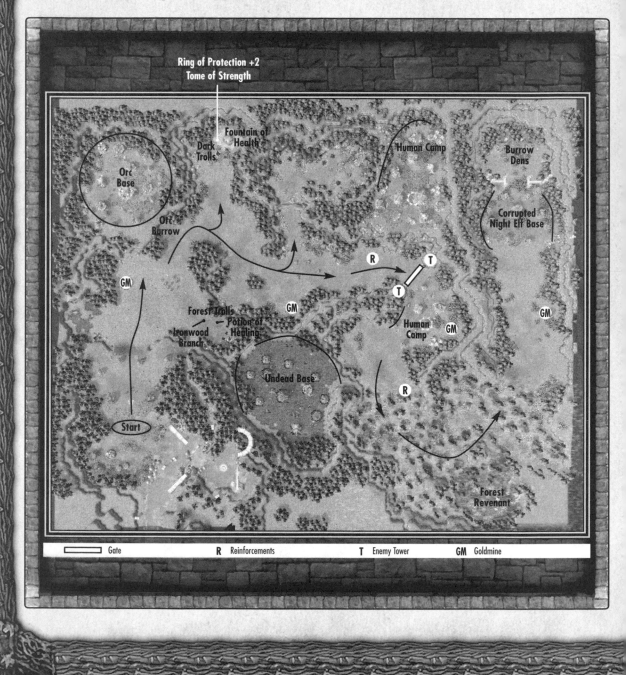

▭ Gate	**R** Reinforcements	**T** Enemy Tower	**GM** Goldmine

AVAILABLE STRUCTURES

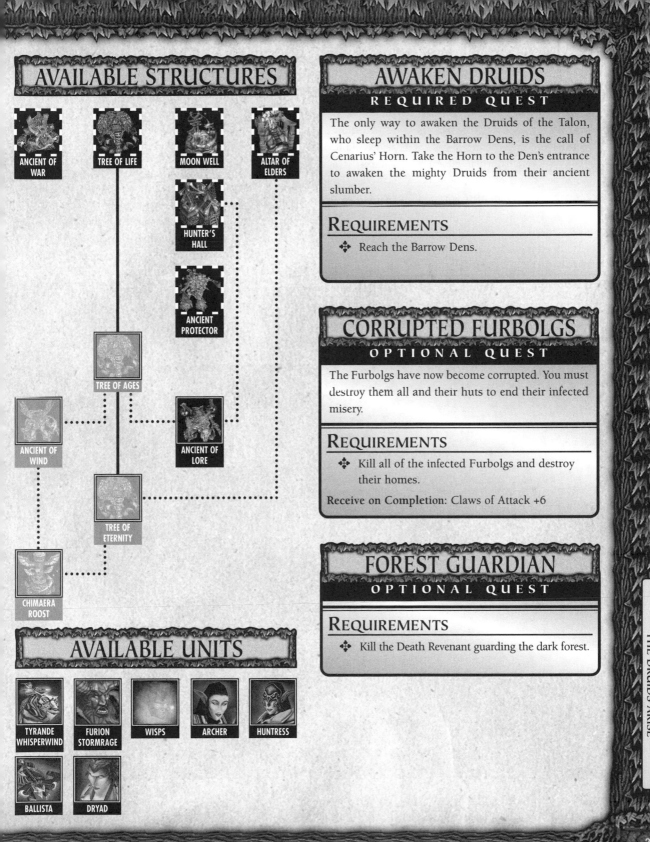

ANCIENT OF WAR

TREE OF LIFE

MOON WELL

ALTAR OF ELDERS

HUNTER'S HALL

ANCIENT PROTECTOR

TREE OF AGES

ANCIENT OF LORE

ANCIENT OF WIND

TREE OF ETERNITY

CHIMAERA ROOST

AVAILABLE UNITS

TYRANDE WHISPERWIND

FURION STORMRAGE

WISPS

ARCHER

HUNTRESS

BALLISTA

DRYAD

AWAKEN DRUIDS
REQUIRED QUEST

The only way to awaken the Druids of the Talon, who sleep within the Barrow Dens, is the call of Cenarius' Horn. Take the Horn to the Den's entrance to awaken the mighty Druids from their ancient slumber.

REQUIREMENTS

✤ Reach the Barrow Dens.

CORRUPTED FURBOLGS
OPTIONAL QUEST

The Furbolgs have now become corrupted. You must destroy them all and their huts to end their infected misery.

REQUIREMENTS

✤ Kill all of the infected Furbolgs and destroy their homes.

Receive on Completion: Claws of Attack +6

FOREST GUARDIAN
OPTIONAL QUEST

REQUIREMENTS

✤ Kill the Death Revenant guarding the dark forest.

THE PATH TO VICTORY

This mission's main quest involves working your way to the Barrow Dens on the far east side of the map. Unfortunately, the amount of Gold is extremely limited, so be very careful when allocating resources. There are a series of Gold Mines that have 1500-2000 Gold per mine—just enough to keep things going, but not enough to provide the power to confidently overcome your enemies.

FIRST GOLD MINE

You begin with all of your base's Treants up and moving. Send the two Ancient Protectors north to support your troops where the Undead and Humans are fighting.

When the Alliance flees the area, don't follow them. Place your Tree of Life near the Gold Mine to Entangle it, then move your Wisps down to harvest the valuable yellow ore.

With the area secure, upgrade your units in the Hunter's Hall and work on building a few more key units to support your fight. Also, have your Ancient Protectors eat some trees to repair themselves, because they will become an important part of the mission going forward. Approach the Forest Trolls in the small pocket to the east of the Gold Mine and destroy them. These creatures yield an Ironwood Branch and a Potion of Healing.

The Ancient Protectors help you defeat the Undead base near the first Gold Mine.

FOUNTAIN OF HEALTH

The Orc base is located in the northwest corner of the map, but you do not have access to it—it sets atop an inaccessible cliff. There is a group of Dark Forest Trolls near the Fountain of Health, including a Forest Troll Warlock. Dispose of them and collect the Ring of Protection +2 and the Tome of Strength, then replenish your forces at the Fountain of Health.

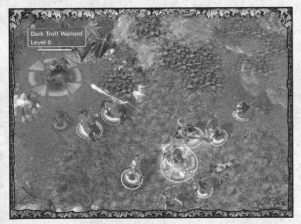

Clear out the area near the Fountain of Health. You need this to repair your wounds, because resources are limited in this mission.

CORRUPTED FURBOLGS

The first quest is given when you venture to the east after clearing out the Fountain of Health. It begins once the Furbolgs attack. Move past the Defiled Fountain of Life up to the Furbolg base and destroy the Furbolgs and their huts. It's a tough battle, so use Furion Stormrage's Force of Nature Spell to raise the Treants to fight by your side. It's best to have these units on the front lines taking hits from the Furbolgs while your Archers, Huntresses, and Dyrads hang back and attack from afar. After defeating the Furbolgs, you complete the quest.

> **NOTE**
>
> While fighting the Furbolgs, Furion or Tyrande may level up. If this occurs, you can upgrade their skills yet again. We recommend investing in skills that help the entire group, not just the Hero. For this reason, Furion's Thorns or Tyrande's Trueshot Auras are the best choices.

The Furbolgs are tough. Use your Treants from Force of Nature to absorb the brunt of their attacks.

Second Gold Mine

After destroying the Furbolgs, move your Tree of Life and your Ancient Protectors down to the Gold Mine to entangle it for another 2000 Gold. This is a relatively calm portion of the quest, so spend some time at your original base ensuring that you have fully upgraded all of your troops.

Human Camp

You gain two extra Huntresses as you move to the east with your attack force. They warn of danger up ahead. Find the Human gate guarded by a pair of Guard Towers. As soon as you break through the gate, Aurrius the Pure, a Human Paladin, appears with his forces. When attacking an enemy town, hit the Guard/Cannon Towers first, then the Barracks, and finally the Town Hall. You must also have a number of troops available for melee combat. Use Furion's Force of Nature to bolster your numbers during the attack, and use a pair of Ballistae to crush the structures.

The Human camp is well protected.

With the camp destroyed, head south for more reinforcements (two Dryads and two Huntresses). You also get the Forest Guardian quest. You can complete this along the way to the final destination. Before venturing into the Dark Forest, move your Tree of Life and Wisps down to the captured Human Gold Mine, and gather any remaining resources.

Dark Forest

The forest to the south is your only path to the Barrow Dens, but it's full of Ghosts, Skeletal Archers, and Giant Skeleton Warriors. Use Furion's Force of Nature to create Treants that can move through the forest ahead of your main group. This helps to deflect the punishment that your troops must endure.

The forest is full of Ghosts and Skeletal fighters. It's a tough fight, but keep your troops together and concentrate on the enemies one at a time.

The Forest Revenant is in the southeast corner of the map. Take him down with all of your troops to complete the quest. He is guarded by a series of Wraiths and Ghosts, which makes your job a lot harder. When the Forest Revenant falls, the area suddenly lightens and becomes uncursed.

The Barrow Dens

Before you make the final push to the Barrow Dens, buff up your forces with the greatest number of units that you can afford based on your remaining resources. You will most likely have to build another Moon Well, so balance the value of having a new Moon Well over the future ability to replace a fallen unit.

Move your troops north to find the last Gold Mine. This one has 5000 Gold in it, which should be enough to rebuild an attack force. Relocate your Tree of Life to this spot to harvest the Gold, then build an attack force of Dryads, Huntresses, and Archers. Also, add a supplementary force of at least four Ballistae and a few Archers. When you're ready, move your troops north and have the Ballistae attack the Ancient Protectors. The remaining troops should focus on the defending Satyrs.

Move up, leveling the corrupted Night Elf buildings one at a time until all of the defensive structures lie in ruins. With the unit-producing and defensive structures destroyed, the path to the Barrow Dens is secure and the mission ends.

The corrupted Night Elf base is well defended with Ancient Protectors and Satyrs. If you attack the base properly, however, you can defeat it without heavy losses.

CHAPTER 5

BROTHERS IN BLOOD

The next morning, within the subterranean Barrow Deeps of Mount Hyjal, Furion and Tyrande arrive to find and awaken the Druids of the Claw.

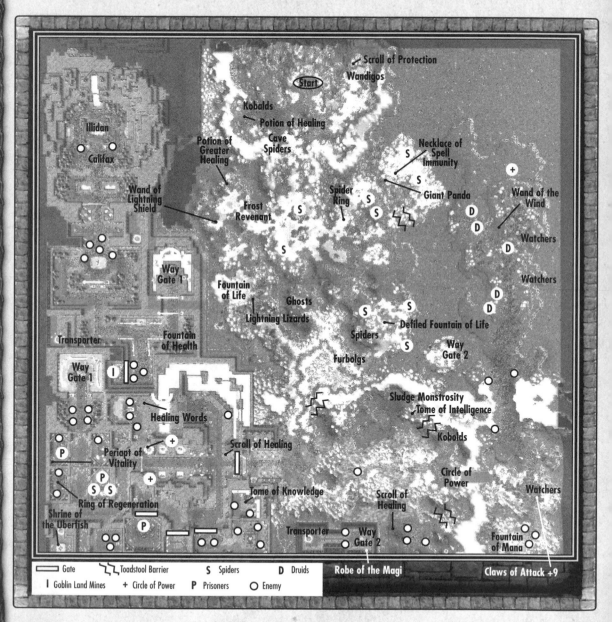

Start

Scroll of Protection

Wandigos

Kobalds

Potion of Healing

Cave Spiders

Illidan

Califax

Potion of Greater Healing

Necklace of Spell Immunity

Giant Panda

Wand of the Wind

Spider Ring

Wand of Lightning Shield

Frost Revenant

Watchers

Watchers

Way Gate 1

Fountain of Life

Ghosts

Lightning Lizards

Defiled Fountain of Life

Transporter

Fountain of Health

Spiders

Way Gate 2

Furbolgs

Way Gate 1

Sludge Monstrosity

Tome of Intelligence

Healing Words

Kobolds

Periapt of Vitality

Scroll of Healing

Circle of Power

Watchers

Tome of Knowledge

Scroll of Healing

Ring of Regeneration

Shrine of the Uberfish

Transporter

Way Gate 2

Fountain of Mana

| | Gate | | Toadstool Barrier | **S** | Spiders | **D** | Druids | Robe of the Magi | Claws of Attack +9 |
| **I** | Goblin Land Mines | **+** | Circle of Power | **P** | Prisoners | ○ | Enemy | | |

AVAILABLE STRUCTURES

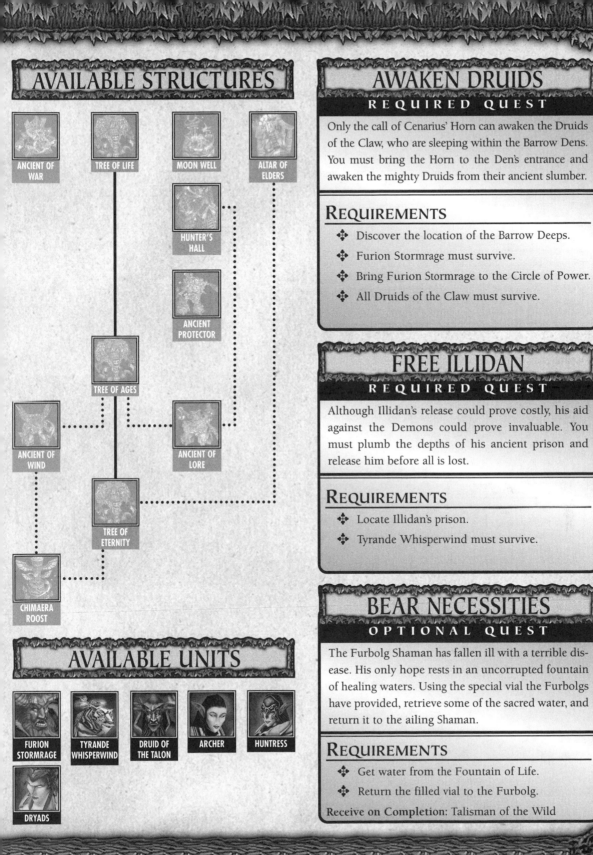

ANCIENT OF WAR

TREE OF LIFE

MOON WELL

ALTAR OF ELDERS

HUNTER'S HALL

ANCIENT PROTECTOR

TREE OF AGES

ANCIENT OF WIND

ANCIENT OF LORE

TREE OF ETERNITY

CHIMAERA ROOST

AVAILABLE UNITS

FURION STORMRAGE

TYRANDE WHISPERWIND

DRUID OF THE TALON

ARCHER

HUNTRESS

DRYADS

AWAKEN DRUIDS

REQUIRED QUEST

Only the call of Cenarius' Horn can awaken the Druids of the Claw, who are sleeping within the Barrow Dens. You must bring the Horn to the Den's entrance and awaken the mighty Druids from their ancient slumber.

REQUIREMENTS

❖ Discover the location of the Barrow Deeps.

❖ Furion Stormrage must survive.

❖ Bring Furion Stormrage to the Circle of Power.

❖ All Druids of the Claw must survive.

FREE ILLIDAN

REQUIRED QUEST

Although Illidan's release could prove costly, his aid against the Demons could prove invaluable. You must plumb the depths of his ancient prison and release him before all is lost.

REQUIREMENTS

❖ Locate Illidan's prison.

❖ Tyrande Whisperwind must survive.

BEAR NECESSITIES

OPTIONAL QUEST

The Furbolg Shaman has fallen ill with a terrible disease. His only hope rests in an uncorrupted fountain of healing waters. Using the special vial the Furbolgs have provided, retrieve some of the sacred water, and return it to the ailing Shaman.

REQUIREMENTS

❖ Get water from the Fountain of Life.

❖ Return the filled vial to the Furbolg.

Receive on Completion: Talisman of the Wild

THE PATH TO VICTORY

This mission has several components. It begins with Furion and Tyrande leading a band of fighters into the caverns, but it quickly diverges into two separate portions with Furion leading one team to the Druids and Tyrande leading another team to free Illidan. This is a long and complicated mission that covers the *entire* map.

> **TIP**
>
> Just because you're below ground doesn't mean that Furion can't create Treants with his Force of Nature spell. Target the giant toadstools in the cave and transform them!

SPIDERS

When the mission begins, you're faced with a large cavern that stretches out in many directions. Use the map to help get through the area and find some of the bonus areas. Move south until you reach the large concentration of Spiders, then destroy them and continue south.

> **TIP**
>
> There is a Giant Panda that can be accessed only by using Furion's Force of Nature spell to knock down the toadstools. After destroying the Panda, you get a Necklace of Immunity.

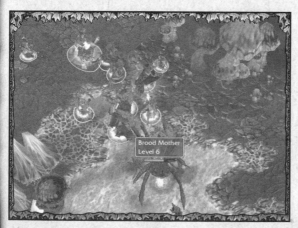

There are Spiders aplenty in this cavern.

Work through a narrow passage past the Defiled Fountain of Life, until you reach a group of Furbolgs.

BEAR NECESSITIES

The Furlbolgs ask your help in healing their fallen Shaman. By retrieving some water from the nearby Fountain of Life, you can help save him. Get your troops ready, then move west toward the Fountain of Life. It's guarded by Lightning Lizards, creatures that can inflict considerable damage in a short period of time. The best way to defeat them is to attack one at a time with *all* of your troops. After the fight, replenish your units' health and get the water to help the Furbolgs.

The Fountain of Health is protected by Lightning Lizards.

For your help, the Furbolgs give you a special Talisman that enables you to summon a Furbolg to fight by your side for 180 seconds. The Talisman permits the Hero to summon this three times.

AWAKEN DRUIDS

Move through the maze until you reach the gates that lead to the west side of the map. At this point, a cinematic shows that Tyrande wants to free Illidan, a powerful Night Elf warrior. She breaks with Furion and goes after her old friend, while Stormrage takes the remainder of the troops to awaken the Druids of the Claw.

Move Furion and his troops to the east to find a Circle of Power. Stand on it to form a bridge, then continue toward the Druids. There are a series of Watchers on the other side of the bridge that want to prevent you from reaching the Druid's Circle of Power.

Move north along the narrow bridge, keeping an eye out for Dragon Welps. Eventually, you come to an area where two Druids of the Talon are controlling two Druids of the Claw with Cyclone. Your quest has been updated, so you now must make it to the Circle of Power *without* destroying any of the Druids of the Claw. You have two tools to accomplish this task. First, your Druids of the Talon can use Cyclone to lift the Druids of the Claw so you can move past them. Second, Furion can use Entangle to immobilize them. Using either technique, provides enough wizardry to keep all the Druids safe. When Furion steps on the Circle of Power, his half of the mission ends.

TIP

There's a secret area to the south that you can access only with Furion's Force of Nature spell. The spell reduces a barrier of trees and eventually leads to a group of Skeleton Archers and Warriors. To the north of the Circle of Power is an area that is also closed off by Toadstools. Transform the fungus into Treants so your troops can fight the Sludge Monstrosity and collect a Tome of Intelligence for Furion.

Stand on the Circle of Power to make the bridge appear.

ILLIDAN

After Furion awakens the Druids of the Claw, the mission switches to Tyrande's attempt to free Illidan. The Priestess and her group start in the western portion of the map. Destroy the nearby Sentinels, then turn south and bash through the gate. Continue through the next gate to get a Tome of Knowledge.

It's not imperative to explore this area, but there's a Tome of Knowledge to pick up.

Continue west until you see a Circle of Power. Hit it twice to open the gate that holds three prisoners. Move your troops up and around to the second Circle of Power (see map). There are several Sentinels and Skeleton Warriors to fight along the way. There's also a set of Healing Wards; just destroy some crates in the area.

After activating the second Circle of Power, destroy the gate to free the prisoners. You must now move your troops through a dangerous area, a place in which a set of four statues blast icy showers as you move past. Enter the southern room, which contains three Sleepers. Destroy the enemies, then continue to the north until you reach a set rooms on either side of the path. Two of the four rooms contain prisoners, the rest are occupied by enemies and items. Eventually, you'll reach a Way Gate. Enter it and transport to the northern portion of the map.

There are Slippers of Agility +3 in this room.

Stop at the Fountain of Health on the other side of the Way Gate to heal up before moving onward. There's a secret area on the far west edge of the map. Inside is something that resembles a Circle of Power, but when you step on it, it transports you to the Shrine of the Uberfish.

To get to the transporter on the far western edge of the map, you must move down this narrow corridor.

CALIFAX

Continue to the north until you reach Illidan's prison, which is guarded by Califax and two other Watchers. After defeating these foes, Tyrande can free Illidan to fight as an ally to the Night Elves and the mission ends.

To defeat Califax and his Watchers, use your Healing Wards to keep your troops constantly regenerating. It doesn't matter if Tyrande is the only unit left standing; as long as she is alive when the area is cleared of enemies, you will still complete the mission.

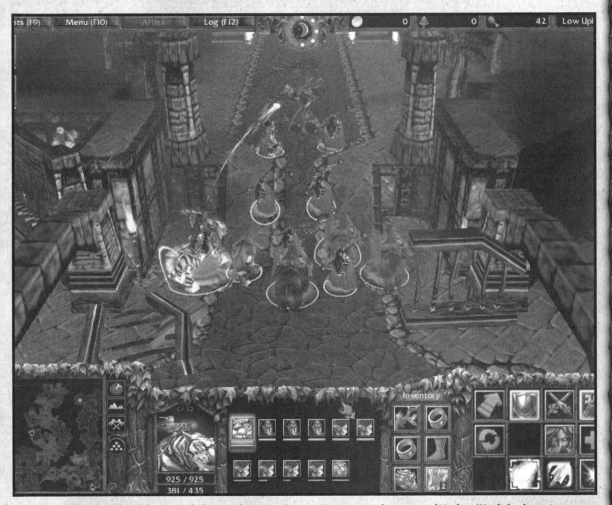

The final battle with Califax is tough, because he raises Treants. However, a judicious use of Healing Wards leads to victory.

CHAPTER 6

A DESTINY OF FLAME AND SORROW

The following evening, deep in the corrupted forests of Felwood, Illidan is still bitter. Arthas approaches him and they fight head-to-head. Ultimately, it's clear that no one will win. Arthas asks Illidan to capture the Skull of Gul'dan and destroy it.

AVAILABLE STRUCTURES

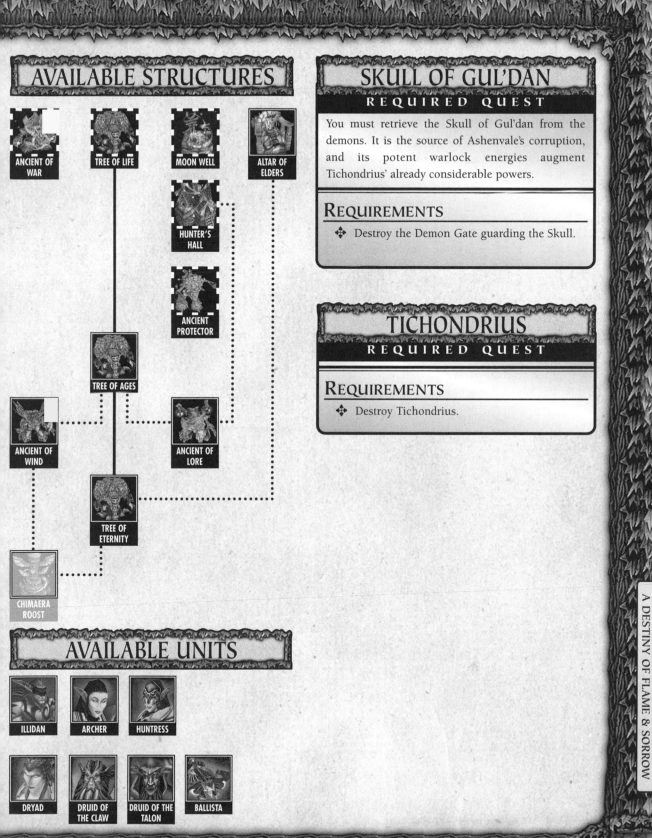

ANCIENT OF WAR

TREE OF LIFE

MOON WELL

ALTAR OF ELDERS

HUNTER'S HALL

ANCIENT PROTECTOR

TREE OF AGES

ANCIENT OF WIND

ANCIENT OF LORE

TREE OF ETERNITY

CHIMAERA ROOST

AVAILABLE UNITS

ILLIDAN

ARCHER

HUNTRESS

DRYAD

DRUID OF THE CLAW

DRUID OF THE TALON

BALLISTA

SKULL OF GUL'DAN

REQUIRED QUEST

You must retrieve the Skull of Gul'dan from the demons. It is the source of Ashenvale's corruption, and its potent warlock energies augment Tichondrius' already considerable powers.

REQUIREMENTS

❖ Destroy the Demon Gate guarding the Skull.

TICHONDRIUS

REQUIRED QUEST

REQUIREMENTS

❖ Destroy Tichondrius.

THE PATH TO VICTORY

This is a two-part mission. First, Illidan must capture the Skull of Gul'dan. With this objective complete, Illidan can't control himself, and he will harness the power of the Skull for his own uses. After absorbing its powers, he can defeat Tichondrius and destroy him in the second half of the mission.

BUILD BASE

The base is mostly complete as the mission begins. However, you need to build an Altar of Elders and upgrade the Tree of Life to a Tree of Eternity. You will also likely need at least a pair of extra Moon Wells to handle the increased troop load.

While building your base, set your Moon Wells to Autocast their Replenish ability, and pour your resources directly into upgrading everything. The enemies constantly attack, so having the Moon Wells Autocast nearby helps heal your troops while they are defending your base.

The base will endure multiple attacks.

It's critical to get most of the upgrades in place before venturing away from the base. When you're ready to leave with an attack force, build several Ancient Protectors to help with base defense, then leave in any direction. If you'd like some items for the road, visit the Goblin Merchant in the southwest corner of the map.

THE SKULL OF GUL'DAN

While the two main objectives in this mission rest squarely in the northwest and northeast corners of the map, there are other things available throughout the land. When your upgrades are complete, build an attack force of Druids of the Claw, Archers, Huntresses, Dryads, and Druids of the Talon in two groups totaling at least 20 units. You also need a group of three Ballistae to battle the Corrupted Ancient Protectors that stand between you and the Skull.

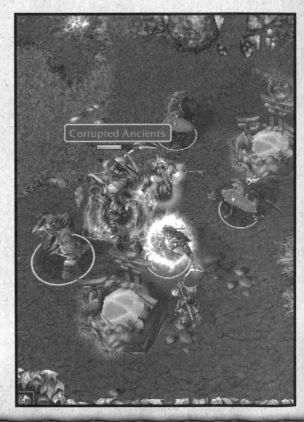

When you're ready, follow the path leading north on the map.

There are several well-defended corrupt Night Elf bases on the map. Although you can attack them, you may also bypass them completely. We suggest you follow the path described here, because the enemy bases are *very* tough to destroy while still defending your home base.

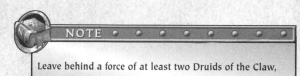

NOTE

Leave behind a force of at least two Druids of the Claw, two Archers, and two Huntresses (all nearby Moon Wells with Autocast activated) to defend your base.

Move your attack force toward the area defended by Doom Guards, Infernals, and Skeleton Archers/Warriors. Make sure your troops have a pair of Scrolls of Protection to help with the battle. After the first area of Doom Guards, you face one more next to the Skull with two Infernals. After destroying them, the mission pauses and moves into its second phase.

The Skull of Gul'dan is very well defended.

NOTE

If you have a keen interest in patrolling the rest of the map and scooping up all of the available items, do so *after* Illidan captures the Skull, but *before* he takes on Tichondrius.

TICHONDRIUS

Tichondrius awaits in the far northeast corner of the map. He is also guarded by Doom Guards, and there are two Demon Gates through which pesky enemies emerge until the gates are turned to dust. By this point in the game, you will likely need to move your Tree of Eternity (or build another) beside a new Gold Mine (there are two nearby) to access the resources necessary to replenish your troops.

To defeat Tichondrius, you need Illidan (in Demon form) and a group of Dryads, Druids of the Claw, Huntresses, and a pair of Archers. Move the group from your base back to the area around the Skull of Gul'dan (where it used to be), then head straight across the map (from west to east) along the top edge. This takes you to a pair of Infernals that are no match for your troops.

Two Infernals are usually tough, but not against a buff group and Illidan.

After passing the Infernals, you can demolish the two Demon Gates or go straight for Tichondrius. If you go after the gates, you may need to replenish and heal your troops before the final push.

When you get close to Tichondrius, use a Scroll of Protection (if you have one) and focus all of your attacks on him. It's a tough battle and you may have to attack a second time. When he dies, the mission ends!

Illidan
So be it... brother.

Tichondrius must die for you to win.

CORRUPTED NIGHT ELF CAMPS

If you're looking for more fights, then go after the two main Corrupted Night Elf bases on the map. Keep in mind that this isn't recommended. To do so, use the two-pronged fighting approach discussed throughout this guide—

one group for melee attack and another comprised of Ballistae that follow behind and concentrate solely on crushing enemy buildings. The Gold Mines in the bases are loaded, especially the one in the west. After destroying the bases, Tichondrius sends multilpe Doom Guards and Felhounds. It should be noted, however, that the resources needed to destroy those bases is huge, so the Gold you recover from them will be *necessary* to continue the mission.

We don't recommend you do this, but you can battle the Corrupted Night Elf bases if you yearn to fight.

CHAPTER 7

ARCHIMONDE'S ASCENT

The next morning, near Hyjal Summit, the Night Elves, Orcs, and Humans gather to plan their defense of the mountain against the final assault of Archimonde's forces.

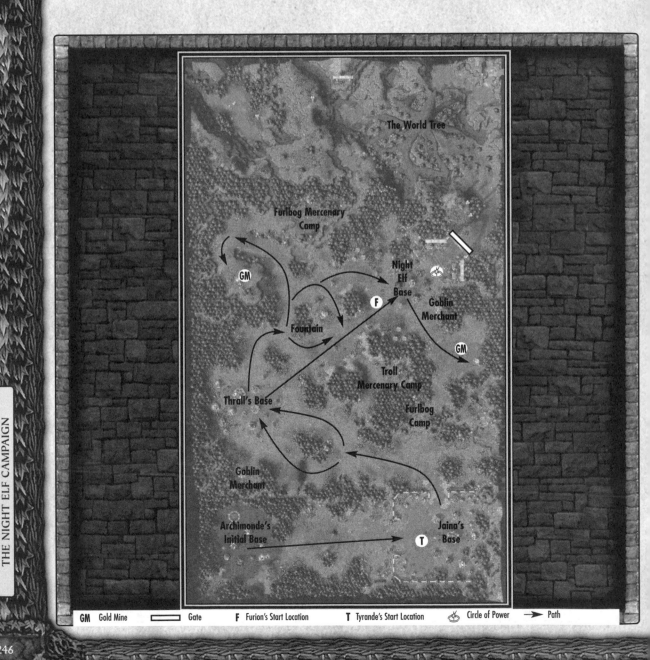

AVAILABLE STRUCTURES

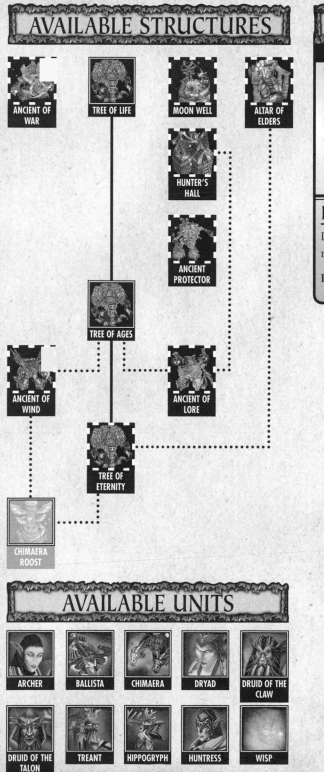

ANCIENT OF WAR

TREE OF LIFE

MOON WELL

ALTAR OF ELDERS

HUNTER'S HALL

ANCIENT PROTECTOR

TREE OF AGES

ANCIENT OF WIND

ANCIENT OF LORE

TREE OF ETERNITY

CHIMAERA ROOST

AVAILABLE UNITS

ARCHER

BALLISTA

CHIMAERA

DRYAD

DRUID OF THE CLAW

DRUID OF THE TALON

TREANT

HIPPOGRYPH

HUNTRESS

WISP

DELAY ARCHIMONDE

REQUIRED QUEST

You must attempt to slow Archimonde's ascent to the Hyjal Summit by throwing everything you can at him and his elite forces. By doing this, you will buy Furion the time he needs to implement his mysterious plan for the World Tree's defense. Though many of your brethren may fall, their sacrifice will secure the future of the world itself.

REQUIREMENTS

Delay Archimonde for 45 minutes. Archimonde must not reach the World Tree.

Receive on Completion: Warcraft III Victory

THE PATH TO VICTORY

The goal of this mission is to prevent Archimonde from reaching the Circle of Power at the Hyjal Summit. Archimonde follows a preset path through the map, moving through Jaina's base, then Thrall's, before hitting yours in an attempt to reach the World Tree. While both Jaina and Thrall put up a significant defense, it definitely behooves you to help first Jaina, and then Thrall, defend their bases. As soon as Archimonde conquers a base, he immediately commandeers the area and builds up a base of his own. It is from this location that he prepares his attack on the next base. For this reason, you must be aggressive or all may fail.

SET UP INFRASTRUCTURE

Your first priority is to get your infrastructure up and running so that you're harvesting Gold and Lumber in sufficient quantities to support the battle with multiple troops. You also need to upgrade at a frantic pace in order to be ready for the final defense against Archimonde. Move very quickly to establish your resource gathering—immediately take control of the two expansion Gold Mines (see map).

It's also important to get the available Forest Trolls and Furbolgs in three areas (see map). These reinforcements are a welcome addition. We suggest you save them until late in the mission when you'll need every unit you can get your hands on. Have your damaged units retreat to the Fountain of Health (see map), and visit the Goblin Merchants to purchase items such as Scrolls of Protection for your Hero.

Anetheron has some powerful spells up his sleeve.

Make sure you get plenty of reinforcements.

> **TIP**
>
> All of that we've mentioned so far *must* be done very quickly so that you can get to work helping Jaina defend her base. Don't waste one second—just set everything up as fast as you can so that resources continue to pour into your coffers.

JAINA'S BASE

Archimonde begins in the southwest corner of the map, and eventually moves his troops east to attack Jaina's base, which is defended with both walls and towers (along with her Human troops). Once you have prepared your main base, you can train extra Wisps to move down and build a pair of Ancient Protectors at Jaina's gates. This helps to stem the initial tide from Archimonde's forces.

> **NOTE**
>
> Archimonde throws several Heroes at you throughout this mission, although not all at once. Here they are:
>
> **Azgalor, Level 10 Pit Lord—** Uses Thunder Clap, Shockwave, Reincarnation, and a devastating Earthquake spell.
>
> **Anetheron, Level 10 Dreadlord—** Uses Carrion Swarm, Rain of Chaos (summons multiple Infernals), and Sleep.
>
> **Winterchill, Level 10 Lich—** Uses Frost Nova, Frost Armor, Dark Ritual, Death and Decay, and Finger of Death (this spell does massive damage to a single target, but cannot be used on Heroes).
>
> **Archimonde, Level 10 Warlock—** Remains in his base until the final moments. Uses Dark Portal (summons multiple Felhounds and Doom Guard), Rain of Chaos, Bash, Finger of Death, and Spell Immunity.

It's also a good idea to move (or build) an Ancient of War or two in or near Jaina's base so that your units can be replenished closer to the action. We recommend, however, that you build these just to the north of Jaina's base. That way, when Archimonde destroys her base, you can simply uproot them and move them north where they can continue to produce units.

Winterchill uses his dark magical powers to ravage your forces.

The enemy attack waves consist of Banshees, Necromancers, Doom Guard, Infernals, Meat Wagons, Felhounds, Abominations, Frost Wyrms, Gargoyles, and Crypt Fiends. Mix the unit type of your army, since the waves come very close together, and both land and air units are thrown at you constantly. The Doom Guards have War Stomp, Dispel, Rain of Fire, and Cripple, while the Felhounds use Mana Burn. The Banshees Possess your units when given the chance. Archimonde also sends three Heroes at you, usually only one or two at a time, with the attack waves.

Azgalor is another one of the deadly Heroes that Archimonde unleashes on you.

When Jaina's Castle falls, it's time to head for Thrall's camp.

Jaina's base is surrounded by walls and is defended by Towers (a few of each kind), Riflemen, Footmen, Knights, Sorceresses, and Priests. She also uses Water Elementals and Blizzard often. Move your troops into her base in volume and do whatever you can to stem the evil tide that washes up on her shores.

Inevitably, Archimonde will overwhelm Jaina's base, so be ready to face defeat here despite your best efforts. Remember, you are only trying to slow Archimonde down, not defeat him entirely at this location. When Jaina's Castle is destroyed, her whole base simultaneously faces destruction. Archimonde then establishes a new base and begins sending attacks at Thrall's base. Therefore, when it becomes clear that Jaina's base is finished, uproot any nearby Ancients and move them (and your units) up to Thrall's camp to the northwest.

THRALL'S BASE

After Jaina's base falls, Thrall is Archimonde's next target. The Demon Lord's new headquarters is in the spot where Jaina's once stood, thereby adding insult to injury and shortening the distance that his units must travel to attack Thrall's positions.

Placing Ancient Protectors around Thrall's base is a good strategy, but be warned that Meat Wagons accompany almost every attack from Archimonde's forces, and they specifically target these defensive structures. In order to prevent the Meat Wagons from turning your Ancient Protectors into hamburger, you must intercept them with melee troops before they can do their damage.

Thrall's camp has a solid defense, but eventually faces defeat.

TIP

If you want to make a stronger defense in Thrall's base, avoid sending quite as many units/structures into Jaina's base and take a little more time (and resources) for building up Thrall's defenses. Still, you're basically borrowing from Peter to pay Paul, but this strategy does give you more time to develop a cohesive force at Thrall's camp.

Purchase Goblin Land Mines at the nearby Goblin Merchant (see map) to provide an extra layer of defense around Thrall's base. Thrall's troops cast Bloodlust and heal your Night Elf troops, but this will not be enough. Use the Druid of the Claw's Rejuvenation to further mend your embattled troops.

(see map)

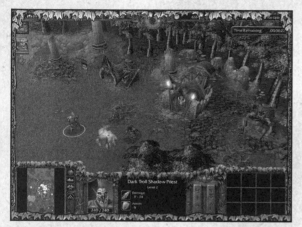

Hire some Trolls to supplement your forces.

TIP

Whenever a unit or group of units takes heavy damage, move them back to the Fountain of Health for them to heal. By doing this *before* your troops bite the dust, you can save considerable resources. This tactic also creates a 'circuit' of sorts where units are constantly coming and going from the Fountain of Health and back to the front lines.

Again, when Thrall's base falls, you must fall back to the final stronghold of good—your Night Elf base. If it looks like Thrall's camp is finished, have your troops retreat hastily, then set them up in a line to defend your base and the Circle of Power.

THE FINAL DEFENSE

Archimonde eventually claims Thrall's base for his own. Although there will be some initial attacks on the Night Elf base, Archimonde won't make his attempt on the Circle of Power until the final few minutes of the mission. If you've slowly built up the defenses around the Circle of Power while fighting Archimonde in Jaina's and Thrall's bases, then you are in a good position to win.

NOTE

The mission is lost if Archimonde gets to the Circle of Power, but you can also lose the mission if all of your structures are destroyed.

Archimonde
At last! The way to the World Tree is clear! Witness the end, you mortals! The final hour has come!

The final minutes of the mission are a massive defensive battle to prevent Archimonde from reaching his goal. This is the time to uproot all Ancients to help in the defense of the area. It's also not a bad idea to bring your Wisps in so that they can Detonate themselves and prevent the use of magic near the gate. Use everything you've got to hold Archimonde at bay—it'll be close. If you can do it, however, you will drink from the chalice of ultimate victory!

Furion Stormrage
We are its protectors, and through it we were granted immortality and power over nature. Now, at last, it is time we gave that power back.

MULTIPLAYER BASICS & TACTICS

This chapter includes the key information about the Creeps, Items, and Neutral Structures in Warcraft III: Reign of Chaos. It also contains exclusive tips and strategies straight from Blizzard.

ITEMS

The item collecting aspect of *Warcraft III: Reign of Chaos* makes it a complex and rich gaming experience. Only Heroes can pick up and use items, and each Hero can hold only six.

Items range from the practical (like potions of health) to the magical (like a Cloak of Invisibility). You can obtain items in one of two ways. First, you can pick them up after defeating Creeps (Neutral enemies). You can also acquire them at the Goblin Merchant.

The following list of items includes pertinent information, such as what each item does and what it costs.

CHARGED ITEMS

Charged items are limited-use items—between one and five uses, depending on the item. Examples include the Crystal Ball and a Wand of Negation.

CONSUMABLE ITEMS

Consumable items are also single-use commodities. These items disappear as soon as they're used. Examples include Potions and Scrolls.

PERSISTENT ITEMS

Persistent items always remain in the Hero's inventory until he/she throws them away. Some examples include the Gauntlets of Strength and the Orb of Frost, both of which are constantly in use as long as they're in the Hero's inventory.

ITEM	ACTION	COST (GOLD)
Red Drake Egg	Summons Red Drake to fight	400
Periapt of Vitality	Increases maximum Hit Points	325
Pendant of Energy	Increases Mana Capacity	325
Orb of Frost	Gives +10 Frost Damage Bonus	325
Orb of Fire	Gives +10 Fire Damage Bonus	325
Lion Horn of Stormwind	Generates +1 armor aura for the Hero	500
Warsong Battle Drums	Gives Attack Bonus	500
Ancient Janggo of Endurance	Gives 45% attack speed and +10% movement speed	400
Legion Doom-Horn	Nearby units heal and move more swiftly	400
Boots of Speed	Increases the Speed of wearer	250
Gloves of Celerity	Increases Attack Speed	250
Ring of Protection +2	Increases Defense Bonus +2	250
Claws of Attack +9	Increases Attack Bonus +9	325
Gauntlets of Strength +3	Increases Strength Bonus +3	250
Soul Gem	Allows theft of Hero's soul	Quest
Tome of Power	Increases Hero's Level by 1	650
Tome of Knowledge	Increases all Attributes +1	400

ITEM	ACTION	COST (GOLD)
Tome of Strength +2	Increases Strength +2	325
Tome of Dexterity +2	Increases Agility +2	325
Tome of Intelligence +2	Increases Intelligence +2	325
Manual of Health	Permanent Hit Point Bonus from charged item	150
Tome of Strength +1	Increases Strength +1	150
Tome of Agility +1	Increases Agility +1	150
Tome of Intelligence +1	Increases Intelligence +1	150
Necklace of Spell Immunity	Gives Magic Immunity	1000
Scroll of Restoration	Restores Hit Points and Mana	650
Potion of Restoration	Restores Hit Points and Mana	500
Crown of Kings +5	Gives +5 to all Atributes	1000
Ankh of Reincarnation	Reincarnates wearer after death	400
Ring of Protection +5	Defense Bonus +5	800
Scroll of Resurrection	Resurrects up to six fallen friendly warriors	500
Scroll of Animate Dead	Raises Skeletal Warriors from fallen warriors	500
Scepter of Mastery	Get permanent control of non-hero unit	1000
Mask of Death	Attack drain 50% attack damage from life	650
Ring of Protection +4	Defense Bonus +4	650
Periapt of Health	Increases Hit Points of wearer	500
Pendant of Mana	Increases max Mana	500
Claws of Attack +15	Attack Bonus +15	800
Belt of Giant Strength +6	Strength Bonus +6	650
Boots of Elvenkind +6	Agility Bonus +6	650
Robe of the Magi +6	Intelligence Bonus +6	650
Ring of Regeneration	Increases Hit Point Regeneration	325
Sobi Mask	Increases Mana Regeneration	400
Talisman of Evasion	Enemies have chance of missing hero	400
Cloak of Flames	Deals 10 points of fire damage per second	500
Ring of Protection +3	Defense Bonus +3	400
Claws of Attack +12	Attack Bonus +12	500
Circlet of Nobility	Gives +2 to all Attributes	400
Demonic Figurine	Summons a Doom Guard to fight for you	650
Inferno Stone	Calls Infernal	650
Stone Token	Creates a Rock Golem	500
Spiked Collar	Creates a Vicious Hound	400
Slippers of Agility +3	Agility Bonus +3	250
Mantle of Intelligence +3	Intelligence Bonus +3	250
Scourge Bone Chimes	Gives Vampiric Aura	500
Khadgar's Pipe of Insight	Gives Brilliance Aura	400
Alleria's Flute of Accuracy	Gives Trueshot Aura	400

ITEM	ACTION	COST (GOLD)
Wand of Cyclone	Cyclone Spell	400
Antibody Potion	Anti-Magic Shield	150
Claws of Attack +6	Attack Bonus +6	250
Potion of Greater Healing	Heals 500 lost Hit Points	250
Potion of Greater Mana	Restores 500 lost Mana	250
Book of the Dead	Summons Skeletal Warriors	325
Potion of Invulnerability	Makes Hero invulnerable for a short time	200
Scroll of Town Portal	Transports Hero and nearby units to Town Center	350
Ring of Protection +1	Defense Bonus +1	200
Scroll of Healing	Divides 100 Hit Points equally between nearby units	200
Scroll of Roar	Gives Roar Attack Bonus +25%	250
Scroll of Protection	Increases Armor Rating for a short time	200
Claws of Attack +3	Attack Bonus +3	200
Scroll of Mana	Restores Mana to nearby units	150
Wand of Illusion	Creates duplicate fake Hero (or other unit)	250
Wand of Negation	Dispels all nearby Magic	200
Potion of Healing	Heals Hero	100
Potion of Mana	Restores Mana	100
Gem of True Seeing	Allows Hero to see invisible units	200
Healing Wards	Heals all units around it for a set time	400
Potion of Greater Invisibility	240 seconds of Invisibility	200
Potion of Invisibility	180 seconds of Invisibility	100
Cloak of Shadows	Shadow Meld	200
Potion of Speed	Increases Hero's Speed	75
Wand of Lightning Shield	Gives Lightning Shield	325
Crystal Ball	Gives Hero five views on the map	200
Goblin Land Mine	Land mine that blows up when enemies are near	225
Amulet of Recall	Teleports units to the user	250
Wand of Sentry Ward	Sentry Ward	200
Goblin Night Scope	Gives Hero the Ultravision Upgrade	200
Talisman of the Wild	Summons Furlbogs to fight for you	325

NEUTRAL STRUCTURES

There are a number of Neutral structures, many of which are useful to Heroes. There are also many inconsequential structures; these include huts, tents, or other buildings on any given map. These buildings may occasionally hide an item, but are otherwise not important.

DRAGON ROOST

This is where you can obtain powerful Dragons to fight by your side. These creatures are excellent in multiplayer action.

FOUNTAIN OF HEALTH

A constant source of health for your non-mechanical units. Simply place your units near the fountain to heal 100% of their hit points. Obviously, it can be a huge advantage to fight near one. In fact, there are multiplayer missions with a Fountain of Health in the middle of the action.

ARTHAS: This must be the shrine the old man spoke of. Any man who drinks from these light-blessed waters will be healed.

FOUNTAIN OF MANA

This replenishes your units' Mana. When using plenty of spells, Fountains of Mana are very important. On maps like The Crucible (multiplayer), you can use the Fountain of Mana as a pit stop between your base and battle.

GOBLIN LABORATORY

Sells several key units, including the Goblin Zeppelin, which can carry up to six units anywhere on the map. Use Goblin Zeppelins to drop units into inaccessible or obstructed areas.

GOBLIN MERCHANT

Sells an assortment of items that can vary between Merchants. As a rule, you can always get Health and Mana Potions, Scrolls of Town Portal, Potions of Invisibility, Wands of Negation, as well as Scrolls of Protection. Although there are a finite number of items in the Goblin Merchant, they are replenished over time.

MERCENARY CAMP

These are places where you can exchange Gold for fighting units, who will then join in the fight for your side! Oftentimes, the Mercenaries are Ogres, Berserkers, or Shadow Priests. However, any Creep can appear in a Mercenary Camp, making your usual enemies valuable allies.

MINE

Serves as the primary source of Gold in the game; as a result, they are indestructible. When a mine runs out of Gold, it collapses and disappears.

WAY GATE

More commonly seen in the single-player game, but they can appear on any map. Way Gates are gateways through which your units can pass and transport to another Way Gate somewhere else on the map.

HUTS/ZIGGURATS/TENTS

These miscellaneous structures dot the maps of the single-player missions (and some multiplayer maps). As noted earlier, they usually serve no function other than to hide an odd item (which appears when the structure is destroyed). Nerubian Ziggurats, Murloc Huts, Infected Granaries, Gnoll Huts, Furbolg Huts, and Tents are all examples of miscellaneous structures. All the hidden items in structures that appear in the single-player game are noted on the maps in this guide.

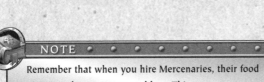

NOTE

Remember that when you hire Mercenaries, their food requirements become your problem. This prevents you from buying 16 Ogres (four food each).

CREEPS

These creatures inhabit single-player and multiplayer maps. Creeps attack you *and* your enemies; in essence, they are the keepers of the map. Sometimes they defend areas or structures (such as Goblin Merchants or Gold Mines), while other times they simply wait in certain areas.

MERCENARIES

Mercenaries are all taken from the Creep pool. Therefore, any Creep can be a Mercenary, which is why these two groups are lumped into the same area.

LIST OF CREEPS

- Ancient Sasquatch
- Ancient Wendigo
- Apprentice Wizard
- Assassin
- Bandit
- Bandit Lord
- Berserk Elemental
- Berserk Owlbear
- Black Dragon
- Black Dragon Whelp
- Black Drake
- Black Spider
- Blue Dragon
- Blue Dragon Whelp
- Blue Drake
- Brigand
- Bronze Dragon
- Bronze Dragon Whelp
- Bronze Drake
- Brood Mother
- Burning Archer
- Centaur Drudge
- Centaur Impaler
- Centaur Khan

- Centaur Outrunner
- Centaur Sorcerer
- Centaur Archer
- Corrupted Treant
- Dark Troll Berserker
- Dark Troll High Priest
- Dark Troll Shadow Priest
- Dark Wizard
- Dark Troll
- Dark Troll Trapper
- Dark Troll Warlord
- Death Revenant
- Deceiver
- Dire Wolf
- Doom Guard
- Dragon Hawk
- Elder Sasquatch
- Elder Wendigo
- Enforcer
- Enraged Elemental
- Enraged Owlbear
- Fallen Priest
- Felhound
- Fire Revenant

- Forest Troll Berserker
- Forest Troll High Priest
- Forest Troll Shadow Priest
- Forest Troll
- Forest Troll Trapper
- Forest Troll Warlord
- Frost Tevenant
- Furbolg
- Furbolg Champion
- Furbolg Elder Shaman
- Furbolg Panda
- Furbolg Shaman
- Furbolg Tracker
- Furbolg Ursa Warrior
- Ghost
- Giant Spider
- Giant White Wolf
- Giant Wolf
- Gnoll Assassin
- Gnoll Brute
- Gnoll King
- Gnoll Poacher
- Gnoll Robber
- Gnoll Warden
- Granite Golem
- Green Dragon
- Green Dragon Whelp
- Green Drake
- Green Spider
- Harpy Hag
- Harpy Queen

- Harpy Rogue
- Harpy Scout
- Harpy Witch
- Heretic
- Ice Revenant
- Ice Troll Berserker
- Ice Troll High Priest
- Ice Troll Shadow Priest
- Ice Troll Trapper
- Ice Troll Warlord
- Ice Troll
- Infernal
- Kobold
- Kobold Geomancer
- Kobold Leader
- Kobold Tunneler
- Lightning Lizard
- Lightning Revenant
- Mud Golem
- Murloc Fisherman
- Murloc Flesheater
- Murloc Huntsman
- Murloc Mutant
- Murloc Nightcrawler
- Murloc Plaguebearer
- Nerubian Queen
- Nerubian Seer
- Nerubian Spider Lord
- Nerubian Warrior
- Nerubian Webspinner
- Ogre Lord

- Ogre Magi
- Ogre Mauler
- Ogre Warrior
- Owlbear
- Plague Treant
- Poison Treant
- Quillboar
- Quillboar Hunter
- Razormane Brute
- Razormane Chieftain
- Razormane Medicine Man
- Razormane Scout
- Red Dragon
- Red Dragon Whelp
- Red Drake
- Renegade Wizard
- Rock Golem
- Rogue
- Rogue Wizard
- Salamander
- Salamander Hatchling
- Salamander Lord
- Salamander Vizier
- Sasquatch
- Sasquatch Oracle
- Satyr
- Satyr Hellcaller
- Satyr Shadowdancer
- Satyr Soulstealer
- Satyr Trickster
- Skeletal Archer
- Skeletal Marksman
- Sludge Flinger
- Sludge Minion
- Sludge Monstrosity
- Spider
- Spiderling
- Spitting Spider
- Storm Wyrm
- Thunder Lizard
- Timber Wolf
- Wendigo
- Wendigo Shaman
- White Dire Wolf
- White Wolf
- Wraith
- Zombie

CRITTERS

There are also some Critters that just wander around the maps. You can kill them and use their corpses, but for the most part they just sit around and look pretty. Here's a list of the Critters in the game.

- Stag
- Dog
- Pig
- Rat
- Seal
- Sheep
- Vulture

GENERAL TACTICS

This section covers general gameplay tactics and tips. These tips were gleaned from hours and hours of gameplay, as well as from the Blizzard QA Team. Many thanks to those who helped out, including: Zach Allen, Nicholas Pisani, Michelle Elbert, Manuel Gonzales, Dennis Lam, Andrew Brownell (Andrew contributed a great deal), John Yoo, Mike Kramer, Mike Nyguyen, and Kenny "Dodger Dog" Zigler.

FIGHTING CREEPS

- When attacking Creeps with ground troops, push them toward your troops with a small group of air units. (Zach Allen)

- If you have a Hero who can summon an Elemental, Treant, or Dire Wolf, then do so and have them take the brunt of the Creeps' attacks rather than units you've created from scratch. In the long run, this will save resources.

- If you fight Creeps and they leave items that you won't use, use your Meat Wagon/Catapult/Mortar Team to destroy the items before the enemy can get to them! (Manuel Gonzolas)

UPGRADING HEROES

- The Creeps are there to help you level up your Heroes so you can acquire more powerful spells later on. It's important early in any game (either single-player or multiplayer) to get your Hero out to the Goblin Merchants, Gold Mines, and other Creep areas. You need to level them up and get as much experience as possible.

MATCH ABILITIES WITH NEEDS

- Always attempt to match abilities with needs. For example, the Human Archmage has a Brilliance Aura that increases the Mana regeneration rate of nearby units, including allied units. Therefore, if a group of Priests is healing allied units, it would be wise to have an Archmage nearby to increase their functionality.

DEFENSIVE TACTICS

- Each race has base defenses that can turn the tide of battle. If you're playing as the Humans, control group (hotkey) your Town Hall so you can quickly use Call to Arms. Likewise, if you're playing as the Orcs, control group all the Orc Burrows so you can quickly call Battle Stations. (John Yoo)

GENERAL

❖ Place your siege units into a separate control group along with some Peons to repair them (for the Humans, this would be Mortar Teams and Priests). This provides more space in your main attack group for melee units. It's also a beneficial tactic when attacking an enemy base, because your siege units can assault buildings while your main attack group hits the enemy units. (Nicholas Pisani)

UNDEAD AND THE IMPORTANCE OF CRITTERS

❖ Remember that you can kill the Critters you see wandering around the single-player and multiplayer maps (usually with just one hit) and they leave corpses. This is particularly helpful if you're playing Undead.

If you're raising skeletons with your Necromancer, Rat and Sheep corpses give you the same result as if it were used on a Tauren, or any other felled unit. The same is also true for the Ghouls' Cannibalize skill, so save the corpses of more powerful units for your Death Knight's Animate Dead skill. Critters, it's what's for dinner! (Michelle Elbert)

BUILDING CONTROL

❖ Control group your buildings and set rally flag to hero. This prevents the hassle of returning to your base and queuing up units. By control grouping your buildings and rally pointing them to your hero, you can continually control your army and create more units without having to lose focus on your army. In addition, you can queue up units in battle without having to return to your base. (John Yoo)

KNOW WHEN TO RETREAT

❖ If you're losing, don't let your troops continue to fight until your army is completely destroyed. Know when you are defeated, and retreat by running away or using your Scroll of Town Portal to return to your base. The earlier you can realize the onset of defeat, the better the chance you have at regrouping your forces. (John Yoo)

LEARN YOUR HOTKEYS

❖ Hotkeys are essential tools in micromanaging your army quickly and efficiently. If you haven't mastered hotkeys and your enemy has, you are in deep trouble. The same is also true when playing against the computer in single-player games.

DON'T EXPAND TOO EARLY

❖ Expanding too quickly may lead to early attacks. Spending resources on gatherers and an expansion can result in getting caught with your "pants down" if your enemy decides to focus on building troops. If this occurs, they will outnumber your army and quickly destroy your base. You need to expand but only after you're confident that your army can repel an enemy attack. (John Yoo)

CONCENTRATED FIRE

✤ Concentrate your attacks on a specific target and drop it as soon as possible. Then you can distribute the damage evenly through your opponent's army, because the enemy is still inflicting full damage even though they are hurt.

However, they won't cause damage if they are already dead, so concentrate on one at a time. This approach is especially effective with Archers and other ranged weapons that can fire en masse from multiple angles. Also, it's a good idea to eliminate your enemy's Hero as soon as possible with concentrated fire.

A good player can run his or her Hero away to avoid attacks. If this happens, focus on your enemy's troops so that you can take out the weaker troops compared to the Hero. Also, if the enemy has artillery, take them out first, followed by the range units, and then the melee units. Artillery units cause big damage but are very weak.

The range units aren't quite as strong as the Artillery, but they're still fairly weak. The melee units are better at absorbing damage, so save them for last. (John Yoo)

USE YOUR HEROES

✤ To be successful, you must use all of the Heroes' skills. Don't let skill points pile up; use them and keep your Hero involved in as much of the action as possible because a Hero's abilities will ultimately make the difference in the game.

PREVENT EXPANSION

✤ If your opponent has good base defenses and you can't penetrate it without losing lots of troops, wait outside the base and amass Artillery. Keeping your enemies in their base prevents them from expanding. It will also eventually give you the edge, since you can out-resource and out-produce your opponent. (John Yoo)

THE HUMAN ADVANTAGE

✤ If you want to expand in a hurry, choose to play as the Humans. Take advantage of their ability to have multiple Peasants build a structure. An effective expanding tactic is to send out five Peasants and command them all to build a Town Hall. In no time at all, they will complete it and automatically start mining.

MULTIPLAYER TACTICS

Starting a multiplayer game and getting connected is covered in the game manual. Because the multiplayer experience is so dynamic and the maps (and, in some cases, the rules) will change as the game evolves, it's just not possible for us to discuss each multiplayer map.

We do, however, have access to the folks who have been religiously playing the game—the Blizzard QA Team. They've offered some of their tips and strategies for multiplayer gaming. The contributors include: Zach Allen, Nicholas Pisani, Michelle Elbert, Manuel Gonzales, Dennis Lam, Andrew Brownell (Andrew contributed a great deal), John Yoo, Mike Kramer, Mike Nyguyen, and Kenny "Dodger Dog" Zigler.

HIT-AND-RUN

Use hit-and-run tactics to make your opponent waste their Town Portal Scrolls or run back to their bases and expansions. Orc Raiders and Human Steam Tanks are very effective at this, because they cause siege damage, which enables a small number of them to deal lots of damage to a base or expansion in a hurry. (Andrew Brownell)

TIMING

In large multiplayer games, coordinate the timing between allies when using Town Portal Scrolls. When done at the same time, Town Portal Scrolls can teleport multiple armies on top of enemy armies, which can be devastating to your opponent's attack. When done separately, you will just allow a large army to defeat each of your team's armies one at a time, making them even more powerful by leveling up their Heroes. (Andrew Brownell)

RUSH STRATEGY

This strategy works well in two-on-two and one-on-one games. The strategy only works when the number of players in the game is at the maximum for the map and no more than two teams. (Dennis Lam)

1. When using the Orcs, send three of your five starting Peons toward an enemy base and have the remaining Peons gather resources (one for Gold and one for Lumber). Then using three Peons, build three Orc Burrows scattered around the enemy's base but within range to attack the Town Hall (Necropolis, Tree of Life, etc.).

2. Keep creating Peons at your own base, and build Burrows for defense. Send a few extra Peons to the enemy's base and put the Peons *inside* the Burrows. They'll immediately start attacking the enemy.

3. If one of the Burrows you're building in the enemy base is near destruction, cancel it at the last moment to save the resources from it!

4. Have an ally play as the Night Elves, and have him/her send two Wisps to build two Ancients. When finished, uproot them and attack the enemy base.

5. You can support this nefarious attack by sending a Hero in as support. A Far Seer with some Dire Wolves can help the situation a great deal!

6. The reason this is successful is that the enemy is rarely prepared for someone to build an Orc Burrow in *their* own base right away! What tends to happen is that the enemy builds fighting units one at a time, which is very inefficient.

BASE MANAGEMENT

❖ Avoid making too many of the same building. You will never need more than two of any unit-producing buildings (i.e., Barracks); oftentimes, one will be enough.

❖ Control group (Ctrl + #) each of your important unit-producing buildings (such as Barracks or Ancient of War). Produce units while moving around the map. It's important to remain focused on your main army instead of your base. You'll waste lots of time by constantly returning to your main base to make units or upgrade.

It's a good idea to create your own way of controlling your buildings. By using the hotkey system, you know exactly what key to press to access a particular building. With a little practice, you can reinforce your army, research new spells, and increase your units' armor while in the middle of a battle.

❖ Don't branch out too far in your selection of units. Instead, pick a few units early on and invest in maxing out the upgrades/research to make those units the best.

❖ Get your starting build order for each race into exact steps that you can do over and over, to make the few units and upgrades you want, as fast as you can. It's important to get a reliable build order to maximize your efficiency during the early part of the game with each race. (Andrew Brownell)

UNDEAD NUKING STRATEGY

Lich: Frost Nova. Dreadlord: Carrion Swarm. Death Knight: Death Coil. Concentrate on getting these skills as high as possible. Then when you're in a battle, target the enemy Hero and cast all three spells. As the cooldowns for the spells run out, continue to cast the spells on Heroes or tightly clustered groups of units.

Use the Death Knight's Death Coil to finish off a large unit or Hero. When used effectively, the constant barrage and the large area of damage decimate your opponent so quickly that he/she typically cannot recover fast enough. (Andrew Brownell)

SHARING HEROES: TEAM GAME STRATEGY

In a team game, have both players play as the same race and set the control of the units to shared control. Have both players build the same two Heroes, then have them swap Heroes. This gives each player two of the same Hero. (Andrew Brownell)

Two of the same Hero is usually better than one. For example, two Paladins allow for unstoppable healing to that player's army and Paladins (usually major targets) who just will not die due to their ability to heal one another. Here's is a list of very effective uses of this technique:

- ❖ Two Paladins with Holy Light

- ❖ Two Mountain Kings with Storm Bolt

- ❖ Two Archmages with Water Elemental

- ❖ Two Farseers with Feral Spirit or Chain Lightning

- ❖ Two Death Knights with Death Coil

- ❖ Two Lichs with Frost Nova

- ❖ Two Keepers of the Grove with Force of Nature

- ❖ Two Demon Hunters with Mana Burn

> **TIP**
>
> When attacking, *always* use the attack move command by pressing "A" on the keyboard and targeting an area. This enables your units to auto-acquire enemy units to their destination. This is *very* important, and helps keep your units from taking damage without fighting back.

UPGRADE

Upgrades are extremely important. If you and your opponent's armies are equal in strength, upgrades determine the outcome of the battle. Upgrade when the opportunity arises, especially when it comes to armor. (John Yoo)

SET A PLAN

If you know what you want to do early in the game (for example, rush your opponent), decide what you want to buy with your starting resources. Many gamers quickly build an Altar and then produce a Hero who can antagonize the enemy and establish their position before they have a chance to get set up. Either way, decide where you want your resources to go to avoid waiting for resources or food.

WORK AS A TEAM

When playing on teams, work as a team. Have one player create melee units and upgrade only their abilities, then have another player create and upgrade only ranged units.

If there are more than two players, the others can create high-end units like Tauren or Chimeras. Then when you're ready to attack (or defend), the combined upgraded strength of the multiple allied groups will be great. If these sacrifices are made (only upgrading one side of the tech tree), the players *must* work together!

HERO STRATEGY

Three Heroes are much better than one. If you can create three Heroes early in the game, spend some time leveling them up. Remember, however, that Heroes require more experience to level up at higher levels then they do at lower levels. Therefore, if your Heroes stay alive, they will be a much stronger force than your opponent's lone Hero.

For example, suppose your opponent has a level 8 Paladin, but you have a level 5 Paladin, a level 4 Mountain King, and a level 4 Archmage using the equivalent amount of experience. In this situation, your opponent has eight skills points to invest in skills, but you have 13 skill points! (Andrew Brownell)

SAPPER ATTACK

Another very effective tactic that is used frequently at Blizzard is the use of Goblin Zeppelins and Goblin Sappers.

To employ this strategy, fill a Goblin Zeppelin with Sappers and drop them on your enemy's base. Two Sappers can destroy a Barracks or a Town Hall, thus wreaking havoc on the enemy and giving *you* the edge. (Dean Shimonishi)

FIRST HERO

When choosing your first Hero, select a tough melee Hero. Humans: Paladin, Orc: Tauren Chieftain, Undead: Death Knight, Night Elf: Demon Hunter. You fight Creeps at the start of the game, so you need a Hero who can absorb some damage to help keep your other units alive. To make things even better, choose a Hero who can heal (like the Paladin/Death Knight). (Andrew Brownell)

ZEPPELIN DROP

Using this strategy, you can transport your troops behind enemy lines and attack them where they least expect it. To do so, follow these steps:

1. In any map, find a Goblin Laboratory and hire a Zeppelin. Fill it up with as many units as possible.

2. Drop the units behind enemy lines and attack the Peons/Peasants mining gold and harvesting Lumber.

3. It takes a few minutes for the enemy to get their Peasants/Peons back to harvest resources. This delay *alone* can make the difference in a multiplayer game.

4. This works well with one Hero (preferably one who can heal) and several basic units. It's best to use this with allies.

5. Hear the cries of your opponents when their production stops. (Manuel Gonzales)

UNDEAD SHADES

If you really want to track the movements of your enemies, have a Shade get near your opponent's Hero, then right-click on the Hero (for the Shade to follow). The Shade will follow the Hero wherever he/she goes, which gives you access to your enemy's most important movements!

THE
APPENDIX

HUMAN

Here's a look at how the Human Heroes stack up against each other in various categories.

AGILITY

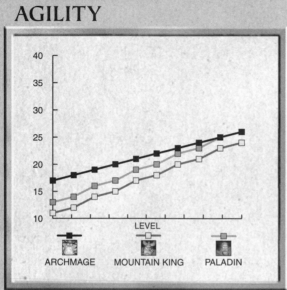

ARMOR

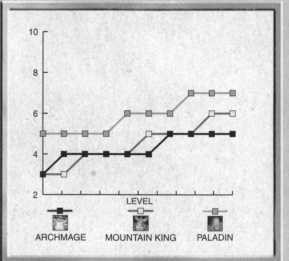

GROUND ATTACK

HIT POINTS

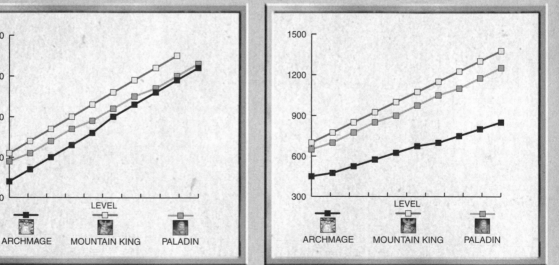

HEROES

INTELLIGENCE

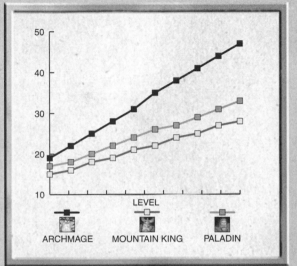

MANA

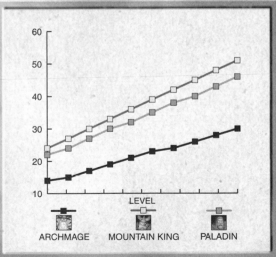

STRENGTH

CONCLUSIONS

❖ The Mountain King may be the best bet for an early choice in Heroes. He's the strongest and most durable of the three, and has a great attack. Although he falls short in Agility and the magical stats, he's ideal for fending off early rushes.

❖ Don't count the Paladin out as an early Hero. In contrast with the Mountain King, this Hero focuses on Armor and comes in a close second for Hit Points, Attack Rating, and Strength. The Paladin is a well-rounded character, whereas the Mountain King's stats focus on crushing the enemy.

❖ The Archmage is an incredible mid- to late-game addition to your forces. Although not as strong and protected as the other Heroes, his magic more than makes up for this. Use an already powered up Paladin or Mountain King to protect the Archmage as he gains levels.

UNDEAD

Here's how the Undead Heroes stack up against each other in various categories.

AGILITY

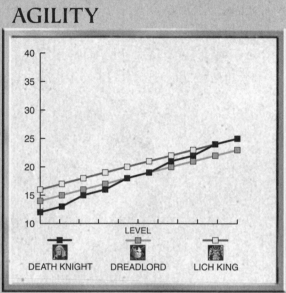

ARMOR

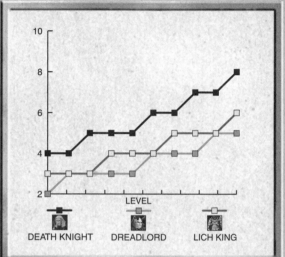

GROUND ATTACK

HIT POINTS

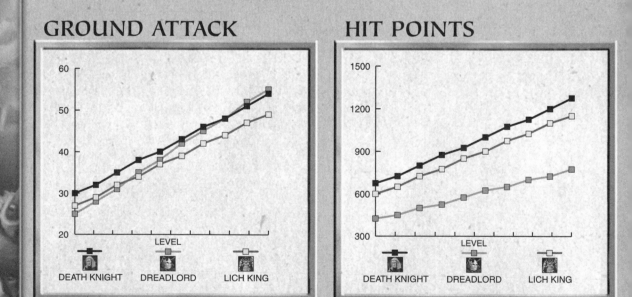

HEROES

INTELLIGENCE

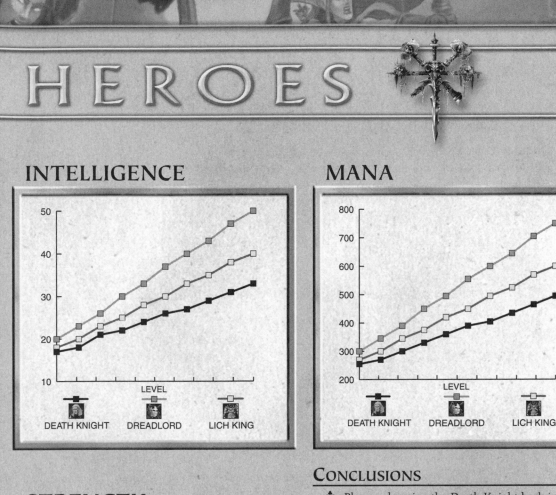

MANA

STRENGTH

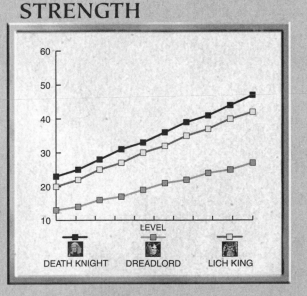

CONCLUSIONS

❖ Plan on dragging the Death Knight back into the land of the living early. He's got great stats in the melee-oriented areas and can withstand a wave of oncoming rushers. He stays tough right to the end, so keep leveling him up and you'll have a fierce warrior to bring against the enemy.

❖ The Lich King is a tough Hero. With a mixture between melee and magic as his base, he becomes a force to be reckoned with. He develops into a great Hero as the game goes on, so keep him in a group and hunt for kills until he's a true monster.

❖ As the Undead's magical Hero, the Dreadlord is a challenge to keep alive. With relatively low Hit Points and average Armor, it may be best to bring him out only when there's a bigger, more powerful Hero around to protect him. When the time comes to introduce the Dreadlord, it will be worth the wait. He's got the most Mana and highest Intelligence in the game.

UNDEAD HEROES

ORC

Here's how the Orc Heroes stack up against each other in various categories.

AGILITY

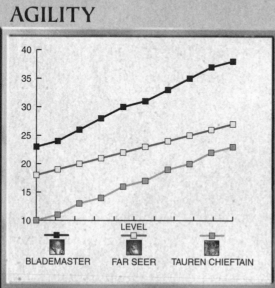

ARMOR

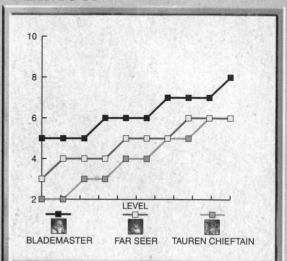

GROUND ATTACK

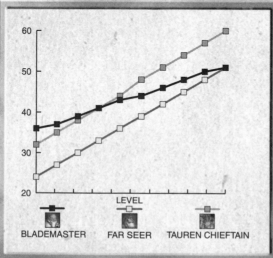

HIT POINTS

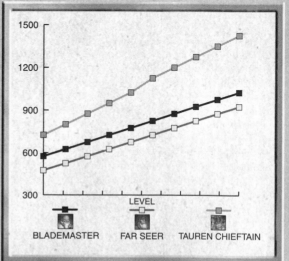

HEROES

INTELLIGENCE

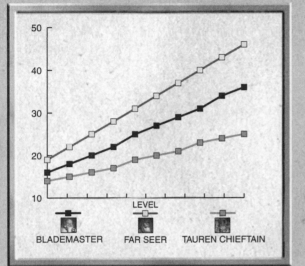

MANA

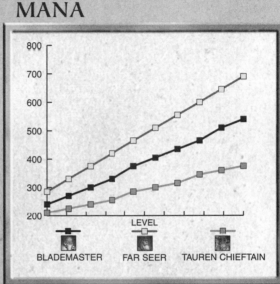

STRENGTH

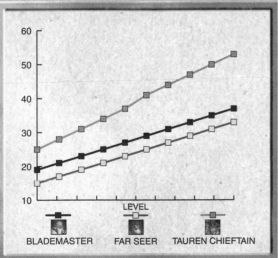

CONCLUSIONS

❖ The Blademaster is your best bet early on. He starts with an attack value much higher than either of the other two Orc Heroes. His Armor value and Agility are above average, as well. Even with mediocre Hit Points, this Hero is well-suited for leading early rushes and defending against them, too.

❖ The Tauren Chieftain is a wonder to behold. With an incredible amount of Hit Points, he's durable and can pound the enemy into submission. His Strength tops the charts and his Attack eventually becomes second to none. However, he's slow and ponderous, making him a poor choice for quick strike teams.

❖ The Farseer is one of the better mages in the game. His attack value eventually matches that of the Blademaster. Although he's not particularly strong, his magic compensates for this shortcoming. He is tough for a magic-oriented Hero, though, so consider him a nice addition in the mid- to end game.

NIGHT ELF

Here's how the Night Elf Heroes stack up against each other in various categories.

AGILITY

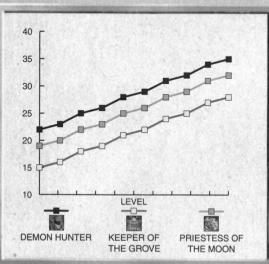

ARMOR

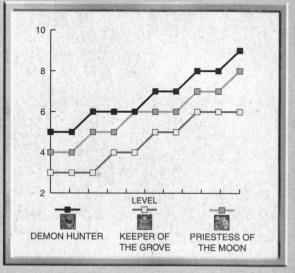

GROUND ATTACK

HIT POINTS

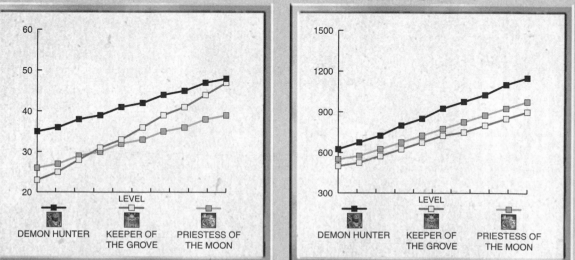

APPENDIX

HEROES

INTELLIGENCE

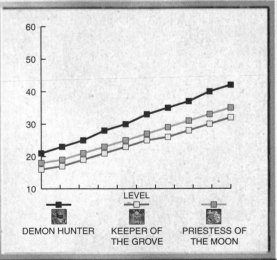

50
40
30
20
10

LEVEL

DEMON HUNTER   KEEPER OF   PRIESTESS OF
                THE GROVE   THE MOON

MANA

800
700
600
500
400
300
200

LEVEL

DEMON HUNTER   KEEPER OF   PRIESTESS OF
                THE GROVE   THE MOON

STRENGTH

60
50
40
30
20
10

LEVEL

DEMON HUNTER   KEEPER OF   PRIESTESS OF
                THE GROVE   THE MOON

CONCLUSIONS

❖ The Priestess of the Moon can dominate in the initial stages, but weakens in comparison as the game progresses. Her abilities will make up for it a bit, but make sure to take advantage of her early on. With decent stats in every category, she is a well-rounded Hero.

❖ The Keeper of the Grove's ability to add extra units to the battlefield makes him a formidable spell-caster. His attack begins low, but ends up just shy of the best—the Demon Hunter's. You can count on this Hero in nearly any situation.

❖ Starting strong and ending strong, the Demon Hunter is a great choice for the mid-game. He lacks an air attack, but that's what your Archers are for! He keeps his focus down to earth and can tear through land units. In addition, his Armor class ends up as the highest in the game. Although his Hit Points aren't as high as some others, his Speed and power still make him a good choice for a rush.

THE RACES

This section takes an average of the three Heroes from each race. A single Hero from a race may have different ratings in certain categories, but these charts give you an overall picture of how each race measures up against the Heroes of the other races.

AGILITY

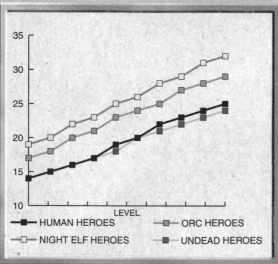

- HUMAN HEROES
- ORC HEROES
- NIGHT ELF HEROES
- UNDEAD HEROES

ARMOR

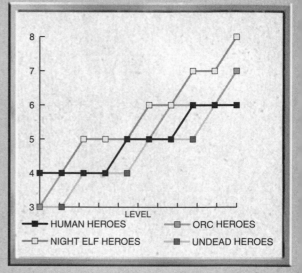

- HUMAN HEROES
- ORC HEROES
- NIGHT ELF HEROES
- UNDEAD HEROES

GROUND ATTACK

- HUMAN HEROES
- ORC HEROES
- NIGHT ELF HEROES
- UNDEAD HEROES

HIT POINTS

- HUMAN HEROES
- ORC HEROES
- NIGHT ELF HEROES
- UNDEAD HEROES

INTELLIGENCE

MANA

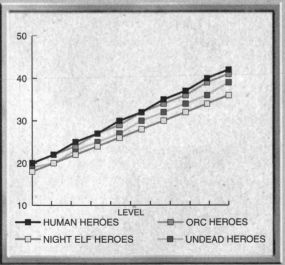

STRENGTH

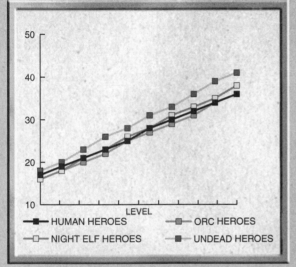

CONCLUSIONS

❖ For strength and power, head for Lorderon—the land of the Humans. As a whole this race has an advantage in Strength and Hit Points. They may be slow, but the Human Heroes don't have to run—they can just stay put and pound their enemies.

❖ When looking for Speed and Armor, look no further than the Night Elves. Their advantage is a quick, precise attack that leaves the opponent reeling. This speed advantage enables them to get away before most units can react effectively.

❖ The masters of magic were once among the dead, and it seems that the Undead's powers were enhanced while taking their dirt nap. This advantage allows them to use their powers constantly without running too low on Mana—unlike the Orcs.

❖ The Orcs are well rounded. They have the best Attack value, and solid stats in all of the other categories except magic. Take advantage of this strength. Get in close and crush the enemy. Don't react to their actions, make them react to yours.

THE RACES COMPARED

HUMAN TECH TREE

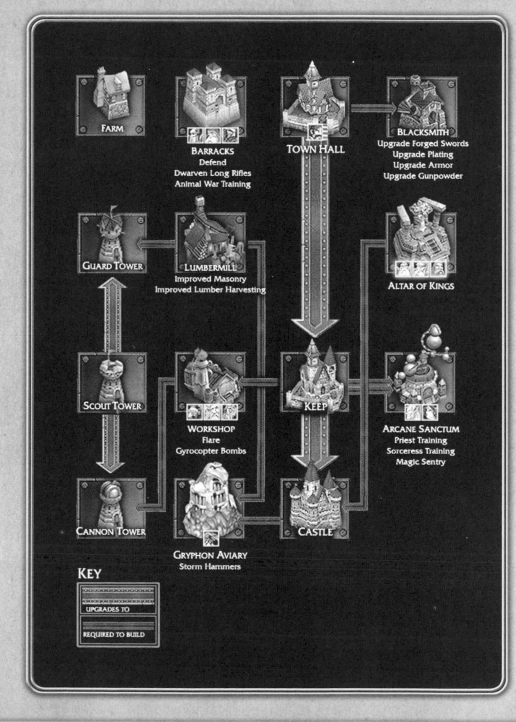

FARM

BARRACKS
Defend
Dwarven Long Rifles
Animal War Training

TOWN HALL

BLACKSMITH
Upgrade Forged Swords
Upgrade Plating
Upgrade Armor
Upgrade Gunpowder

GUARD TOWER

LUMBERMILL
Improved Masonry
Improved Lumber Harvesting

ALTAR OF KINGS

SCOUT TOWER

WORKSHOP
Flare
Gyrocopter Bombs

KEEP

ARCANE SANCTUM
Priest Training
Sorceress Training
Magic Sentry

CANNON TOWER

GRYPHON AVIARY
Storm Hammers

CASTLE

KEY

UPGRADES TO

REQUIRED TO BUILD

UNDEAD TECH TREE

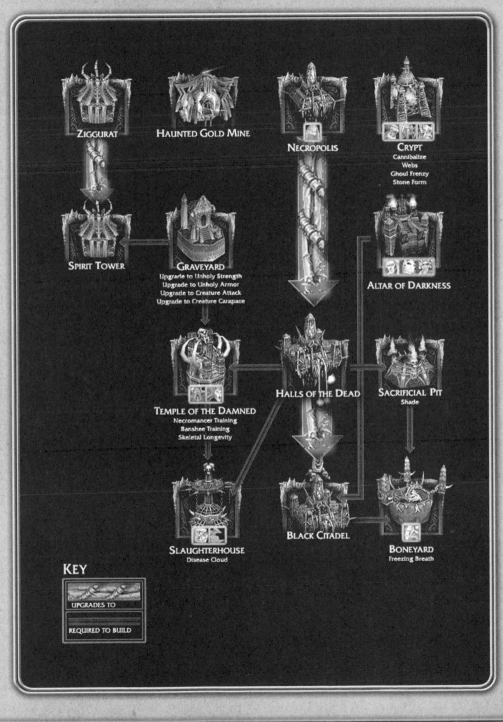

ZIGGURAT

HAUNTED GOLD MINE

NECROPOLIS

CRYPT
Cannibalize
Webs
Ghoul Frenzy
Stone Form

SPIRIT TOWER

GRAVEYARD
Upgrade to Unholy Strength
Upgrade to Unholy Armor
Upgrade to Creature Attack
Upgrade to Creature Carapace

ALTAR OF DARKNESS

TEMPLE OF THE DAMNED
Necromancer Training
Banshee Training
Skeletal Longevity

HALLS OF THE DEAD

SACRIFICIAL PIT
Shade

SLAUGHTERHOUSE
Disease Cloud

BLACK CITADEL

BONEYARD
Freezing Breath

KEY

UPGRADES TO

REQUIRED TO BUILD

ORC TECH TREE

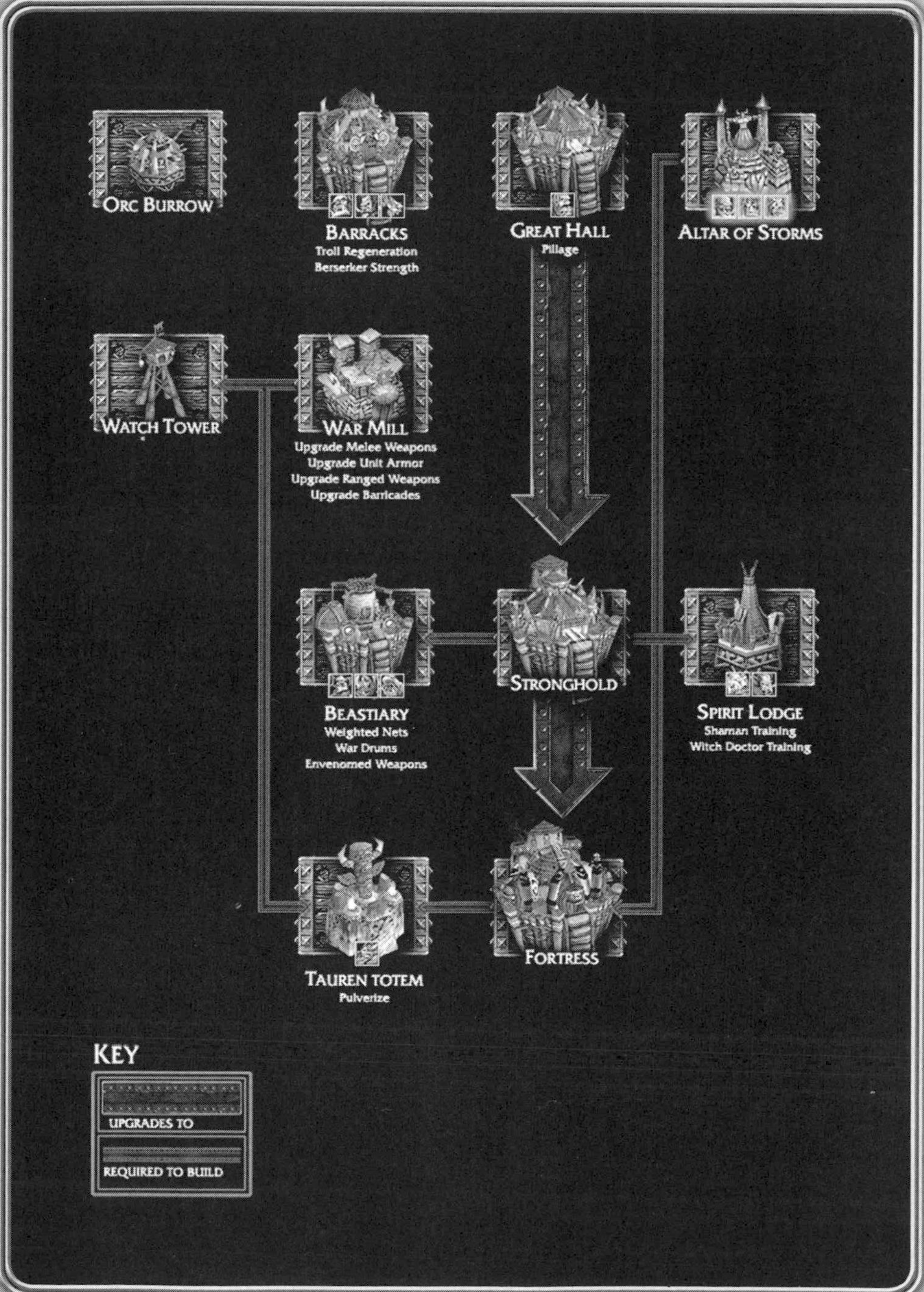

ORC BURROW

BARRACKS
Troll Regeneration
Berserker Strength

GREAT HALL
Pillage

ALTAR OF STORMS

WATCH TOWER

WAR MILL
Upgrade Melee Weapons
Upgrade Unit Armor
Upgrade Ranged Weapons
Upgrade Barricades

BEASTIARY
Weighted Nets
War Drums
Envenomed Weapons

STRONGHOLD

SPIRIT LODGE
Shaman Training
Witch Doctor Training

TAUREN TOTEM
Pulverize

FORTRESS

KEY

UPGRADES TO

REQUIRED TO BUILD

NIGHT ELF TECH TREE

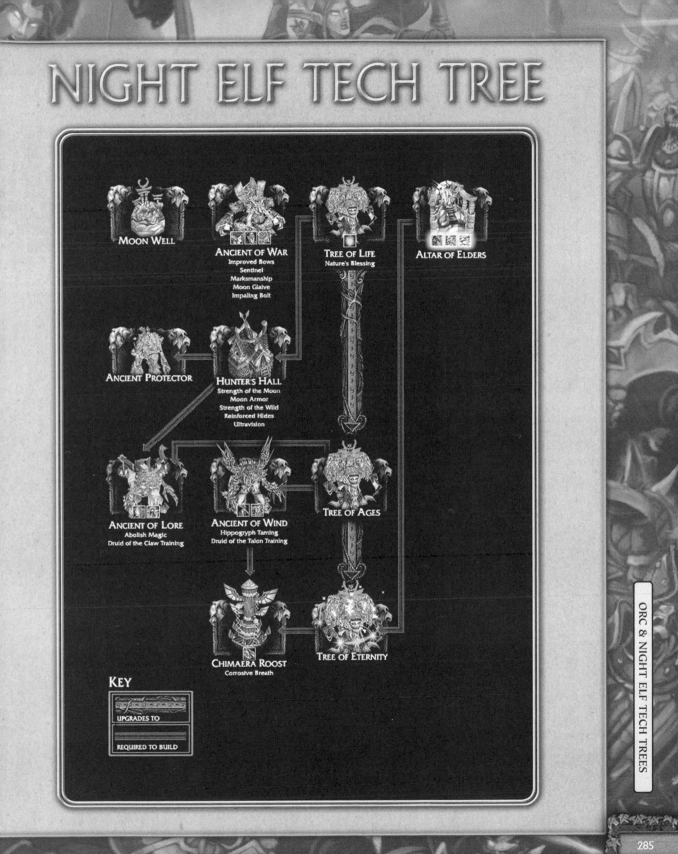

MOON WELL

ANCIENT OF WAR
Improved Bows
Sentinel
Marksmanship
Moon Glaive
Impaling Bolt

TREE OF LIFE
Nature's Blessing

ALTAR OF ELDERS

ANCIENT PROTECTOR

HUNTER'S HALL
Strength of the Moon
Moon Armor
Strength of the Wild
Reinforced Hides
Ultravision

ANCIENT OF LORE
Abolish Magic
Druid of the Claw Training

ANCIENT OF WIND
Hippogryph Taming
Druid of the Talon Training

TREE OF AGES

CHIMAERA ROOST
Corrosive Breath

TREE OF ETERNITY

KEY

UPGRADES TO

REQUIRED TO BUILD

*For generations, mighty warriors have heeded
your command and battled for control of Azeroth.
Now it's your turn. Descend into the World of
Warcraft™ and join thousands of adventurers
in an online world of myth, magic and legendary
chaos. Your definition of epic adventure is
about to be shattered…*

WORLD OF WARCRAFT

COMING SOON...

THE WARCRAFT® UNIVERSE COMES TO LIFE...
in this unique collector's guide.

Rare and never-before-seen images from the *Warcraft* series, from conceptual sketches to finished pieces.

An inside glimpse at the *Warcraft* universe, taking you from the dawn of the Night Elves to the return of the Burning Legion, and beyond.

Exclusive images from the *World of Warcraft*™ game, behind-the-scenes commentary from the Blizzard development team, and much more!

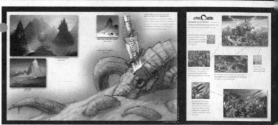

To purchase BradyGames' *The Art of Warcraft*®, visit your local electronics, book, or software retailer. Also available online at bradygames.com.

ISBN: 0-7440-0081-5
UPC: 7-52073-00081-3
PRICE: $24.99 US / $34.99 CAN / £19.99 Net UK

TAKE YOUR GAME FURTHER™
www.blizzard.com   www.bradygames.com